Child Rearing

Child Rearing

An Inquiry into Research and Methods

Marian Radke Yarrow
John D. Campbell
and Roger V. Burton

Jossey-Bass Inc., Publishers
615 Montgomery Street · San Francisco · 1968

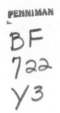

CHILD REARING
An Inquiry into Research and Methods
        by Marian Radke Yarrow, John D. Campbell,
        and Roger V. Burton

Jossey-Bass, Inc., Publishers
615 Montgomery Street
San Francisco, California 94111

Library of Congress Catalog Card Number 68-22785

Printed in the United States of America
by York Composition Company, Inc.
York, Pennsylvania

FIRST EDITION

68057

THE JOSSEY-BASS BEHAVIORAL SCIENCE SERIES

Preface

How firm are the foundations of research in child development? This question has provided the impetus for the inquiry presented in this volume. Our data are data on methods, and our objective is an inspection of methods. We have approached this objective not in general discussion of methodological issues, but in direct examination of these issues as they become manifest in the specific research products. Our analysis uses studies that are replications and near-replications of some of the commonly employed procedures for collection and analysis of verbal data. These studies permit us to seek evidences of consistency in research results, and enable us to assess the methodological adequacy of using such data as basic evidence on parent-child relations and personality development.

This book has grown out of our concern with the nature of the information on which propositions regarding the developmental process have been based. From study of methodological issues, we have been made very aware of the multidetermination of "findings" in our field. We have been made very appreciative of the difficulties in getting good behavioral data, and soberly impressed with the hazards of being other than cautious consumers and cautious producers in our science at the present stage of its technology.

◫ *ACKNOWLEDGMENTS* ◫

This work has been carried out at the National Institute of Mental Health. For the many kinds of tangible and intangible supports provided by its administrative and research staff throughout the conduct of this research, we are deeply grateful. Our research has depended, too, on the collaboration of the staff and parents associated with the National Child Research Center, a private nursery school in Washington, D.C., which served as the source of our subjects. We owe a very great debt to Doris Hawkins, director of the school when this research began; it was through her planning that research with the school was made possible. To Marie Crowley and Dorothy Sandstrom, acting directors of the school in 1962–1963 when the data of this project were gathered, we express our thanks for continuing support of the research. The teachers and school administration were indispensable aides in translating research activities to parents, providing data on the children, and providing the kinds of situations in the school which made data collection a smooth procedure. We also gratefully thank the mothers for submitting to the hours of interviewing which have entered into this research.

As our research evolved from plans to manuscript, we were aided in countless ways by the contributions of many professional colleagues. Particularly, we wish to thank Robert R. Sears, whose own work has served to stimulate our inquiry and from whose helpful questioning and insightful comments we benefited. At the stage of a nearly-completed manuscript, we profited from the constructive suggestions of Thomas Landauer and John A. Clausen. Our colleagues at N.I.M.H. were our constant helpful critics, and to Melvin Kohn, Leonard Pearlin, Carolyn Zahn, Earl Schaefer, and Richard Bell we express our gratitude.

In carrying out this study, we have been blessed with a

skilled and durable staff. The interviewing was done by Jean Darby, Eleanor Monahan, and Barbara Strope. They, along with Doris Hawkins and Janet Turnage, carried out the endless chores of coding and statistical analyses. We are deeply indebted to them for their perceptive and painstaking work. Our thanks go also to Tony Gray and Leonard Montgomery, who smoothed the tasks of data programming and processing by the careful technical assistance they provided, and to Frances Polen, who made an essential contribution through her meticulous attention to the details of manuscript preparation.

MARIAN RADKE YARROW

JOHN D. CAMPBELL

ROGER V. BURTON

Bethesda, Maryland
April 1968

Contents

	Preface	xi
ONE	The Origins of Data	1
TWO	Measurement of Dependency and Its Correlates	21
THREE	Theories and Correlates of Child Aggression	55
FOUR	Conscience and Its Correlates	94
FIVE	Toward Continuity in Developmental Research	125

Appendix A: Identification of
Variables   153

Appendix B: Intercorrelation of
Variables   173

References   191

Index   197

Child Rearing

CHAPTER 1

The Origins of Data

Systematic observation provides the cornerstone of science. When measurements have been repeated and when such repetitions have produced consistent results, scientific "reality" begins and opinion and hypothesis advance to findings. From findings that build upon one another conceptually and empirically, a body of knowledge develops. Results of diverse research efforts become woven into a network of related facts and interpretations, giving an essential continuity to the broad endeavor of research.

That continuing research depends on the observations and theories of preceding investigations underscores the importance of sound and stable predecessors on which to build. Although no simple guarantees against errors in the results and conclusions of research exist, judicious adherence to principles of scientific procedure greatly enhances the likelihood that the evidence produced will be truly solid and believable. Sound measurements are central to this scientific process. They must be reliable, must yield similar research results under similar measurement conditions. Thus the scientist turns to the repetition of his measurements to appraise them and the results generated by them. In the consonance of results from repeated measurements, he derives confidence and a basis for proceeding further. If he fails to find consistency, he begins again, reexamines and revises.

But consistency alone is not enough. For reliable results to be meaningful, they must be valid as well. Procedural adequacy of measurements is an essential condition for the validity of findings. If the gauge is uncertain, its meaning unclear (it may be reliable or unreliable), there can be little confidence in its products. When, by relevant criteria, the gauge is judged acceptable, the prospects brighten for enduring viability of the results. When such a foundation in repeatability and clear interpretability of evidence is lacking, research experience is likely to be noncumulative and chaotic, and knowledge to be "valid" for only a short time. "Advances" in science, beautifully integrated explanatory systems, have been known to perish because they proceeded from unreliable data and proliferated into unwarranted interpretations (see Allport, 1954).

Of any area of research or of any theoretical integration of the empirical data of a field one may ask to what degree the origins of the substance of the field are tested and solid. In the present study we have asked these questions as they pertain to developmental personality theory. Our research is directed to the objectives of examining the measurement procedures from which the evidence comes, and the soundness of findings and conclusions resulting from these procedures. Our domain is not as broad as personality theory; its focus is on a major motif in developmental research—the impact of childrearing experiences on child behavior.

Most of our day-to-day thinking on personality takes for granted that in the environment and experiences of the young organism are to be found the roots of his current and potential response tendencies. Evidence of this belief is ancient as well as new; it is held equally by the naïve layman and by the sophisticated and informed expert. This *assumption* of early effects is common to most of the theories on development. The harder task, however, has been to go beyond the assumption or general indication that influences are present, to the exact identification and measurement of the variables that are necessary and sufficient to produce specific effects. A very considerable quantity of developmental theory centers specifically on the influences of maternal care on child behavior, and empirical studies of child rearing are numerous. But as research investigators (perhaps more than research consumers) are keenly aware, events of child rearing are most difficult to measure, and the possible consequences of these events in child behavior are equally difficult to determine. Advances toward precision depend on conceptual and theoretical strides in the close company of sound methods and techniques. So it is of this particular sector of developmental research that we are inquiring: What is the nature of the evidence that has been accumulated in the field? And are the experiences with research procedures in this area of more general relevance in the conduct of behavioral studies of development?

The field of child rearing is a curious one—one that has interested almost every discipline in the behavioral sciences. The early experiences of infancy and childhood are given a central role in Freudian theories of personality development (Freud, 1930, 1949). Psychoanalytically oriented anthropological writing has viewed the infant and child care practices characteristic of different cultures as keys in explaining the "character structure" and the institutions of these cultures (Kardiner, 1939). Sociologists have marked child-rearing practices as sensitively differentiating attributes of social classes (Kohn, 1963; Clausen and Williams, 1963). Although in the earlier history of American psychology child rearing was generally regarded as a descriptive, nontheoretical field of investigation with "practical" purposes, such as parent education, it gained a stellar role in theoretical psychology, beginning in the 1950's with the upsurge of interest in developmental processes. Since then, conditions of early rearing have received steady attention in both child and animal research.

Two conceptual frameworks, psychoanalytic and behavioristic, in some respects quite divergent and in others quite consonant with one another, have served to provide the theoretical underpin-

nings for a great portion of the psychological research on the influences of child rearing. These two orientations by no means set forth
the same views of social learning; nevertheless they have led to research investigations that have many shared interests. Both have
typically viewed the process of socialization as one in which stimulus
events provided by the caretaker are important determinants of
child behavior. In both orientations the complex effects of rewards
and punishments have been of focal interest. The amount, intensity,
timing, and the scheduling of rewards and punishments, and the
nature of their effects in combination have been emphasized in behavioristic formulations. In psychoanalytic theory an additional hypothesized identification process is viewed as an important determinant in personality development. Characteristics of the caretaker or
parent model and interpersonal dimensions of the parent-child relationship, such as warmth and rejection, have been posited as contributors to the course of socialization. The theoretical positions
adopted by those working in this area are by no means identical, and
such different positions *do* make a difference. Yet from a broad perspective it is reasonable to state that the wide-ranging interests and
positions in this field converge with an almost single purpose and, in
some respects, a single point of view.[1]

Along with this conceptual convergence between different
theoretical formulations, there is similar correspondence in the research methods that have been used in investigating childrearing
influences on personality. Both psychoanalytically oriented research
and research from a social-learning framework (as well as atheoretical studies) have by and large used similar procedures to obtain data
on rearing experiences and on child behavior. There has been heavy
reliance on verbal reports of untrained introspectionists, parents or
children. These reports have generally been the bases of indices of
mother-child interactions that are interpreted as modal or usual sequences of interplay. The dimensions of parental behavior that have
been studied are those specified above as the theoretical concerns:
mainly the kinds of rewarding or punishing attentions from the par-

[1] For detailed presentations of theoretical positions on childrearing influences, see Bandura and Walters, 1963; Becker, 1964; Sears, Maccoby, and
Levin, 1957; Sears, Rau, and Alpert, 1965.

ent, and the warmth or hostility of parental interactions with the child. The hypothesized behavioral outcomes investigated cover the gamut of personality dimensions, depending on the nature of the subjects: infant responsiveness, toddler dependency, adolescent delinquent hostility, adult psychopathology. In the investigation of rearing antecedents of offspring behavior, experimentation or direct observations involving histories of interaction have been used less extensively. Such use is illustrated in animal research in the work of Harlow and Harlow (1962), in infant studies by Rheingold (1960), in clinical studies of pathological family interaction (Wynne, Rycoff, Day, and Hirsch, 1958), and in miniature short-term "histories" of interaction in experimental work with children by Bishop (1951) and by Bandura and Walters (1963). However, verbal reports to date constitute the principal evidence upon which childreading theory and prescriptions for childrearing practice rest.

◘ THE RESEARCH PURPOSE ◘

The present research carves out of this immense field of personality development a very small (yet very large) area for special study: research concerned with the effects of maternal rearing antecedents on the more or less current behavioral characteristics of the young child. This area conforms to the larger field in the nature of its theories and the nature of its empirical data. How then does it come to be the focus of the present study? There are several reasons. It is, first, a field from which there has been a great deal of extrapolation of theory and conclusions to other areas, and, therefore, a field that has had much influence. Many summary appraisals made in textbooks and encyclopedic reviews make it appear that regular and trustworthy findings have been established. Does this appearance coincide with reality? Also, the verbal report findings have been used as a criterion against which to judge other research evidence. Investigators have interpreted experimental findings in terms of parent-child behavior relations presumed to have been established in studies using verbal data. Is this an acceptable strategy? Conclusions from childrearing studies have been made the bases for prescriptions of educational practices, guidelines for institutional procedures, and advice to laymen concerning the treatment of young children, and these conclusions have been again extended to apply to older and to very different populations. Do the methods and findings warrant such translations?

In our present inquiry we have raised questions about the body of knowledge that has been acquired in this field: How robust are the relationships between presumed antecedent childrearing events and consequent child behavior? How thoroughly has the stability of these relationships been established through careful replication? To what extent do procedural attributes contribute to the results obtained? Are the measurement procedures historically associated with childrearing research suited to testing the hypotheses which the theories put forth? To pursue this inquiry, we have designed a childrearing study generally conforming to prototype and have carried it out as a replication of studies in this field; we have repeated measurements within our own study, varying the instruments of measurement but using the same subjects; and we have analyzed the aggregate of evidence in the literature of a delimited area of childrearing research.

▣ REPLICATION, CONSISTENCY, AND CONTINUITY ▣

Each phase of our research is concerned with the processes of appraising the findings from research, through the replication of measurements and the assessment of consonance and continuity in results.[2] There is considerable latitude in views of what constitutes replication of research. One of the more rigorous definitions is that offered by Kendall and Buckland (1960): "The execution of an experiment or survey more than once so as to increase precision and to obtain a closer estimate of sampling error. Replication should be

---

[2] This research is one of three investigations by the authors concerned with methodological issues in research in child development. The foci of the other two are on (1) the congruency of developmental data obtained contemporaneously with those retrieved through recall, and the moderating factors which affect this congruency or lack of it; and (2) the reliability of direct observations of child and adult behavior, and comparisons of such observational records with interview reports of the behavior.

distinguished from repetition . . . by the fact that replication of an experiment denotes repetition carried out at one place and, as far as possible, one period of time." If studies in the behavioral sciences were held to the measure of this pattern, the number of investigations that could thus legitimately be called replications would indeed be small.[3] Fortunately, Kendall and Buckland provide an escape clause by appending to their definition the statement, "Current usage on this point is often rather loose" (p. 249).

Clearly the central core of definitions of replication is *exact repetition*. (For example, note these two further definitions: "replicate: to repeat an experiment or field study precisely as it was first carried out" [Harriman, 1947, p. 168], and "replicate: *v.* to reproduce or copy an original in all essentials; esp., to repeat an experiment with all essentials unchanged . . ." [English and English, 1958, p. 457].) Yet it is equally clear that precise repetition is difficult, if not impossible, to come by. In the strictest sense, replication could only be accomplished if the same measuring instruments were applied to the same subjects, in the same setting. But the "same" human subjects are never really the same; the fact of earlier testing is incorporated as a part of their life experience and, no matter how minutely, they are changed accordingly. When one adds the changes in the organism that are part of development, of growing older, the exactness of any repetition of measurement is again reduced. So, too, the "same" situation may not be truly the same, if only because the passage of time will have its effect. And the instrument itself, as it is administered a second time, or at least as it is interpreted by the subject during his second experience, may reasonably be viewed as lacking complete constancy.

If one adopts as a working premise that one is likely to be working with less than pure replication, what deviations will one

[3] Samuel Stouffer, often attuned to methodological matters, is one of the few behavioral scientists who on one occasion might be said to have met Kendall and Buckland's stringent standards for replication. His study, *Communism, Conformity, and Civil Liberties* (1955), marked the first time in which two independent public opinion polling agencies employed the same interview schedule at the same point in time to obtain information from separate carefully selected cross sections of the American population. Stouffer used the data to examine correspondence in results of the two surveys.

tolerate? To pin this question down to specifics in studies of child development and parental behavior, consider the following: In interview studies, if the schedule used in one study is not identical to that used in another, does this fail to constitute replication because of differences in instruments used? What about changes in the nature of the response categories and in the manner of coding responses; do all of these represent permissible variations, or can none of them be tolerated? Then consider the subjects. Should one accept mothers of preschool children in Memphis as interchangeable with those in Minneapolis, or with those in an Arab village? Or perhaps an even more remote comparison, are fathers' responses to be equated with those of mothers?

The setting poses further problems of constancy when a second sample of families from the same community is studied with the same instruments, but one or ten years later. Both time and untold changes in the larger setting have reduced the identical elements in successive studies. Consider other aspects of setting intertwined with small or large instrument variations: One sample of mothers is interviewed in their homes, while another is seen in a school interview. The interviewers in the two studies have different orientations and training. Do these studies constitute replications?

To all of these and similar questions one might respond that exact and less than exact comparability in repeated investigations provide different kinds of evidence in *consistency* of results, and fulfill different purposes in establishing *continuity* in findings. It is important, therefore, that the investigator's choice between "exact" replication and planned departures from exact repetitions be governed by explicit objectives. A choice of closely comparable procedures under highly similar conditions is desirable when the investigator wishes to establish the basic reliability of his instrument and the stability of the relation found between variables on his first run. If he is dealing with a reliable instrument and with a true relationship between variables, he should expect the consistency of findings to be high. Any differences in findings would reflect only random errors. Attainment of such high consistency should encourage him to go on and even to begin to theorize about his findings. If, on the other hand, he has performed a nearly exact repetition of his pro-

cedures and the outcome spells inconsistency, there is little justification for taking his findings seriously or for theorizing about them.
There is more work to be done on procedures or theory or both. By
replication of this kind, at this stage, he has spared himself the dis-
aster of using an unverified finding as the basis for a next theoretical
step when, indeed, the first step is nonexistent.

Even without evidence on the stability of findings under conditions of exact repetition, an investigator may choose to depart from
close comparability—in methods of data collection, techniques of
data handling, the nature of research subjects or the research setting.
He may reason that by varying the trivial or theoretically unrelated
conditions in his research he can derive assurance that the results
obtained in the first study are not functions of idiosyncratic features
of that study.[4] To ensure that he has hold of a variable or relationship, he may choose to change the form of questions, to move from
a Memphis sample to one in Minneapolis, and so on. If such variations from "exact" repetition result in accord in findings across studies, confidence in the findings gains materially. All is well if such
accord is found. But should discrepancies occur, interpretation grows
exceedingly complex. It must be remembered that the investigator
began his study assuming theoretically *irrelevant* variations in his
approach; under these circumstances departures from consistency
that have *not* been anticipated on theoretical grounds pose a problem for him. When inconsistencies arise in such circumstances, to
what source should he attribute them? Are the dissimilar results due
to methodological variations, or to the general instability of the relationships being considered, or possibly to both? No matter what the

---

[4] That method or apparatus factors exist is well known. We have not,
however, utilized this knowledge to the full. In a discussion of validation procedures in psychology, Campbell and Fiske (1959) cite several instances in
which such factors play a major role. These cover a range: At the level of
animal behavior are data showing that when hunger, thirst, and sex drives
were measured in two different ways (with an obstruction box or with an
activity wheel), the correlations between different drives measured by the
same method were higher than those between two measures of the same drive
obtained by different methods. At the human level they note the similar importance of "apparatus" factors in measurement of social traits by different
methods of sociometric appraisal and direct observation.

source of difficulty, the absence of consistency should both temper his interpretations and bring out the sleuth in the researcher to trace factors contributing to absence of correspondence. It is all too tempting in such circumstances to find an altogether plausible, even exciting, theoretical explanation for the discrepancies. But this is yielding to temptation, and should be resisted.

In order to establish general principles of human development and behavior, the repetition of investigation by extension is, of course, necessary. That is, one must ask what generality does the relationship that has been established with some precision through "exact" replication have? This question can be answered only by introducing theoretically significant variations in the continuing study of a set of relationships. Continuity in science and extension of knowledge into new areas result from this kind of "replication" with variation.

Thus, the kind of contribution to continuity which a new study makes by exact or varied repetition of preceding research is governed by what is required at a given time in the particular area of investigation. When one sees many conflicting findings, it would seem necessary to lean to the side of exact repetition, to cut down on the degree of "leniency" in replication of procedures and in interpretation of consistency in results. Where, as in the domain of child-rearing research, there is so little standardization in concepts, such imprecise measuring procedures, so many exceptions to theoretical expectations, and where interpretive consistency must often lean on tenuous findings, more basic replication and more congruency of results are required.

◙ REPLICATION IN DEVELOPMENTAL PSYCHOLOGY ◙

Replication in the exact sense is not the norm in developmental psychology. Many of the "classics" in the history of the field have never been tested by later studies. There are, of course, many understandable deterrents to carefully defined replication. After having given much in time and energy to his research, an investigator, as Kessen (1960, p. 54) points out, "will be humanly reluctant to begin again before he has stated publicly the results of his work." Also, "Having 'found' a relationship, it is altogether too easy for the researcher to construct a convincing explanation, and his achievement of this step will tend to make doubts and potential criticisms less obvious to him. Moreover, in writing up his results, his commitment to a particular understanding of his data may frequently lead to a further constriction in the range of alternative explanations. . . . we should recognize with great clarity the pitfalls that grow from the human desire to impose order on a set of data. The sole guarantee against error of this variety is the establishment of a new test or the examination of unanalyzed data to determine stability of a relationship."

Still other deterrents come from the scientific community. In developmental psychology and a number of other areas of the behavioral sciences replicative studies have often been neither expected nor required. In the competition for journal space, such a study might often be viewed as low man on a totem pole. Furthermore, should the repeated study not confirm the earlier finding, the burden of proof rests heavily on the second study to demonstrate that it has, indeed, been a faithful repetition and that some quirk in it has not accounted for its failure to produce congruent findings. Therefore, any investigator contemplating the replication of his own research or that of others might well decide that the reinforcement provided by professional peers was not sufficient to warrant the time and energy required.

In addition, the scientist's training may contribute to his attitude concerning the need for replicating research. The natural sciences give the student a built-in indoctrination in replication. The beginning student of chemistry, for example, performs standard laboratory experiments which by their results inform him of his progress as a scientist; he has the concreteness of a standard by which to accept or reject his findings. It is often possible for him to check where and how he "went wrong," why his replication failed to produce the same results. Students of human social behavior tend not to experience this kind of indoctrination in replication in either the construction or use of the instruments of the science.

Compared again with the natural sciences, the consistency of findings in studies of personality and social behavior is less readily assessed. To the extent that the materials and procedures of the chemical experiment can be precisely described and duplicated, results can be quickly verified or refuted independently in different laboratories; but lacking similar standardization of language and procedures in some areas of behavioral research, it is far more difficult to be certain of consistencies in repeated investigations. Yet if replicative inquiries are not frequently undertaken, and if such efforts, when undertaken, do not yield comparable data, then the stance of certain areas of behavioral science may legitimately be questioned.

◙ THE PRESENT INQUIRY ◙

With our major purpose the examination of relations between methods and results and between results and interpretations in childrearing research, we need to delimit our scope at the outset: Which methods and which childrearing results and interpretations? We have chosen representative areas in personality theory, and, for these analyses, we have accepted a formulation of unidirectionality of influence—of parent on child. We have directed our attention to the hypothesized influences of maternal behaviors on the subsequent development of the child. The maternal behaviors have been conceptualized broadly as acceptance and rejection of the child, and reward and punishment of behavior. By considering child dependency and aggression and what has euphemistically been called "conscience" as the behaviors influenced by maternal variations, many developmental hypotheses are sampled. Indeed, investigation of these behaviors constitutes a very large part of past and current research in child rearing.

As indicated earlier, the studies of this field have been relatively homogeneous in their methods. Maternal "antecedent" behaviors have been measured by verbal reports from the mothers; measures of child "consequent" behaviors have come predominantly from mothers' reports of children's behavior at home and ratings made of children's behavior in school. These methods have been our focus.

Although the influences of maternal behavior on the child are not limited theoretically to any single age, early childhood (usually institutionally defined by attendance at preschool) has been the most investigated period of childhood. Within this age bracket we find a relatively homogeneous group of research studies that approximate replications of one another in theoretical interests, procedures, and research subjects.

In this realm of theory, variables, measuring procedures, and subjects we have studied some issues of methodology in research. Our strategy has been to carry out a childrearing study of our own, and to subject its procedures and findings, along with the procedures and findings of published research, to methodological inquiry.

The National Institute of Mental Health study was designed to repeat closely the procedures of the existing research in this field. Our primary model was the survey by Sears, Maccoby, and Levin (*Patterns of Child Rearing,* 1957), a study that has served as the prototype for numerous investigations, and that in many ways stands as a representative of theories, methods, and procedures common to the field. Investigators have followed up hypotheses derived from its theoretical formulations and have repeated its procedures in other subjects. Its findings have often been used to aid in the interpretation of other research. Still a further measure of the impact of this study is the extent to which its findings have been included in Berelson and Steiner's volume (1964), which has attempted to assemble the best-established empirical results from research in the behavioral sciences. Thus, our objective of replicating as nearly as possible the usual research procedures that have been used in the field was reached more easily by having in the Sears, Maccoby, Levin instrument one resource upon which other investigators have frequently drawn.

SUBJECTS

The subjects of our study are 86 nursery school children (43 boys, 43 girls) and their mothers. The families in the sample are Caucasian, native-born Americans, professional and business families living in the Greater Washington area. Ninety-two per cent of the fathers have college or graduate degrees; 74 per cent of the mothers are college-trained. At the time of the study, most of the mothers were between twenty-five and forty-five years of age, the fathers between thirty and fifty years. The mean age of the children at the time of the mother interview was four years, two months (a range of 2–11 to 6–0). All of the children were considered "normal," having no major physical or psychological problem. These sample characteristics do not differ greatly from those of the studies considered in our analyses of the field.[5]

PROCEDURES

Data from the NIMH study derive from three sources: mother interviews, mother questionnaires, and teacher ratings. The wording of questions used to elicit information, descriptions of scoring procedures, and (where relevant) coding reliabilities are presented in Appendix A. Our own interview questions concerning the child's dependent, aggressive, and "conscience" behaviors and maternal practices theoretically related to them were in the main taken directly from *Patterns of Child Rearing*. Information on question wording, scoring, and reliability of coding in that study is also detailed in the appendix; thus the reader who is so inclined may note and compare these aspects of the two studies.

The mother interviews and the mother questionnaires of the NIMH study provide information on both maternal rearing practices and children's behavior. Data from teachers' ratings deal solely with children's behavior within the setting of the school. The nature of the coverage of each instrument is described in the paragraphs that follow.

The mother interview. The type of instrument used as the

---

[5] Middle- or upper-middle-class groups, often university communities, predominate in these studies (for example, Becker, Peterson, Luria, Shoemaker, and Hellmer, 1962; Burton, Maccoby, and Allinsmith, 1961; Sears, Rau, and Alpert, 1965; Sears, Whiting, Nowlis, and Sears, 1953). In studies that include middle-class and working-class groups, a breakdown of findings by class has usually been made (Eron, Walder, Toigo, and Lefkowitz, 1963; Hoffman, 1960; Sears et al., 1957). Except in the Eron, Banta, Walder, and Laulicht (1961); Eron et al. (1963); and Lefkowitz, Walder, and Eron (1963) studies, in which the sample is of a semirural population and of eight-year-old children, the research samples are white, urban nursery school or kindergarten children and their mothers.

principal source of data in the present study has been characterized in *Patterns of Child Rearing* (p. 19) as "somewhere between the flexible, unstandardized, 'depth' interview which is characteristic of clinical interviewing, and the completely structured interview with a long list of multiple choice items." The rationale for the use of such a schedule and the details of interview construction have been fully presented by Sears and his collaborators in that volume. For the NIMH study, as was the case with the Sears, Maccoby, and Levin interview that served as the prototype, most of the interview items are open-ended questions requiring descriptive statements from the mother.

Our interview measures of mothers' *childrearing practices* can be conceptualized in terms of four classes of behavior: (1) maternal functioning in relation to the three aspects of children's behavior most central to our study—maternal responses pertaining to the child's dependence and independence (V's 11 and 12),[6] those pertaining to his aggressive actions (V's 7, 7a, 13, 14, 15, 16, 17, 18, 20e, 21e, and 21f), and those pertaining to his conscience-relevant behavior (V 14a); (2) maternal functioning in relation to other specific aspects of the child's behavior, including modesty training, mealtime behavior, neatness, bedtime routines, and so on (V's 19a-i, 20a-d, 20f, 21a-d); (3) reports of the mother's *general* use of control, disciplinary, and training techniques (V's 1, 2, 3, 4, 4a, 5, 6, 8, 9, 10, 10a, 10b, 19, 19j, 19k, 20, 21, 22); and (4) the mother's affective relationship with her child (V's 23, 24, 25, 26, 26a).

Mothers' reports provide the information on the classes of *child behavior* viewed as the consequent variables: dependency (V's 28, 29, 30, and 31), aggression (V's 32 and 32a), conscience (V's 33, 33a-e, 34, and 35), independence (V 27), and compliance (V's 32b-g). (Detailed consideration of the hypothesized antecedent and consequent measures is an integral part of the chapters that follow.)

The NIMH interviews were conducted at the nursery school by three trained assistants, each with experience in research in child

---

[6] When an NIMH variable is referred to in the text, it is identified by number (for example, V 3, V 47, and so on). The interview source, the coding scale, and the coding reliability of the variable are identified by the corresponding numbers in Appendix A.

development. The mothers were given a general explanation of the research as a study of their experiences in teaching and disciplining their young children. The mothers' responses were tape recorded. In coding the information derived from the interviews, five- or seven-point rating scales were used. Each interview record was coded before another mother was seen. The coding was done independently by pairs of coders (one of whom was the interviewer), working directly from the taped record. In cases of disagreement between coders, an adjudicated score, a joint decision by the particular coder pair, was used. (Each coder was paired with each other coder to assess agreement in ratings. Based on a sample of the total list of variables, the average correlation between coders A and B was $+.79$, between A and C it was $+.74$, and between B and C it was $+.75$. Given this similarity for each of the pairs, coder agreement is presented without further attention to the identity of particular coder pairs.) One sees, by referring to Appendix A, a rather wide range of coding reliabilities (from r's of .93 to .34 in the NIMH data, and from .87 to .33 in *Patterns of Child Rearing*), reflecting the relative ease or difficulty in arriving at coder agreement on the different dimensions and, in the case of low correlations, signaling problems at a very basic level of data.

As the listings in Appendix A demonstrate, some of the questions and analyses in the NIMH and Sears, Maccoby, and Levin studies differ. Such differences generally occurred as a result of our effort to avoid certain problems in data gathering or analysis that had arisen in earlier studies. One example of a procedural modification appears in our questions concerning disciplinary practices. In an attempt to avoid the mother's general set concerning disciplinary techniques, and also to avoid her chance mentioning of some techniques and omitting of others, we asked an open-ended question about how she handled the child's misbehavior in each of the specific settings (mealtime and so on, listed above), and then followed this with standard probes. A specific technique (such as isolation or physical punishment) was then scored as used or not used in each of the situations. A summed standardized score was obtained for each technique based on its use when all of the specific situations were considered. For scoring summary appraisals of restrictiveness

(V 19), severity of punishment (V 20), and emotional expression in punishment (V 21), the child's compliance (V 32b), and dependent behaviors (V's 38, 43), standardized scores were similarly derived by summing the ratings of behavior in the specific situations.

Interview studies of American parents have found it difficult to obtain good indications of rejective feelings by mothers (see Sears et al., 1957, p. 170), therefore it seemed appropriate to introduce a variant procedure for obtaining indicators of maternal rejection. To elicit at least an indirect expression of rejection, we asked the mother, "What kinds of things does X do that get on your nerves?" We reasoned that perhaps negative affect might thus be expressed through an admission of many specific annoyances, and our measure was a count of such annoyances reported. A positive affective relation between mother and child (maternal warmth) has been accorded considerable theoretical importance in socialization theories, and it, too, has been difficult to define and measure and code adequately. To attempt to obtain a simple appraisal in this area, we asked, "What sorts of things do you enjoy about X?" Here, too, the information coded was a count of things enjoyed. In addition, a global rating of warmth based on the total interview response from the mother, the procedure in *Patterns of Child Rearing,* was used.

Mother questionnaires and teacher ratings. While the major interest of the NIMH study was to follow closely the procedures of published studies, a second objective was to *repeat* measurement on the *same* sample but with other research instruments. For this purpose, for a limited number of the variables in the interview, data were also obtained in a written questionnaire form filled out by the mother, and from an interview with nursery school teachers (see Appendix A, V's 36 through 50). The *questionnaire* was filled out by the mother at the time of the child's entrance to the nursery school, about a half year before she responded to the interview. Other information was requested in the questionnaire, such as developmental history data, in addition to the items relevant to this study. The latter were questions on the mother's level of demands on her child regarding mealtime behavior and neatness (V's 36a, b), the child's compliance (V 36), dependency (V's 39, 40, 41), and aggression (V 42). On these items mothers checked one of five possible responses on a scale ranging from "1," "Yes, definitely," to "5," "No, definitely." (For example: on the item, "Child is very demanding of adult's time and attention, wants a lot of help," a mother's response of "Yes, definitely" would indicate that she felt that the description fit her child very well; a response of "No, definitely," that it did not fit her child at all.)

On 58 of the 86 children, *teachers' ratings* were obtained an average of two months after the mother interview. In individual interviews, each of two teachers independently responded to questions concerning the child's dependent, aggressive, and "conscience" behaviors. The questions were very nearly identical to those asked the mother, but dealt with the child's behavior in school. After the teacher had described the child on a given dimension, she was given a card specifying a seven-point rating scale. The descriptions for the ratings were the same as those of the scales used by coders to evaluate maternal interview responses. The teacher selected the appropriate rating category. Ratings of the two teachers were summed to arrive at the child's score.

The modifications in procedures introduced by the questionnaire and the teacher ratings are representative of the different types of replication discussed earlier. They involve both trivial and theoretically significant variations from the interview with the mother. For example, the questionnaire item quoted above on the child's demand for attention was assumed not to tap an essentially different area from that of the parallel question in the mother's interview ("How much attention does X seem to want from you?" [V 29]). The anticipated similarity between responses to the two questions would, therefore, be high. On the other hand, this would not be the expectation for the findings on child aggression reported by mother and by teachers: While instrument differences between mother and teacher interviews are minimal, the situations in which the child is appraised and the person of the appraiser are significant variations in replication procedures. One would on theoretical grounds expect *not* consistency, but a marked and systematic change in findings on aggression from the two measurements. The analyses turn to such issues of interpretation in considering the procedures and results of the NIMH study and the reported literature.

◘ *SCOPE OF THE STUDY* ◘

In summary, from one perspective we have conducted a generally typical study of child rearing; we have at the same time incorporated in our study an attempt at systematic replication of procedures to assess stability of results. Compilation of new data on child rearing is *not* the substance of our concern. Our primary goal is a methodological one; we have directed our inquiry basically to the processes and products of research in child rearing, and to the merits and pitfalls of the techniques by which childrearing knowledge has been obtained. Questions of the relation between parental practices and three areas of child behavior provide the substantive framework in which we examine matters of measurement and interpretation of measurement. Thus, in Chapter 2, it is within the context of a consideration of child dependency and parental correlates of such behavior that several methodological issues are raised. Aggression, in Chapter 3, and conscience formation, in Chapter 4, serve in a similar fashion. Although many of the same issues are common to each of the three content fields (dependency, aggression, and conscience) that we have used in our analyses, we have not followed a uniform course in the analyses of each area. When we have examined a problem that is equally relevant to each substantive area, we have developed it rather fully in one context, and have referred to it more briefly in the others.

This study has as its major purpose the exploration of consistency in research findings. Thus we examine consistency within our own data and also see whether it is the rule in the data of comparable inquiries of others. It is our intention to go beyond a surface appraisal of research results by considering some of the pieces in the often complex machinery of the research process and, in so doing, giving attention to some of the methodological factors contributing to consistency or its lack.

The interrelation of conceptualization and measurement constitutes a fundamental concern throughout this volume. The definition of variables receives more than passing notice, and considerable attention is devoted to the detailed examination of such factors as the conceptual equivalence and interchangeability of measures and the suitability of various indices. Reliability of measurement, naturally enough, enters discussion from several perspectives—coding of interview responses, agreement between independent raters of behavior, consistency of assessment over time, and the impact of unreliability of measurement on subsequent analyses of relations between variables.

Our own data also provide a context in which to explore the potential influence of certain biasing factors on research results. Among the sources of bias examined are halo effects, social desirability factors, and research designs that fail to obtain independent measurement of antecedent conditions and their presumed consequences.

In analyses of our data we have used the bivariate and multivariate procedures commonly reported in the relevant research literature, but in so doing we have noted that bivariate analyses may not be suitable as tests of many of the basically multivariate hypotheses of child development.

Throughout we have raised a number of questions concerning fundamental issues in the use of interviews and questionnaires. We have noted some of the limitations in particular types of interviews, have offered some specific suggestions for developing suitable verbal report methods, and have also considered some alternatives to the interview and the questionnaire as sources of information on the relation between childrearing practices and the development of personality.

The critical issues of research cannot, of course, be restricted solely to the mechanics of data collection and analysis. Also relevant are the communication of research results and the placing of research findings in appropriate interpretive contexts. The desirability and difficulty of full communication concerning the research process, and the special requirements and pitfalls encountered in attempting to synthesize information from diverse research sources are factors considered in this volume. And, finally, since any given research inquiry derives its value not in isolation but as a portion of a larger canvas, we have attempted to specify the characteristics of a general research strategy, a strategy that builds in methodological checks as an essential part of the necessary continuity in research.

CHAPTER 2

Measurement of Dependency and Its Correlates

$\mathbf{T}$he intertwining of conceptualization and method, the reciprocal influence of one upon the other, is relevant in any area of childrearing research. Naturally enough, the formulation of a concept imposes structure on measurement possibilities; the investigator attempts to select measures that are consonant with the ideas basic to his research. At the same time, the measures themselves must of necessity stand as the working definitions of concepts, and as such, to a considerable degree they limit the contribution of particular conceptualizations to the ordering of empirical data. Thus the selection of suitable indices constitutes a difficult and crucial step in the initial phases of a research inquiry.

To inspect this part of the research process and to analyze some of the difficulties that may stem from it, we shall concentrate on dependency as a personality attribute of young children. We shall look as closely as possible at measures subsumed under this label. Then, aided by the information harvested from this examination of dependency indices, we shall ask how consistently these measures are related to certain parental characteristics.

▣ MEASURING DEPENDENCY ▣

During infancy and early childhood, dependency stands as a prime characteristic of the human condition; the gradual emerging of the child as an independent entity is a salient aspect of his social growth. It is no wonder that specialists in personality and child development have been as much enthralled by this process as have parents themselves. Given the relevance of dependency to general issues of personality development, it is natural that investigators have directed some of their energy toward examining the nature of the concept of dependency, developing and assessing procedures used in its measurement, and specifying antecedent and contemporaneous correlates of dependency.

Of various issues concerning dependency, one highly pertinent to matters of measurement is the question whether dependency is a unitary concept: is it a *general* characteristic of an individual, or are we dealing with a multidimensional construct, a series of entities, linked not so much in the functioning of research subjects as in the mind of the investigator? Research support can be found for either view. In one study in which teachers rated five different aspects of dependency in nursery school children, intercorrelations of the different components of dependency ranged from .48 to .83, and the median correlation was greater than .60 (Beller, 1957, p. 299). This gives considerable comfort to supporters of a unidimensional conceptualization of dependency. On the other hand, when in another study trained observers followed a time-sampling procedure to obtain relative-frequency measures of different types of observed behavior displayed by nursery school children, evidence tended to support a multidimensional view: intercorrelations of five measures grouped under the umbrella concept of dependency ranged from −.03 to .71 for girls (with a median less than .19) and −.24 to .23 for boys (with a median correlation less than .04). (See Sears et al., 1965, p. 41.) Indeed, only *one* of the 20 coefficients derived from behavior observations was as large as the *smallest* of those reported in the preceding study.

Choice of method (for example, rating vs. behavioral observation) and choice of components presumed to represent the domain of dependency doubtless both play a part in such conflicting views of the generality or specificity of dependency. Given such differing data, Hartup's (1963, p. 337) appraisal of this issue is appropriate:

> Over-all . . . the evidence concerning generality in dependency and independence is equivocal. Neither those data which support the unidimensional hypothesis nor the findings which support multidimensionality are entirely free of methodological weakness. The generality problem is often ignored and dependency is used repeatedly as a label for a single unitary dimension in personality. There is, however, a distinct possibility that this label has been used to subsume a multiplicity of factors.

An investigator's stand on the specificity-generality issue may influence his methods of research. A proponent of dependency as a unitary general concept would be more likely to rely on overall nonspecific and composite indicators of dependency than would a research worker committed to a multidimensional construct. This suggested causal sequence may, of course, operate just as readily in the reverse order: chosen method may influence theoretical commitment. If halo effects operate when ratings or interview reports of several different components of dependency are given, then intercorrelations of such components are elevated, and the likelihood that the investigator will accept a generalized unidimensional concept of dependency is enhanced. If, on the other hand, an investigator uses behavioral observation of mutually exclusive actions presumed to measure dependency, the fact of mutual exclusiveness might readily be reflected in low intercorrelations among the components, evidence that could lead the investigator away from the acceptance of the generality hypothesis.

In our own research we have made no effort to resolve the generality-specificity issue. Our own data deal exclusively with verbal reports of dependency behavior, and we recognize that under certain circumstances such reports may lead to a spurious conclusion concerning the consistency of behavior. Our use of multiple sources of data and multiple items within each source permits a close appraisal of certain measurement issues common to verbal data-collection efforts of this kind.

In the present study, as has been generally the case in interview and questionnaire assessments in this area, several different items provide measures of children's dependency. The three facets of such behavior about which we have inquired are "attention wanted," "closeness wanted," and "separation anxiety." At two different times measures of each of these aspects were obtained from the mothers of children in our sample, and a similar set of measures has come from ratings made by the children's teachers. The items used on each of the data-collection occasions are presented in Table 1. Clearly the three sets of items do not represent exact repetitions: there are differences in content, in data sources, in the times when the items were asked, and in techniques of eliciting and scoring responses. Yet despite such differences, a presumption that the three sets are attempting to tap into the same components of children's dependent behavior seems, at the outset at least, a reasonable one.

The paragraphs that follow deal with two basic questions concerning the measures of reported dependency used in this study. First, the question of *intra*set consistency: *within* each of the three data sources (mother interview, mother questionnaire, or teacher ratings) how well do reports about several different indicators of children's dependent behavior agree? Second, the question of *inter*set consistency: when presumably comparable indicators of dependency are employed with different data sources, do similar dependency appraisals result?

Table 1

MEASURES OF DEPENDENCY

Source	Attention Wanted	Closeness Wanted	Separation Anxiety
Mother interview	How much attention does X seem to want from you? (V 29)	Does he follow you around and hang on to you? (V 30)	How does X react generally when you go out and leave him at home with someone else? (V 31)
Mother questionnaire	Is very demanding of adults' time and attention, wants a lot of help. (V 39)	Shy in a social situation, loses confidence on his own, stays close to an adult. (V 40)	Gets upset when mother leaves, does not accept her departure readily. (V 41)
Teacher rating	How much attention does X seem to want from you? (V 44)	Does he follow you around, hang on to you, or try to be near you? (V 45)	How did X react in the beginning when his mother left him at school? (V 46)

Mother interviews. Mothers were asked questions concerning the extent to which the child wanted the mother's attention (V 29), the degree to which he followed and clung to her (V 30), and his reaction to his mother's leaving him at home with someone else (V 31).[1] For each of the three areas concerned with dependency, intercoder reliability in application of seven-point scales was satisfactory. (Correlations ranged from .72 to .82.) When adjudicated ratings (see p. 16 for coding procedures) of mothers' responses to each of these questions were correlated to yield information on intraset reliability, the relationships, though not as high as for intercoder reliability, suggested consistency in appraisal from one item to another (from .42 to .57 for the sexes combined).[2] (See Table 2). To provide additional context for these correlations one may note that interitem correlations for the three comparable questions in the Sears,

[1] For question wording, see the first row of items in Table 1. To obtain a flavor of the raw data note the replies to these questions given by one mother.

Attention wanted: "Oh, I don't know if there's too much difference in what each one demands. They both demand an awful lot of attention. They get entirely too much attention. That they're (we're) very conscious of." This was coded 5, the numerical equivalent of a mother's report that her child wanted "quite a bit" of attention.

Closeness wanted: "No, they don't hang on to me, but they like me near. But that's not always the same either. Sometimes I like to get out of the (company of the youngsters) and study and read the newspaper and just have a cup of tea and just be alone. Well, they don't like it. They want to come in with me. They like to be just about where I am. Some days I notice are not as bad as others. . . . But they stick sure close to me. They don't hang on me, that's something I could never take, is hanging on me. They've tried it but I couldn't go along with that." This, too, was rated 5—less than maximum dependency, but clearly indicating some tendency.

Separation anxiety: "I find if I stay very close to them, which I usually do, they resent it very much and I found if I (leave them more often), it doesn't bother them so much. They accept it quicker. Sometimes they both cry terribly. Sometimes it doesn't make any difference." A rating of 4, midway between the two extreme scores, was assigned to this response.

[2] Unless otherwise noted, all intercorrelations reported in our discussion of dependency measures are those based on the combination of data for boys and girls. The intercorrelations for the sexes considered separately are, however, included for reader perusal in Table 2.

Table 2

INTERCORRELATION OF DEPENDENCY MEASURES

(TOTAL SAMPLE, MALES, AND FEMALES)

			Mother Interview				Mother Questionnaire				Teacher Ratings			
Source	Variable Number	Measure	29	30	31	28	39	40	41	38	44	45	46	43
Mother interview	29	Attention wanted	—	58* / 54*	56* / 35*	87* / 78*	24 / 21	12 / 20	15 / 34*	26 / 33*	-02 / 48*	06 / 36	35 / 47*	17 / 62*
	30	Closeness wanted	57*	—	38* / 50*	80* / 85*	27 / 24	23 / 27	54* / 19	51* / 32*	10 / 20	-00 / 08	35 / 19	20 / 22
	31	Separation anxiety	46*	42*	—	79* / 78*	12 / 31*	10 / 13	22 / 35*	22 / 36*	-22 / -10	-12 / -05	50* / 53*	06 / 18
	28	Summed dependency	83*	82*	78*	—	26 / 31*	18 / 25	37* / 36*	40* / 42*	-07 / 26	-03 / 17	50* / 52*	17 / 45*
Mother questionnaire	39	Attention wanted	21*	23*	20	27*	—	-04 / 25	23 / 37*	62* / 73*	04 / -24	-09 / 00	16 / 19	05 / -02
	40	Closeness wanted	15	24*	11	20	12	—	20 / 28	59* / 70*	-09 / -05	16 / 06	32 / 20	17 / 10
	41	Separation anxiety	25*	34*	28*	35*	30*	25*	—	74* / 76*	20 / 24	19 / 21	45* / 33	37* / 37*
	38	Summed dependency	28*	37*	28*	39*	68*	66*	75*	—	08 / -07	12 / 10	50* / 33	30 / 17
Teacher Ratings	44	Attention wanted	19	16	-18	06	-09	-09	19	-01	—	82* / 61*	16 / 11	86* / 82*
	45	Closeness wanted	20	08	-09	08	-07	08	13	06	74*	—	19 / 01	87* / 77*
	46	Separation anxiety	40*	28*	50*	50*	17	25	39*	39*	14	11	—	58* / 53*
	43	Summed dependency	35*	23	10	29*	01	11	32*	20	84*	83*	56*	—

Maximum sample sizes on which correlations are based: Mother Interview and Mother Questionnaire, 86 (43 boys, 43 girls) ; Teacher Ratings, 58 (30 boys, 28 girls). Data on total sample are below the diagonal. In each cell above the diagonal the correlations for girls are indicated immediately beneath those for boys. Correlations significant at or beyond the 5 per cent level are indicated by an asterisk in this and all other tables of the text.

Maccoby, Levin schedule (questions 30, 30a, and 31) ranged from .17 to .50 (1957, p. 524). Such interitem correspondence makes the idea of a single summated measure of reported dependency combining responses to these three items quite reasonable. Thus, in addition to using measures indicative of responses to the separate items, subsequent discussion includes a score (V 28) based on the summation of standardized scores for each of the three items. A correlation of such summed scores for these items appraised by independent coders yields the sizeable coefficient of .87. Further, each item shows a reasonably strong relation to a score that is the summation of the other two. (For our total sample these correlations range from .50 to .62.[3]) Such an appraisal, at once more conservative and more meaningful than one in which each item is related to a score of which it is itself a part, continues to support the view that, whatever these mother-interview items are measuring, they seem to represent different facets of what is essentially one concept. Do our other two sets of dependency appraisals present the same picture when we examine their intraset consistency?

Mother questionnaires. Several months prior to being interviewed, mothers filled out a questionnaire. As a part of this process, for each of the three dependency items listed in the second row of Table 1 mothers checked one of five possible responses (from "yes, definitely," to "no, definitely"), indicating "how well the following descriptions fit your child." The intraset correlations of these items reveal a picture at variance with the measures resulting from the interview questions that permitted the mother a considerably more open response (see Table 2). Only two of the three item intercorrelations are statistically significant (the smallest is .12; the larg-

[3] It is possible, of course, to correlate each separate item with the overall measure of which it is a part. (These correlations, ranging from .78 to .83, appear in the appropriate cells of Table 1.) Such an approach is, however, at best problematic; it leads to a spuriously high coefficient. As is well known, if n items have equal variances and are independent of one another, the correlation between the scores on any item and the summed scores of which it is itself a part is $\dfrac{1}{\sqrt{n}}$. Thus, given three such items summed to provide a single score, the correlation between one of these items and the summated score is $\dfrac{1}{\sqrt{3}}$, or .58.

est, .30), and when each item is correlated with a summed score of the other two, the three correlations range from .22 to .38. (Two of the three items assessing dependency were located next to one another near the beginning of a series of 26 requiring similar check-list responses, the third appeared in the latter half of the series. As an inspection of correlations revealed, however, this matter of item location was clearly not a major factor influencing the magnitude of interitem relationships.) Such information suggests that a composite score based on these particular questionnaire responses should be used with considerable caution; though the aspects of reported dependency here measured have something in common, they nevertheless do not blend together in a straightforward unidimensional mix.

Teacher ratings. In individual interviews, each of two teachers independently used seven-point rating scales to characterize two aspects of the child's current dependence on her (attention wanted and closeness wanted) and to indicate the nature of the child's reaction to separation from the mother at the beginning of the school year. As one may see in Table 1, the questions addressed to teachers were very nearly identical to those of the mother interview.

A dimension-by-dimension comparison of the ratings of the two teachers shows that for two of the three areas of dependency considered, the child in the eyes of one teacher yielded an impression similar to, but not identical with, the impression held by the other. (Interteacher reliability of ratings of the amount of attention the child wanted from the teacher was .44; that for closeness wanted, .42—both significant correlations, but not high enough to indicate identity of measurement.) For the third item, that concerned with teachers' ratings of the child's reactions to separation from the mother, the coefficient was substantially higher, .67.

Interitem correlations (combining information from the two raters of each child) range from .74 (for the relation between teacher ratings of the child's attention seeking [V 44] and his attempting to be near the teacher [V 45]) to the exceedingly modest correlations of .14 and .11 denoting the relation of each of these items to the teachers' appraisals of the child's reaction to separation from his mother at the beginning of the school year (V 46) (see

Table 2). Such slight correlations as these latter two argue against the suitability of a score combining these three items,[4] yet such a combination, paralleling the additive combinatorial procedure followed for mother interviews and mother questionnaires, can be made. When such summed scores obtained from each teacher separately are correlated with one another, the between-teacher reliability coefficient is .47. When the two teachers' ratings of each separate item are pooled and the ratings on each item are then correlated with the sum of the other two, the values are .53, .44, and .13. The lowest coefficient of the lot is the one relating teacher appraisal of the child's reaction to separation from the mother with a score summing two items concerned with the child's dependency on the teacher. Given the pattern of intercorrelations presented in this paragraph, we are left with an uncomfortable feeling that this single composite measure of dependency derived from teacher ratings falls well short of adequacy as a unidimensional appraisal.

Intraset consistency: A summing up. Given three sources of data on dependency (two from mothers and one from teachers), for only one of these, the mother interview, is there clear indication of consistency in the components of an overall measure intended as an assessment of a single conceptual entity. What accounts for the strange behavior of these three sets of items that purportedly measure the same phenomenon, the general dependency of the child? Some steps toward an answer can be taken by considering certain general aspects of each set of items.

Paradoxically, a type of specificity and a type of generality may work together to produce the consistency evident in the mother-interview responses. On the side of specificity, note that each of the three items in the set inquires about one and the same relationship, that between the mother and the child. The situation is clearly defined, the behavioral dimension appropriately specified, and the

---

[4] If one relies only on the ratings made by the head teachers (who had more teaching experience than their assistants), the nature of the item intercorrelations remains practically unchanged; the corresponding values are .71, .15, and .09, respectively. That teacher ratings of children's reactions to separation from their mother show both greater inter-rater reliability and less interitem correspondence is a matter that warrants further consideration at another point in our discussion (see p. 33).

mother is asked explicitly to characterize the child's behavior in relation to herself. As for generality, this is resident in the nature of the responses elicited. The mother freely replied to each question. This open report was later coded along a seven-point continuum. In such circumstances, a halo effect may manifest itself in two ways: The mother herself may communicate a general impression of the child that then gets reflected in the subsequent coding; and the coder, too, may form a general impression that has an impact on the precise ratings assigned in the scoring of the mother's statements about her child.

In contrast to the interview, of the three dependency items to which the mother responded on the questionnaire, only one (that concerned with the child's reaction to separation) dealt explicitly with mother-child relations. Another item, though intended as a measure of reported dependency, might well prove to be a mix of several variables, since the mother was asked to encompass in one reply the extent to which this description, "shy in a social situation, loses confidence on his own, stays close to an adult," characterized her child. Thus, at least after the fact, the lack of striking interitem consistency in this set appears not too remarkable.

Two of the three ratings made by the teachers dealt with the child's dependency on the teacher (wanting attention and wanting closeness). Inter-*rater* correspondence was definitely less on each of these two items than for teachers' ratings of the child's reaction to separation from the mother, even though the latter item required a retrospective report five to seven months after the fact. Yet, when ratings of pairs of teachers were combined on each of the items, interitem correlations were far greater for ratings of attention wanted and closeness wanted from the teacher than the correlation of either of these items with the rating of the child's reaction to separation from his mother. These two pieces of evidence suggest that both *relation-specific* and *situation-specific* factors contribute to consistency (or its absence) in such measures of reported dependency. To the extent that these two potential sources of variation do indeed exist, even highly reliable reports on such behavior might not lead to correlations much different from those obtained.

Our data show that the patterning of relationships among

the items used to measure dependency varies in each set. We have suggested factors that might possibly account for such variations in intraset consistency. The necessary next step is an appraisal of the consistency among presumably similar measures coming from different data sources.

INTERSET CONSISTENCY

This portion of our exploration of verbal reports of dependency approaches the material from a perspective that considers the nature of the correspondence *across* our three sets of data: mothers' interview responses, their replies on a questionnaire, and teachers' ratings.

Summated ratings. Although our data have tended to cast doubt on the uniform utility of a summated (and hence a presumptively unidimensional) appraisal of dependency, let us nevertheless see how such measures separately derived from maternal interviews, check-list questionnaire responses by mothers, and teacher ratings relate to one another. Such overall ratings from mother interviews (V 28) are significantly correlated with those from mother questionnaires (V 38) ($r = +.39$, $p < .01$). Also significantly related, but not as highly correlated, are the summated dependency scores of mother interviews and teacher ratings (V 43) ($r = .29$, $p < .05$). In the right direction, but not significant, is the $+.20$ coefficient indicating the relation between the summated dependency ratings from mother questionnaires and those from teacher ratings.

Three possible contributors to such differential consistency are the nature of the items, the information source, and the time intervals between the collection of the several sets of data. We cannot directly assess the impact of these factors, but it is pertinent to note that the greatest correspondence occurs in the summated scores coming from a single source, the mother. This is the case despite the fact that the average time interval separating the mother interview and mother questionnaire (seven months) was considerably greater than that separating the mother interview and teacher ratings (two months). Further, the lowest overall correspondence occurred when summated ratings from mother questionnaires were compared with those from teachers; here, the longest time interval (nine months on the average) as well as difference in source and in items may all be exerting some weight.

Specific items. Cross-set comparison of items presumed at the outset to be tapping the same aspects of dependency has two possible contributions. It provides a perspective on the extent to which given items, with their differing formats and their differing response sources, yield the same pictures on each child considered. Moreover, such comparisons may clarify some of the factors involved in determining the level of reliability of the summated appraisals of dependency.

When one looks at the measures of interset consistency among the several items, two major conclusions can readily be teased out. First, the items demonstrating greatest cross-set reliability possess these two characteristics: they deal with one very specific relationship, that of mother and child, and they deal with one unambiguous set of behavioral circumstances, the child's reaction to separation from his mother. The three intercorrelations that result from the comparison of items eliciting information about the child's reaction to separation from the mother put appraisals in this area head and shoulders above the other interitem comparisons. (Mother interview [V 31] and teacher ratings [V 46] correlate .50; mother questionnaire [V 41] and teacher ratings, +.39; and interview and questionnaire, +.28. In our data on dependency no other cross-set comparison of presumably similar items yields a correlation coefficient as high as the lowest of these three.)

The second conclusion (that in a sense is a further clarification of the first) that can be drawn from scanning these measures of interset consistency among the specific items is this: The items that show the least correspondence across the several sets are those in which the teacher is appraising the child as he relates to the teacher herself, while the mother describes the child either as he relates to the mother or as he relates to adults in general. One lesson to be drawn from such comparisons as these is readily apparent. Mothers and teachers may be imprecise measuring instruments at best. This imprecision is compounded when we, either in our measurement of given characteristics or in our assessment of reliability of such measurement, use items that are inappropriate because of their omnibus nature (their attempt to capture in one net several facets of a very broad conceptual entity) or that are equally inappropriate because they fail to require assessment dealing with a specific type of behavior manifested in a specific situation or a specific relationship.

This scrutiny of our measures of dependency suggests that their use should be contemplated with considerable caution. Yet since these techniques bear a close resemblance to those often used by others in interview, questionnaire, or rating assessment of dependency, it is reasonable now to ask the two following questions: Do our measures of dependency show any systematic link with interview measures of presumed antecedents of such behavior? How do the results of such an analysis of correlates of dependency compare with the findings and interpretations of others?

◼ REPLICATION OF FINDINGS ◼

Despite the fact that a major motif in children's development is one of increased independence with advancing age, not every child moves toward autonomy at the same rate and in the same style. To account for such variations has been a goal pursued by numerous investigators. A matter of some strategic significance is the decision concerning the point or points on the developmental continuum that are most relevant to the appraisal of conditions leading to dependent behavior. Should primary emphasis be placed on current parental practices and other contemporary factors, or should one principally confine one's quest for causation to examination of early treatment of the infant? Theory suggests that a child's early developmental experiences and here-and-now influences may alike be relevant.[5] In our own methodologically oriented efforts to confirm some of the findings in this area, however, we have limited our attention to *current* correlates of child dependency. Although we present no data assessing effects of infant experience, it is worth noting that evidence on the role of such influences is by no means clear-cut, consistent, and unambiguous.[6]

[5] For a brief summary of theoretical issues in the study of dependency, see Hartup, 1963, pp. 345–347.

[6] In pulling together their own research findings, Sears et al. (1957)

Much of the recent work on contemporary correlates of dependency is based on the principles of social learning that were briefly presented in Chapter 1. Such research has frequently had as its point of departure the effort to examine social stimulus events that might be viewed as causal agents in children's dependent behavior. Four classes of variables that have been hypothesized, either singly or in combination, as potential influences are the following: (1) the general nature of the affectional bond linking mother and child, (2) parental response to dependency, (3) general techniques of discipline and control, and (4) the handling of aggression to parents. For each of these areas we ask first, does our own research evidence give clear and convincing support to a link with the measures that here serve to index various facets of reported dependency? Second, do our data parallel the results of other inquiries?

PROCEDURE FOR SUMMARIZING DATA

Showing the relationship of each of several potential correlates of dependency to each of several measures of reported dependency is a formidable task: Three specific measures of dependency (attention wanted, closeness wanted, and separation anxiety) and a fourth, a summated dependency measure, have been obtained for three different sets of data (mother interviews, mother questionnaires, and teacher ratings). Correlating any single presumed antecedent variable with each of these measures of dependency yields twelve coefficients. If, in addition to looking at the information from the total sample, we also examine the magnitude of the relationship for each sex separately, we need to appraise a total of 36 correla-

---

appropriately characterized the state of the art when they said, "In sum, we have found little to indicate that there are massive effects of the infant experiences we have examined, so far as later dependency is concerned" (p. 160). And in a subsequent volume (Sears et al., 1965), in which parental reports of their children's infancy experiences are viewed as possible antecedents of dependency as objectively measured in observation of behavior, an essentially similar conclusion is reached: ". . . amount of reinforcement in infancy may or may not be influential for later dependency; present measurements of both child-rearing and child-behavior variables are unable to demonstrate or refute any such influence" (p. 47).

tions for each of 15 variables that we would like to relate to dependency, or 540 correlations in all. Rather than bombarding the reader with such a quantity of correlation coefficients, we shall simply report the extent to which the three different sources of data show a *consistent* relationship with each variable in question for any given index of dependency and any group of subjects (that is, correlations with the same sign, regardless of magnitude), and consistent or not, the extent to which *any significant* correlations are present.[7] (Examining for consistency of sign appears to us to be a fairly lenient criterion for suggesting the plausibility of a relation between variables; statistical significance is a somewhat more rigorous one. Sheer magnitude of correlation might, of course, have been chosen as a criterion, but without an assessment of significance, this would beg the question of the stability of the relationship.) Quite clearly, this represents an extensive milking of the data. And if both current conceptualizations of dependency correlates and the methods here employed to measure dependency and its presumptive correlates are reasonable, this should result in a veritable flood of significant relationships. The reader may rest easy on that score, however; such a flood will not take place.

[7] Our appraisal of consistency is based on the comparison of the signs of the three correlations specifying the relationship of a given independent variable to a given index of dependency as this latter is separately derived from each of the three data sources. The *presence* of such consistency is indicated in Table 3 by the notation *C;* the *direction* of such consistent correlations is conveyed by a plus or minus sign preceding the indication of consistency. When any *significant* correlation between a presumed dependency antecedent and a given dependency measure from a particular data source occurs, this is noted in the appropriate column and row of the table by an abbreviated specification of the data source (MI, MQ, or TR) with the sign of the coefficient preceding it. For example, if the dimension to be associated with dependency is affectional demonstrativeness (V 24), and if the measure of dependency is separation anxiety (V's 41, 31, and 46), Table 3 shows that these dimensions were consistently positively related to one another in the findings for the total sample (that is, separation anxiety, as appraised by mother interview, mother questionnaire, and teacher ratings, in *each* instance correlated positively with affectional demonstrativeness). Similar consistency occurred in the data for boys, but not for girls. It is evident that none of the 12 correlations examined for this portion of the table reached the 5 per cent level of statistical significance.

DEPENDENCY AND THE AFFECTIONAL BOND

Four variables that characterize the mother's orientation toward the child are maternal warmth (V 23), affectional demonstrativeness (V 24), "maternal acceptance" as measured by the number of things the mother reports enjoying in her child (V 26), and "rejection," a report of the annoying things in the child (V 25).[8] Of these, only one—that of maternal warmth—shows any major indication of a systematic relation to our data on dependency (see Table 3). Even here, "major" is a relative matter, one to be viewed in the context of the generally inconsistent and impoverished relationships revealed by the other variables. With four dependency indices (three specific measures and a summated index) and three groups of subjects (the total sample, and boys and girls viewed separately), 12 *consistency* appraisals can be made for associations with warmth. For eight of these, consistency in the signs of correlations is the case; warmth is associated with dependency. And for seven of the 36 correlation coefficients, the 5 per cent level of significance was reached. (This trend is not as marked among the girls. In two of four cases, consistency is evident, but not one of the 12 correlations involved reaches the 5 per cent level.) A general appraisal of our data suggests that a link between reports of a child's dependency and his mother's characterization of the affectional bond is a possibility.

This possibility loses much of its momentum when we note findings reported in some other studies concerned with maternal correlates of child dependency. Becker, Peterson, Luria, Shoemaker, and Hellmer (1962, pp. 522–523) found no significant relation between interview-based ratings of warmth or hostility of the mother and two maternal interview measures of dependency of the child. Kagan and Moss's (1962, Appendix 10, p. 314) examination of the Fels data showed no significant relation between observational rat-

---

[8] Each of these measures derives from interview information provided by the mother. Intercorrelations ranged from pronounced (.67) to negligible (.00) (see Appendix B). Four of the six intercorrelations were statistically significant. Warmth showed a sizeable relation to each of the other variables. "Rejection" was the one measure that fitted relatively poorly with the others in the set; only with warmth was it significantly associated.

Table 3

CORRELATIONS OF DEPENDENCY MEASURES WITH MEASURES OF REPORTED MATERNAL BEHAVIOR

Variable Number	Reported Maternal Behavior	Summed Dependency			Attention Wanted			Closeness Wanted			Separation Anxiety		
		Total Sample	Boys	Girls	Total Sample	Boys	Girls	Total Sample	Boys	Girls	Total Sample	Boys	Girls
	Affectional relations:												
23	Warmth	+C +MI	+C +MI	+C	+MI	+MI		+C	+C		+C +MI +TR	+C +MI	+C
24	Affectional demonstrative-ness				-MQ	-MQ		+C	+C		+C	+C	
25	Annoying things about child						+C	+C	+C				
26	Things enjoyed in child						+C					+C	
11	Response to dependency	+C		+C +TR	+C +MQ	+MQ	+C				+C		+C
	General techniques of control:												
1	Isolation		-C	+C	+MI		+C	+C		+C		-C	
2	Love withdrawal	-TR	-TR		-TR	-TR		-TR	-C -TR		+MI	+MI	
4	Tangible rewards					-TR					+MI	+MI	

38

#	Scale							
5	Deprivation of privileges		−C			+C	−MQ	−C, −MQ
6	Physical punishment	+TR	+TR	−C	+TR	−C	+TR	
19	Restrictiveness: overall	+C	+C	+C	+TR	+C	+C	+C
20	Severity of punishment: overall		+MI	+C, +MQ				+C
	Techniques of control for aggression to parents:							
7	Physical punishment for aggression to parents	+TR		−C			+MI, +TR	+C, +MI, +TR
13	Permissive of aggression to parents	+C			+C, +MQ	+C	−TR	
14	Severity of punishment for aggression to parents	+TR	+TR, +TR, +C		+TR	+C	+C	

Directionally consistent correlations across the three data sets are indicated by a table entry, C. Data sets yielding significant correlations are denoted by the following entries: MI (mother interview), MQ (mother questionnaire), and TR (teacher ratings). Directionality of consistent or significant correlations is indicated by the appropriate sign. In this and other tables presenting our data, the direction of the scales is such that the label indicates the high end of the scale; for example, restrictiveness, interval 7 means a high degree of restrictiveness.

ings of dependency of boys and girls at age three to six and ratings of maternal hostility at that same time. Sears, Maccoby, and Levin found that their interview measure of maternal warmth was essentially unrelated ($r = .08$) to mother's reports of dependency (pp. 168 and 372), although they also reported that both affectional demonstrativeness and maternal rejection of the child were significantly correlated with their dependency measure ($r = +.13$ and $+.12$ respectively) (pp. 168 and 525). The data from Sears et al. (1965) clearly do not supply the empirical support needed to strengthen the notion of a strong tie between childhood dependency and the affectional bond linking parent and child. Given six different behavioral measures of dependency and another six variables readily classified in the domain dealing with the mother's expression of affection and warmth, only one out of 36 correlations reached statistical significance for the girls, and only three of 36 for the boys (1965, pp. 51, 54, 56, 59, 60, and 65).[9]

With such absence of consistency in the results of other research inquiries and a somewhat similar lack of consistency in our own data, the safe conclusion at present is that no strong support for the view that child dependency simply and directly relates to the affectional bond between parent and child has been mustered. Whether the difficulty lies in methods of data collection, data handling, or theory, or possibly some combination of the three cannot be specified. But the central fact remains: the relationship has not been established. This somewhat disheartening state of affairs is a harbinger of the picture that emerges when other potential correlates of dependency are considered. The two dominant themes that result from this replication-oriented examination of data are that in our own research, correlations presumed to measure given antecedent-consequent relationships are neither strong nor directionally in ac-

[9] The dependency measures (and their associated variable numbers) considered by Sears, Rau, and Alpert were negative attention seeking (187), reassurance seeking (188), being near (221), touching and holding (220), positive attention seeking (219), and total observed dependency (224). Verbal data appraisals relevant to the mother's expression of affection are mother's warmth (118), affectional demonstrativeness (120), hostility (140), and her warmth factor score (174). Observation of mother-child interaction yielded additional scores of mother warmth (330) and hostility (343).

cord with one another; and further, a close look at the evidence provided by other studies yields little indication of hypothesis-supporting results that are systematically consistent across studies.

Parental response to dependency. Mothers' impressions of their handling of dependency were gauged in our own study by interview questions concerned with maternal reaction to the child's following or clinging, his attention demands when busy, and his efforts to solicit aid when none is needed. Mothers' replies were coded on a single seven-point scale ranging from a strong positive response, approval or reward of dependency, to a strong negative response (V 11).[10] How does this measure relate to the several indicators of dependency employed? Our data provide a mildly consistent picture of a slender relation between dependency (as appraised by mother and by teacher) and reported *low* permissiveness of dependency. Although this holds true for the total sample, the tendency results principally from the more consistent associations between these variables among girls than among boys. (Three of four sets of correlations are consistent for girls; none is for boys.) However real this trend may be, we should not overestimate its strength, since only three of 36 correlations that entered into these appraisals reached the 5 per cent level of significance.

To what extent have other studies reached the same conclusion? The nearest procedural parallel is that of Sears et al. (1957).[11] They interpret their data as showing that maternal irritation with and punishment for dependency ". . . made children more dependent than ever" (p. 171). "The more the mother behaved in this negative way when the child was dependent, the more dependent he was likely to be ($p < .01$; $r = .28$)" (p. 172). Their measures of reported reward and permissiveness of dependency, however, showed no relation to the interview-derived dependency index (p. 172).

---

[10] For question wording, see Appendix A, V 11. Coding reliability was poor; the reliability coefficient is .60. Only five of the seven possible score values were used; both extremes went untouched. Over four-fifths of the code judgments were concentrated in the three middle categories.

[11] Our own study has used interview questions identical to those employed by Sears, Maccoby, and Levin to tap mothers' handling of dependency.

From further analyses they noted, "Only when punishment was superimposed upon a fair amount of reward was there an increase in the child's tendency to show the very behavior he was being punished for" (p. 173).[12]

Data reported by Kagan and Moss (1962) yield a clear picture of results. But this does not fit with the limited pattern noted in our own inquiry, nor does it closely match that of Sears, Maccoby, and Levin. Observational ratings of "maternal protection" (a measure of reward of dependency and prevention of independent development) when the child is in the three-to-six-year age range showed a strong positive association with dependency (.48 for boys, .44 for girls) in the preschool children of the Fels study (p. 314).

Partially in line with the Fels data is information from the Sears, Rau, and Alpert (1965) inquiry, yielding some evidence that girls observed to be high on dependency were those whose parents were characterized (in interview and observational data) as rewarding or not punishing dependency. Again, however, the evidence, though suggestive, does not provide solid support for theory. Six measures of dependency and five of mothers' reward, punishment, or permissivity of dependency yield 30 correlation coefficients, of which only five were significant among the girls; and none of the 30 reached a statistically significant level for the boys.[13]

To further complicate the picture, it should be noted that yet another study, that of Sears, Whiting, Nowlis, and Sears (1953), presents a picture of "a positive relation, in boys, between preschool dependency behavior and current non-nurturance and frustration,"

[12] Since we employed only one coded measure of maternal response to dependency in our study, we cannot examine our data to see whether the dual appraisal of reward and punishment would yield results similar to those obtained by Sears, Maccoby, and Levin. Such a state of affairs is, of course, clearly in line with the hypothesized strengthening role of conflict presented by Whiting and Child (1953).

[13] For dependency measures, see footnote 9, this chapter. Mothers' reports of their reactions to dependency (with associated variable numbers) were permissiveness for dependency (124), use of reward for dependency (126), and use of punishment for dependency (128). Observation of mother-child interaction provided additional measures of the mother's use of reward for dependency (328) and her use of punishment for dependency (329). See Sears et al. (1965), pp. 51, 54, 56, 59, 60, and 65 for relevant tables.

and "a negative relation between these variables in girls" (p. 193). (Although their results are generally in accord with the quoted statements, here too it should be noted that the data are not consistent throughout.)

Since there does not appear to be a consistent picture emerging from the results of such studies as those here reported, it is premature to suggest that any sort of clear relation between children's dependency strivings and parental responses to such behavior has been established by relevant research data.

REPORTED DEPENDENCY AND PARENTS' TECHNIQUES OF CONTROL

Table 3 lists seven general control techniques whose relations to measures of reported dependency have been obtained. For that portion of the table 252 correlations have been examined.[14] Of these, only 18 reached the 5 per cent level of significance. Eight of these significant correlations occurred when love withdrawal (V 2) was the control technique under consideration. And of these eight, six stemmed from teachers' ratings of dependency: children whose mothers' interview responses indicated use of love withdrawal as a disciplinary measure were rated by teachers as less dependent. (These significant results apply to the total sample and to the boys; no similar results obtained among the girls.) As usual, the picture becomes clouded by the addition of a few more strokes: The other two significant correlations between dependency measures and reported use of love withdrawal are in a direction opposite to the six deriving from teacher ratings. Mother-interview reports of separation anxiety are positively associated with reports of the use of love withdrawal for the total sample, and this is especially evident in the data for boys.

Unproductive of significant findings, but worth noting because of the consistency displayed is the overall restrictiveness measure (V 19). Children of mothers who were scored high on the dimension of restrictiveness were generally appraised by mothers and

[14] Each technique has been correlated with four different measures of reported dependency from each of three data sources, and these correlations have been computed for the total sample, and for boys and girls considered separately.

teachers as high on dependency. (Once again, as Table 3 indicates, such consistency holds principally for boys.) The magnitude of the correlations is not sufficient, however, for one to wax enthusiastic about the firmness of the findings; only one of 36 correlations was statistically significant.

No other one of the general control techniques included in our appraisal led to a possibility of a systematic link between the reported use of such techniques and the several measures of dependency. Mothers' reported use of physical punishment (V 6), deprivation of privileges (V 5), isolation (V 1), tangible rewards (V 4), and a measure of severity of overall punishment (V 20) yielded only nine significant correlations out of 180, and directional consistency of the correlations (whether significant or not) was not noticeably present.

From our evidence, then, any support for a hypothesis concerning a simple linear relation between reported dependency and reported general parental control practices is at best equivocal. Moreover, data from other studies, when carefully examined, do not in fact lead to an interpretation noticeably at variance with that presented here.

For discussion economy, let us deal primarily with information pertinent to parental restrictiveness and love withdrawal, the two areas in the disciplinary realm that showed possibilities of a relationship with measures of child dependence in our data. Sears, Maccoby, and Levin found that mothers who reported using withdrawal of love as a disciplinary technique were significantly more likely than others to characterize their child as dependent (p. 525). Our own data partially support this finding; mothers' interview reports of children's separation anxiety were significantly related to reported use of love withdrawal (in the total sample and among boys, but not for girls). The weight of this evidence is lessened, however, when we observe that for other facets of maternal reports of child dependency (attention wanted, closeness wanted, and the summed dependency appraisal) correlations are not only not significant, they are not always even in the same direction as the two significant associations reported. That the teachers' ratings of high dependency are in six of twelve instances significantly associated with maternal reports of *low* use of love withdrawal, and that all 12 of the correlations of such teacher ratings of dependency are in the same direction certainly alters the picture. At the very least this would suggest situational variability in dependent behavior. Clearly the fact that teacher ratings of dependency and mother reports of the use of love withdrawal were made independently places these latter correlations on a different conceptual level from those in which the mother alone is the source of information about both the dependent and the independent variable.[15]

Is the generally consistent positive relation between reported dependency and maternal restrictiveness, a pattern evident in our own results, consonant with data from other studies? Not to any appreciable extent. Marshall (1961, p. 61) found no strong link between observational assessments of children's dependence on teachers and mothers' scores on a parental attitude inventory scale of suppression and distance, a measure conceptually similar to (but not identical with) maternal restrictiveness. Indices (with their associated variable numbers) used by Sears, Rau, and Alpert (1965) that might be viewed as falling in the domain of maternal restrictiveness are the following: mother's pressure for conformity to standards (45), strictness of mother (76), mother's nonpermissiveness factor score (173), and mother's pressure for obedience as rated from observation of mother-child interaction (341). When, for boys and girls considered separately, these measures were related to the six observational measures of dependency, only four of the 48 correlations reached a statistically significant level (1965, pp. 41, 54, 56, 59, 60, and 65). And Kagan and Moss's (1962, p. 314) data show only a slight, clearly nonsignificant relationship between dependency and maternal restrictiveness during the three-to-six age span.

Thus, once again it appears that there is evidence of a lack of consistent and statistically significant research results when one inspects information from several studies.

[15] For consideration of the issue of independence or lack of independence in sources providing presumed antecedent and consequent measures, see p. 80.

REPORTED DEPENDENCY AND THE HANDLING
OF AGGRESSION TO PARENTS

Sears, Maccoby, and Levin found (as did we) no systematic correspondence between dependency measures and mothers' total reported use of physical punishment, deprivation of privileges, and isolation. But when they examined the relation between the mother's report of child dependency and her punishing the child for aggressive acts directed toward the parent, they found a small ($r = .15$) but statistically significant relationship (p. 525). They proffered the following logical explanation:

> We suspect that the reason punishment for aggression proved to be significant here is that the child's aggression toward the parent is in itself an action which threatens the affectional bond between them. Possibly the parent's response has the quality of a response in kind—it may mean "All right, if you don't love me, I don't love you either." Such implications evidently provide a stimulus . . . for the child to seek reassurance that his parent does in fact still love him (p. 171).

Data from our effort at replication do not, unfortunately, give unambiguous support to the Sears, Maccoby, Levin finding, though some support is indeed there. When maternal interview measures of permissiveness of aggression to parents (V 13), use of physical punishment for such aggression (V 7), and severity of punishment for aggression toward parents (V 14) are correlated with measures of reported dependency deriving from mother interviews, mother questionnaires, and teacher ratings, the signs of such correlations are only infrequently consistent across the three data sources. And when such cross-set consistency does obtain, the direction of the relationship is not always in accord with theory.

As can be seen in Table 3, the following sets of consistent correlations do fit the hypothesis that punishment for aggression to parents leads to high dependency: (1) the correlation linking physical punishment for aggression to parents with boys' separation anxiety as measured in each of our three data sets; (2) severity of such punishment correlated with attention wanted by girls; (3) severity of punishment and separation anxiety in the total sample; and (4) severity of punishment and boys' separation anxiety. Yet in four other instances of cross-set consistency, correlations of dependency measures and parental techniques for handling aggression toward parents are not in accord with the hypothesis.

Those correlations that reach significance do, however, in the main fit the proposition that punishment and dependency are positively associated. Ten of the 11 significant correlations are in line with the Sears, Maccoby, and Levin formulation, but these are only ten out of 108, so the strength of whatever relationship is revealed is not overwhelming.

In viewing our data on the association between reports of dependency and techniques of handling aggression toward parents, two additional observations need to be made. First, to the extent that there is evidence supporting the notion that there is a link between these measures, it manifests itself primarily in *teacher* appraisals of dependency. In 26 of 36 correlations examined, children whose mothers were classed as restrictive, using physical punishment, or severely punishing the child for aggression toward parents were generally rated by the teachers as more dependent (eight of these correlations were significant). Of the 72 relationships involving dependency measures deriving from *mother* report, only 28 were directionally in accord with the hypothesis, and of these 28, only two were significant. This suggests that perhaps the view offered by Sears, Maccoby, and Levin could be modified in the following manner: If the child interprets the mother's handling of parent-directed aggressive action as evidence of maternal rejection, he may seek reassurance in a dependent relationship with another maternal figure, his teacher.

The second relevant point is that the posited relationship is more pronounced among the boys than among the girls. For example, six significant correlations were noted for the boys, and 21 of the 36 were in the appropriate direction. For the girls, only 14 of the 36 had signs in accord with the hypothesized direction of the relationship, and there were no significant associations. This pattern may bear some kinship to part of the conclusion by Sears, Whiting,

Nowlis, and Sears (1953, p. 202) that "Maternal punitiveness was positively correlated with dependency in boys and negatively in girls." It has some correspondence as well with data from Sears, Rau, and Alpert in which the significant results show this same pattern of sex differences. The weight of the possible interstudy correspondence becomes much diminished, however, when we recall that the mother's *general* reported use of physical punishment (that is, not exclusively confined to punishment for aggression toward the parent), the measure more comparable to the index of Sears, Whiting, Nowlis, and Sears, showed no such similar systematic sex-related pattern of correlations. And, to continue the necessary qualification, it should be noted that only two of 48 correlations dealing with dependence and mothers' handling of aggression toward parents reached a significant level in the Sears, Rau, and Alpert study.[16]

In this area, then, as in several others, we must conclude that impressive stability of findings across studies simply does not exist.

◙ SOME METHODOLOGICAL ISSUES ◙

For the investigator interested in discerning a pattern in studies concerned with current correlates of dependency, the picture is discouraging, if the evidence presented here is at all representative. When one compares several studies attempting to uncover decisive maternal contributors to the dependent behavior of young children, the threads of systematic agreement from one study to another are slender. Thus it is not surprising that within our own data consistency of results is far from pronounced: When a measure of a presumed antecedent of dependency correlates significantly with a measure of dependency coming from one data source, such as the mother interview, it is not safe to predict that the same antecedent variable also shows a greater than chance association with measures of de-

---

[16] The four measures dealing explicitly with mothers' handling of aggression toward parents are mother's permissiveness for aggression toward parents (58), mother's use of punishment for aggression toward parents (60), and maternal attitude scales of punitiveness for aggression toward parents (168) and permissiveness for aggression toward parents (169).

pendency coming from our other sources, the mother questionnaires and teacher ratings.

Such failure to replicate could clearly stem from several factors: there may be deficiencies in conceptualization and theory; the difficulties could reside in data-collection procedures, instruments, and chosen approaches to data handling; or *both* method and theory could be implicated. We have ruled out extensive consideration of theory; although detailed conceptual critiques are clearly warranted, our own scope is more limited; we have confined our attention to problems of methodology as these can be explored by an appraisal of our own data and those of others.

To the extent that failure to replicate stems from problems in measurement of relevant variables, the difficulties could reside either in assessments of presumed causal factors, or consequent factors, or both. In this portion of our discussion we pay more attention to measures of dependency than to its presumed antecedents, for our alternative sources of dependency estimates have permitted an exploration that our measures of independent variables cannot provide. Thus, once again let us consider our three sources of data on dependency: mother interviews, mother questionnaires, and teacher ratings.

Is there a way of assessing the relative payoff of these three? If one assumes that the presumptive antecedents are indeed linked to dependency, and that inadequacies in measurement of such antecedents should not work differentially to the detriment of relationships with any one of the sets of dependency appraisals, a crude measure of relative performance exists. It is possible simply to inspect Table 3 to note the number of significant correlations obtained with our several sources. It is evident that mother interview, mother questionnaire, and teacher measures were not uniformly successful. Out of 540 correlations examined, only 41 reached a statistically significant level. Of these 41, eight resulted when measures of dependency were derived from mother questionnaires; 13, when such measures came from mother interviews; and 20, when teacher ratings served as dependency appraisals.[17] Reasons for such differences in yield are

[17] To achieve statistical significance, the correlations with TR's had

doubtless numerous. The design of our inquiry does not permit any clear separation of factors accounting for such variation in effectiveness, yet several plausible possibilities can be put forward for consideration.

One potential contributor to the poor payoff performance of the questionnaire is the temporal factor. This looms important for two reasons. First, the time interval separating questionnaire measures of dependency and interview measures considered childrearing correlates of dependency is sufficient to permit appreciable changes in behavior. The typical child in our sample was about three and one-half years old when his mother filled out the initial questionnaire; at the time of the maternal interview he was over four and had had over four months experience in his school group. The nature of his social experiences and development during the seven months that, on the average, intervened between the two measurements might be something other than a mere extrapolation of his developmental level at the earlier point in time. Furthermore, information on the presumed *antecedent* variables was obtained in the interview, *after* questionnaire reports on the presumed *consequent* dependency behavior. Only if mothers' functioning vis-à-vis their children is relatively unmodified during such intervals would such correlations be at all logically justified. Part of the low yield from the questionnaire-derived measures may also be the result of measurement error due to the lack of specificity in two of the items that has already been alluded to (see p. 31).

Why did the mother interview, that wheelhorse of research in child development, not prove more effective? It was employed in our study much as in a number of other inquiries, but it brought in little other than a random harvest. Perhaps one of the "virtues" of this instrument as it was used in our study is also one of its major

---

to be greater than that for MI's or MQ's, since TR's were available for only two-thirds of the cases. Thus, if sheer magnitude of correlation is used as a criterion, teacher ratings are still further differentiated from the other two sources of dependency measures. For example, of the 39 correlations equal or greater than ±.30, MQ measures account for only five; MI, for ten; and TR the remaining 24.

vices. Although questions were precisely formulated, open responses were sought. The rationale for this approach was the conventional one, that further structuring, including the use of check-list responses, would inhibit rapport and would fail to capture the subtle and unique character of parent-child relations in particular families. But unique responses remain unique responses. Their necessary reduction to quantifiable data presents problems of coder unreliability, and such unreliability has not been negligible in childrearing studies. One may inquire how much the nearly random nature of the relationships examined so far is attributable to this source of measurement error. This question will subsequently be examined in the context of childrearing studies of aggression.

For those instances in which the correlations from the interview appear systematic and stable, the possibility of a built-in measurement bias cannot be discounted, since both antecedent and consequent measures are alike derived from the mother's responses on a single interview. A specific example: Mother interview appraisals of child dependency entered into 180 correlations with interview reports of maternal behavior; for 13 of these the correlation coefficients were statistically significant. As is evident in Table 3, six of these correlations resulted when maternal warmth was considered as the antecedent variable. This unequal contribution of maternal warmth is perhaps most parsimoniously explained when one notes that material from *any* part of the interview could be used by the coder to score this characteristic of the mother. Thus, at the very least, a halo effect may be contributing to the number of significant correlations obtained. Some actual contamination of measurement may have resulted from the fact that the presumed antecedent and consequent measures were not independent of one another. (This issue of nonindependence receives fuller treatment in Chapters 3, 4, and 5.)

That teacher ratings of dependency yielded a few more significant correlations with interview reports of maternal functioning than did dependency measures from either the mother questionnaires or interviews might be viewed as an instance of methodological virtue triumphant (provided, of course, that we recognize that the triumph is a small one). Several factors support an argument that use of teacher ratings is procedurally more defensible than is the use of either of the other two sources of dependency appraisals. First, teacher-based measures are independent of the mother-interview measures used as antecedents, so any significant correlations of these estimates of maternal functioning and child behavior cannot be attributed to possible systematic bias deriving from a common source of information. Second, teacher-based measures show at least a degree of stable consensus; between-teacher correlations were roughly twice the size of correlations relating mother-interview and mother-questionnaire measures of dependency. Third, the technique of obtaining teacher ratings was one whereby the teacher, after formulating her general response to each question, then made a rating on a seven-point scale with associated descriptive labels for each scale point; this provided a standardization of approach not evident in our mother interviews and presented a descriptive specificity of rating points not possible in the maternal questionnaires. Admittedly, this rating procedure forces the teacher to fit her appraisal to a limited set of response categories. But this may be more of a virtue than a vice; such a Procrustean bed may well serve until a better Theseus comes along.

The better yield with the teacher ratings should not obscure the fact that even here results were meager. Only 24 of 180 correlations of teacher ratings of dependency and maternal variables derived from the mother interview were equal to or greater than .30. With relationships of this magnitude, how much have we explained? The answer to this question can be found in the well-known fact that the square of the correlation coefficient gives the proportion of the total variance that can be predicted from variations in the other. With a correlation of .30, that proportion is a slender one, just .09.

◘ *CONCLUSION* ◘

This discussion has focused in large part on problems in measurement of one of the variables in child development research, on a detailed analysis of components employed as indices of dependency. Our evaluations clearly raise questions concerning the adequacy of data dealing with this aspect of the child's behavior. Confidence in these indices and, perhaps, in the nature of the conceptualization of the variable has been undermined in two respects: First, different pieces of data from the same informant, presumably dealing with a single construct, do not yield uniformly consistent appraisals. Thus at the very least, the unitary nature of the concept, or the interchangeability of its measures, has been placed in doubt. Second, the impressions of different reporters do not coincide. If one assumes that each is reporting accurately, then the entity to be measured is not constant, or it is many-faceted and each reporter is referring to different aspects. Or, if one assumes that the entity has constancy, then one must conclude that the reporters serve as imprecise yardsticks. For several reasons, then, doubts remain concerning how substantially and consistently children can be ordered by verbal appraisals of this characteristic.

When one turns from measurement of dependency to developmental questions concerning its antecedents in maternal behavior, what has emerged? Slim and doubtful are the relations detected in our data and those of parallel studies in the field. Indeed, the methodologically oriented researcher may have concluded in advance that, given such demonstrated uncertainty in the measurement of the dependent variable, the search for systematic associations with maternal characteristics was in itself a foolhardy pursuit. But concentrated effort leading to a sound means of gauging dependent behavior would not alone clarify our understanding of the way parental practices shape this (or any other) aspect of the child's functioning. Additional questions are obviously relevant: Are the difficulties in finding satisfactory indices unique to dependency? May the insubstantial associations between these measures of dependency and their presumed antecedents be attributable in part to similar limitations in measurement of the independent variables? May analysis procedures also be inadequate for their intended task? Since only bivariate relationships have here been examined, hypotheses suggesting that child behavior is a resultant of complex learning contingencies remain untested.

These questions have their counterparts in other areas of personality development and will be among the issues treated in subsequent discussions. Although not to be discounted is the possibility that theory, rather than method, may be at fault, we would emphasize that satisfactory tests of relevant theoretical propositions can only be made when suitable measurement and analysis procedures are employed.

CHAPTER 3

Theories and Correlates of Child Aggression

As in our analyses of dependency data, the focus continues to be on the contributions of the methods of research to its findings. Within this broad issue, the specific questions we shall raise here in the context of aggression are: How adequate are the measures that have been used to tap the concepts of aggression and the theoretically relevant "antecedent" dimensions of maternal behavior? How equivalent are the various measures that are subsumed under the same conceptual labels? How regular and convincing are the "antecedent-consequent" findings? Are spurious positive relations as well as false negative findings built into research conclusions by the ways in which data are obtained, coded, and interpreted? How well suited are these data to the testing of antecedent-consequent hypotheses?

Aggression is an especially good area for methodological probings because there is an extensive body of research that has been pursued programmatically within the framework of an integrated set of hypotheses. Because there is similarity in design, instruments, and subjects, it is possible to examine closely the correspondence of findings across studies when procedural differences are at a minimum (when correspondence should be greatest). Furthermore, when measurement variations of different kinds exist, their contributions to the findings can be assessed.

▣ HYPOTHESIZED ANTECEDENTS OF AGGRESSION ▣

Since the beginnings of systematic child study, the aggressive responses of young children have interested investigators. Few dimensions of children's social behavior have received as much attention in psychological research. Although there has not been unanimity of viewpoints concerning the origins of aggression or the ways in which it is socialized, most of the studies have been formulated in a common key. The parents' (particularly the mother's) handling of the young child has been assumed to be a major factor determining variations of children's aggressive characteristics.

The explanatory framework that has become most familiar in childrearing studies of aggression and is common to most of the studies that we shall be reviewing is social learning theory. Its origins are in the Yale frustration-aggression research of the 1930's (Dollard, Doob, Miller, Mowrer, and Sears, 1939), which is the offspring of psychoanalytic and learning theories. This body of childrearing research covers a time span from the 1940's to the 1960's. Over this time there have been some changes in emphases and interests, reflecting changes in learning theory in general psychology. Throughout its history, however, research on aggression has focused on certain common factors in the child's socialization, namely the frustrations and punishments in the child's experience and the permission and reward he receives for aggressive behavior. These conditions, translated into rearing practices, are the restraints and demands imposed by the parent, the giving and withholding of nurturance or reward by the parent, and the methods used to control and discipline the child. An overview of the theoretical framework underlying the studies of this area will identify the set of interrelated hypotheses that has guided research on the conditions of maternal handling presumed to influence aggression in the child.

In their pioneering research in 1953, Sears, Whiting, Nowlis, and Sears approached the development of aggression and dependency in young children from the orientation of Hullian behavior theory. This was among the first major research efforts to treat child development data within a framework of general psychological theory. In this formulation frustration and punishment are the hypothesized instigations to aggression; the more severe the frustration or punishment, the stronger the hypothesized aggressive drive. Although severity is expected to strengthen drive, it is not necessarily expected to increase the frequency of overt aggressive behavior. Expression of aggression is conditional upon a number of factors. Thus, when punishment is severe, the specifically punished acts and aggressive acts toward the agent of punishment are likely to be inhibited. Aggressive responses may be manifested in other circumstances, however, in which the likelihood of punishment is reduced. Severe punishment may also lead to generalized inhibition of aggression, particularly in circumstances similar to those of the original punishment. Aggression, it is hypothesized, is also influenced by reward and permissiveness, both presumably serving to increase aggressive responses.

The frequency and intensity with which aggression appears in child behavior are viewed, then, as determined by both excitatory and inhibitory factors, and by conflict-produced drive arising from the combined presence of these factors. Under conditions of excitation and inhibition, of approach-avoidance conflict, it is hypothesized that not only is there a decrease in aggression toward the punisher (the mother), but there is also an increase in aggression toward other persons not in the agent's presence. The strength of these displaced responses will be greater than the strength of those directed to the original instigators.

Although this general theoretical scheme has influenced most of the subsequent investigations of childrearing antecedents of aggression, none of the studies has undertaken to test this entire set of hypotheses. The Sears et al. (1953) monograph came closest to such an attempt. Almost all of the studies have been designed to examine only bivariate relationships; very few have been directed to the more complex, conflict-produced effects emphasized in the theory. Further, the hypotheses that have been tested, and the interpretations and summaries of findings in the field have tended to simplify the antecedent-consequent relation to one of severity of punishment and frequency of expressed aggression. Situational and inhibitory influences have received much less attention.

In examining methodological issues of this research area, we have used these specific hypotheses to organize our discussion. The analyses are directed to the status of the empirical evidence judged by methodological criteria, rather than to the correctness of the hypotheses. Some of the issues are strongly reminiscent of problems identified in the dependency data; others are especially pertinent to the ways in which aggression and its presumed antecedents have been conceptualized and measured.

◙ DEFINITIONS AND MEASURES OF AGGRESSION ◙

Aggression at the conceptual level presents little difficulty. It has usually been defined as actions that bring injury to a person or object, or have the intent to injure. Considerable discussion and debate have been spent on whether or not to include *intent* in this definition, but it is not always clear in examining the empirical data how much this conceptual distinction has actually influenced measurement. There tends not to be any concern about this issue in the choice of behavioral indicators or in the interpretation of child responses or in the review of findings. Aggression is sometimes conceived as a generalized disposition or motive, and sometimes as a set of specific overt acts. But again, this distinction is confined to conceptual discussion and is not very visible in measurement and interpretations.

When we turn attention from the *concept* of aggression to

the *specific behaviors* that have been used as measurements, we are quickly aware of great diversity. The items vary in the directness with which they "bring injury," the intensity with which injury is inflicted, the object toward which it is expressed. One is led to ask whether these items tap the underlying concept equally well and whether they tap the same phenomenon. One may speculate that in some actions more than others one is likely to be dealing with "intent" or general motivational tendencies. Some behaviors more than others are influenced by situational factors. Some kinds of acts may represent the only behavior available to the child (the hitting out of a very young child when he encounters interference may be this kind of behavior), while other aggressive responses are highly adapted, calculated, and chosen from varied alternatives at the disposal of the subject. These issues present complexities in research. Are these different measures interchangeable in testing hypotheses of aggression? When can studies and findings be viewed as replications? Identical measures, applied to similar subjects, in independent studies present little ambiguity as tests of replicated evidence. When various behavioral measures have been used as representative of the same conceptual entity, can findings be interpreted as constituting replication? Are they even stronger evidence for a general principle? When investigators using the same concepts, indexed by different behavioral components, obtain divergent results, does this constitute nonreplication? One is confronted many times with these questions in appraising the evidence of aggression.

Our first analysis, then, concerns the specific "injurious" acts that have been used in assessing the child's aggression and the degree to which they represent a unitary entity. Since young children are likely to "hit out" at the environment openly and directly (by shouting, kicking, biting, and the like), it is not surprising that many of the studies include these direct forms of expression in their measures of aggression. More varied and less direct expressions, such as quarreling, threatening, asking special privileges, destroying property, getting into trouble, "tattling," are also often included in the net. In studies of doll play even more attenuated forms of aggression are used, such as the creation of accidents in play themes, "mischief," the attribution of illness or sadness to the doll. It is apparent, then, that the raw materials subsumed under the label of aggression may vary considerably across studies, among children within the same study, and across settings (home and school) within the same or different studies. Thus one child rated high on aggression hits and kicks and bites, while another rated equally high shows little of such behavior but asks for special privileges or "tattles" or quarrels with his peers. Once the identical scale-label of "high aggression" has been applied, differences in the raw data become dimmed, and measures tend to be viewed as interchangeable and equivalent tests of the same "antecedent-consequent" relations. While an argument can be made for assuming that all of these items of behavior are, at some level of abstraction, similar and are tapping the same phenomenon, it is also important to determine how these data elements relate to one another and how they relate to parental behavior.

Sears, Rau, and Alpert (1965, p. 361, Table K1) supply very relevant data in this regard in their report of intercorrelations among different forms of aggressive expression observed in preschool children. Forty children were observed in nursery school; the categories of observation (parenthetically identified by their associated variable numbers) included direct physical acts of aggression, such as hitting or using force (189), direct verbal acts, such as name-calling or threatening (191), and less direct forms of aggression: mischief (193), tattling (197), verbal disapproval (196), and injury to objects (192). Fairly substantial correlations were found by these authors between *direct physical* and *direct verbal* aggressive acts (+.50 for boys and +.66 for girls). Correlations among the four *less direct forms* range from −.18 to +.63; only one out of six correlations reaches statistical significance for the boys; two out of six reach significance for the girls. Associations between *direct* and *less direct* forms of aggression show a similar range, from −.31 to +.61. Only six of these 16 comparisons are statistically significant at the 5 per cent level. When we extend our examination of intercorrelations to include not only different behavioral indices in the same situation, but also different indices in different situations, the picture grows more disconcerting. In the data from Sears et al., mother-interview reports of children's direct aggression toward adults at home (variable W) and scores of direct aggression toward mother as observed in an experimental situation (variable Y) are correlated −.03 for the boys and +.28 for the girls (p. 124). Scores on direct aggression at home also show little relation to two summary scores of aggression in the nursery school (194, 214): +.01 and +.11 for boys, and +.36 and −.20 for girls. Findings from NIMH data in similar comparisons of home and school aggression (V's 32, 47) are +.39 for boys and +.25 for girls. It is evident from these patterns of intercorrelations that one can confidently expect to find different children in the ranks of "high aggressors" if the bases of rating change to different behavioral items, from the same, or from different settings of behavior. One cannot expect the same "antecedent-consequent" relation between a given parental variable and the different indices of aggression. The absence of correspondence among indices of aggression is important for our methodological considerations in signaling caution in interpreting different studies as replications of identical "antecedent-consequent" relations when the indices of aggression differ, and when aggression has been measured in different situations.

If the preceding intercorrelations are representative, we are led to conclude that interpretations of findings need to keep a closer tie than is usual to the specific components of the aggression measures, specifying the kind of aggression and the stimulus setting that has been studied. The course chosen by some investigators (Sears et al., 1965) is a good one, namely one of measuring, at the same time, a broad and representative range of types of responses, and investigating the influences of maternal antecedents on this range of (possibly) consequent behavior.

MEASURES OF AGGRESSION IN THE NIMH STUDY

Let us turn now to indices of aggression used in the NIMH study. Two assessments were made by the mother, one in an interview and the other on a questionnaire. A third assessment came from the teachers, who were interviewed about the child's aggression in nursery school. All of these measures (in the interest of replicating on the same indices) focus on the more direct, overt forms of behavior. The question in the interviews, taken directly from the Sears, Maccoby, and Levin schedule (question 42c), is: "How much of a problem have you had with X about shows of temper, angry shouting, and that sort of thing around the house?" The mother's response was coded on the frequency of the child's expression of temper tantrums, anger, deliberate throwing of breakable objects, hitting, shouting, and sassing. Aggression toward siblings was excluded. (This interview question does not seem to be ideally designed to elicit a statement of frequency of aggression for it is prefaced with a troublesome phrase, "how much of a problem have you had . . ." One mother who is highly sensitive to negative behavior in a child and another mother who is very tolerant of such expression could have children with identical behavior, yet these mothers would [theoretically] be reporting quite differently on this behavior, according to how much of a problem the child's behavior presented to them.) The nursery school teachers were asked the same question that the mothers had been asked, but with reference to the child's aggression toward adults and children in school. After describing the child's behavior to the interviewer, the teacher made her own rating, using the same categories for rating as were employed by the coders of the mothers' interview responses. On the questionnaire, mothers were asked to check on a single five-point scale the extent to which their child could be characterized as manifesting the same kinds of direct forms of aggression (temper, kicking, hitting, screaming, biting).

RELIABILITY OF MEASURES OF AGGRESSION

The meaningfulness of measures depends in part, of course, on their reliability. With the three indices of aggression in the NIMH study, it was possible to look at several kinds of reliability, each of which is crucial for interpretations of different kinds. The first reliability measure is the kind found generally in the literature, which refers to the correspondence between coders' interpretations of the same interview protocol. Such coder agreement in the NIMH study is respectable at $r = .80$ (V 32). This tells the investigator something about the competence of the coders and/or about the degree of ambiguity in the verbal report on which he has imposed a particular coding framework. But is this the reliability in which the investigator is most interested? Does he not want and need to know the reliability of repeated measurements of the same individuals? The childrearing literature offers little on the essential reliability question referring to the consistency of repeated reports from the mother, or the consistency of information from independent reporters. In the present study an attempt was made to obtain reliability estimates of these kinds. First, mothers' agreement with themselves in describing child aggression was investigated by comparing their descriptions in the interview and on the questionnaire. Although instrument differences and the lapse of time between administrations (an average of seven months) would lead one to anticipate some differences in responses, the correlation of +.29 between mothers' reports on the interview (V 32) and on the questionnaire (V 42) suggests more serious problems. It suggests that one may be dealing with behavior that is not particularly constant for the child even over relatively short periods in his development. Or, if one looks for sources of unreliability within the mother, one may wonder about the representativeness of her description on a single test occasion, and about the immediate factors influencing her responses in the test situation. It reminds us that we are dealing with a single test item as an index of a behavior trait.

A second exploration of reliability involves the consistency of reports on the child from different observers. In our study, comparisons were made of ratings by two teachers, and of teachers' combined ratings with mothers' reports. The teacher-pairs were responding to identical questions about the child, concerning his behavior in the same settings and at the same point in time—in other words, optimal conditions for obtaining consistent appraisals of him. Their independent ratings are correlated +.65 (V 47), clearly indicating similarity in perceptions well above that found in comparing the mother with herself on the interview and questionnaire, yet being far from perfect in agreement. When the combined teacher ratings on the child's aggression are matched with ratings of aggression from the mother's interview (V 32), the correspondence drops to a correlation of +.33. The same interview questions, different observers, different situations of behavior, and different procedures for coding enter into consideration in this comparison. When further instrument differences and the passage of a half year of time are added, that is, when teacher-interview ratings and mother-questionnaire responses are compared, association between the two sets of appraisals all but vanishes ($r = +.05$). These findings lead to more questions than can be answered in the present data: Are teachers better able than mothers to report objectively on child behavior? Does the situation which the teachers observe evoke less variable day-to-day behavior from the child than is the case in the home, thereby making it easier to assess his behavior in school? Does the group of children give the teacher a comparative scale on which to assess children, thereby sharpening her acuity to differences? Are the young child's aggressive responses so very strongly situationally determined that seeing him at school gives little information about his aggression at home? This close look at measures of aggression leads to a number of conclusions that bear directly on the analyses that follow. In asking of research in childrearing how much replicating evidence exists, one needs to be mindful of the specific indices being used and the situations to which the behavior ratings refer. Each factor puts limits on the interchangeability of evidence. Further, the magnitude of "true" relations between child aggression and maternal behavior will be somewhat difficult to estimate, given the degree of unreliability in the measures.

The examinations that we have beamed on measures of aggression are equally applicable to the maternal measures—the frustration-producing demands in rearing, the severity and techniques of punishment, and the quality of affectionate relations. The measurement characteristics of the indices of these concepts will be described in the discussions of the specific hypotheses that involve them.

◙ REPLICATION OF FINDINGS ◙

We are accepting the theoretical orientation described earlier and we are looking at the "returns" from the many inquiries that have proceeded from this point of view. We have followed the research approach that relies chiefly on verbal reports and ratings of general dispositions and characteristics of mother and child. Our analyses are based on childrearing studies in which conceptualizations, measurements, and kinds of subjects studied are generally very similar. In four of these studies, definitions of variables, interview questions, and coding categories are very nearly identical: The procedures developed by Sears, Maccoby, and Levin have been repeated and adapted in studies by Burton (1959);[1] Sears, Rau, and Alpert (1965); and NIMH. In a fifth study by Becker, Peterson, Luria, Shoemaker, and Hellmer (1962), an adapted form of the same interview schedule was employed. The interview data on maternal behavior from the Sears, Maccoby, and Levin volume was used by Levin and Sears (1956). Similar maternal dimensions were measured with open-end interview questions in investigations by Sears, Whiting, Nowlis, and Sears (1953) and by Hoffman (1960). A precoded parent interview was employed by Eron, Banta, Walder, and Laulicht (1961), Eron, Walder, Toigo, and Lefkowitz (1963), and Lefkowitz, Walder and Eron (1963). Information on the child's aggression was supplied by the mother in the first five studies referred to above and in Eron et al. (1961). Ratings or observations by teacher or observer were made in the investigations by Sears et al. (1965), NIMH, Becker et al. (1962), Sears et al. (1953), Hoffman (1960); by peers in Eron et al. (1961, 1963), and Lefkowitz et al. (1963). Observations of doll play behavior provided measures of aggression in the Hollenberg and Sperry (1951), Levin and Sears (1956), Sears et al. (1965) studies. The same children are the subjects in several of the studies: Children from the same sample are represented in Eron et al. (1963) and Lefkowitz et al. (1963). Sears et al. (1957), Sears (1961), and Levin and Sears (1956) report on the same samples. Hollenberg and Sperry's (1951) analyses are based on subjects in the Sears et al. (1953) study.

FRUSTRATION AND AGGRESSION

The questions we haved posed for ourselves will be examined first in relation to hypotheses regarding the effects of frustration on the young child's aggressive responses. The proposition that frustrations in the child's current circumstances ("interference with

---

[1] These are additional analyses based on unpublished data collected as a part of a doctoral dissertation, *Some factors related to resistance to temptation in four-year-old children.*

his on-going actions or a disruption of his state of well-being," Sears et al., 1953, p. 205) contribute to increased aggressive behavior seems to fit one's common-sense notions about behavior and one's experiences with young children. This proposition has been tested in seven of the childrearing studies (Hollenberg and Sperry, 1951; Sears et al., 1953; Sears et al., 1957; Eron et al., 1961; Becker et al., 1962; Sears et al., 1965; NIMH), frustration being measured quite uniformly in terms of mother's reports on her demands, restrictions and pressures on the child to conform to standards in the routines of eating, sleeping, personal cleanliness, and household neatness. The only alternative indices of frustration reported in childrearing studies have been global measures of nurturance and of permissiveness of dependency. Assuming a strong dependency need in the young child, low nurturance and a nonpermissive attitude toward dependent behavior might be interpreted as dependency frustration. Extensive analysis of the findings on frustration is not necessary to arrive at the conclusion that there is convincing consistency in finding no significant associations between these measures of frustration and measures of child aggression. Data from the NIMH study are presented in Table 4. Correlations between three measures of aggression (aggression to parents as measured in the interview [V 32], aggression to parents as measured in the questionnaire [V 42], and aggression in school [V 47] and three indices of frustration or its absence (degree of general restrictiveness [V 19], rewarding or punishing response to child's dependent behavior [V 11], and warmth or coldness in the relationship between mother and child [V 23]) are without a single significant relationship.

The results, typical of findings in the field, can be interpreted variously. One may accept them as evidence against a simple frustration-aggression hypothesis, or one may wonder how much low coder reliability may cover up any "true" relationships that may exist. (Coder reliabilities for none of the three presumed antecedents reach highly respectable levels: .72 for a summary score of restrictiveness, .60 for response to dependency, and .65 for warmth. The NIMH reliability figures are *not* unlike those of other investigations.) Or one may question whether the measures are good indices of the concept of frustration. Stringent requirements in table manners, bed-

Table 4

CORRELATION OF MEASURES OF CURRENT FRUSTRATION WITH CHILD AGGRESSION

Variable number	Child Behavior	Maternal Restrictiveness 19			Maternal Response to Dependency[a] 11			Maternal Warmth 23r		
		Total Sample	Boys	Girls	Total Sample	Boys	Girls	Total Sample	Boys	Girls
32	Aggression to parents (MI)	−02	−09	09	−10	−14	−02	−11	−08	−17
42	Aggression to parents (MQ)	−14	−23	−10	00	15	−11	08	13	01
47	Aggression in school (TR)	04	−07	22	−06	−08	−05	−02	−08	09

Maximum sample sizes on which correlations are based: 86 (43 boys, 43 girls) for MI (mother interview) and MQ (mother questionnaire); 58 (30 boys, 28 girls) for TR (teacher ratings).
[a] High score = approval of dependency; low score = punishment of dependency.

time routines, and similar activities are not necessarily interferences with the child's on-going actions or disruptions of his state of well-being. The effects of such requirements on the child would seem to be inextricably bound up with the meaning of the parental expectations and the manner by which the child is taught the behavior; these factors may be of very considerable importance in determining the interference quality of the requirements. For example, a sleepy child regularly put to bed at precisely eight o'clock with a bedtime story and the full attention of his mother may be experiencing reward in this high-demand regimen. Another child nagged and threatened and punished into compliance may be experiencing frustrations. It seems quite possible, then, that as investigators we may not have succeeded very well in capturing a sampling of frustrations. If we are inclined to believe this, we must conclude that the hypothesis on the effects of frustrating childrearing experiences has not been tested. No review of this field has really strongly concluded that frustration has no effects, which would be the conclusion if the weight of evidence were accepted at face value.

The overall picture of findings on frustration thus leaves us in doubt as to the test of the hypothesis in childrearing research, but confident as to the absence of an empirical relationship between reported parental demands and restrictions and child aggression.

PUNISHMENT AND AGGRESSION

A major hypothesis regarding the maintenance and increase of aggressive behavior concerns the severity and kinds of punishment used in rearing the child. The conclusion that punishment of young children begets aggression has been accepted with a considerable degree of finality in much of the childrearing literature, in both the original research reports and the secondary sources. While some unresolved complexities and differences are noted, the positive association of punishment and aggression is viewed as quite firmly supported. This generalization, it should be observed, is consonant with experimental work with animals in which it has been concluded that punishment does not eliminate the punished behavior, but acts only as a temporary suppressant of the punished responses, after which there is compensatory recovery (see Skinner, 1938; Estes, 1944).

The confidence that comes from this confirmatory evidence may be unwarranted, however. Solomon (1964) has described this interpretation as a persistent legend about punishment. Recent empirical investigations (Boe, 1966; Boe and Church, 1966; Church, 1966) have also challenged the earlier conclusion and have, in fact, tended to support the opposite interpretation: punishment of a response does decrease its strength (or future probability). The conclusion on punishment effects that is drawn from childrearing research may also require reexamination.

Evidence on punishment and aggression in the childrearing studies of this survey comes from two types of research designs. The first design relies on the mother's reports of the punishment she uses and also her reports of the child's direct aggression toward adults in the home. We shall refer to this as the contaminated design. In the second design there are independent sources of maternal and child data: The reports of punishment are obtained from the mothers; the ratings of child aggression are provided by teachers, peers, or observers. Child aggression measured in studies of the second design occurs outside the home, not in the presence of the mother (punisher), is directed toward other persons or objects, and may include indirect as well as direct forms of aggressive expression. Thus, the two types of designs vary in several dimensions simultaneously, thereby muddying comparisons of data from them.

The data in our analyses have been presented in the tables according to the design and instruments used in the studies. In Table 5 are presented the results deriving from the contaminated design. In Tables 6 and 7 are findings of investigations with independent sources of child and maternal data. The measures of punishment and aggression have also been grouped into like classes in the tables. Punishment is specified as: severity of punishment specifically for aggression to adults in the home, overall ratings of severity of punishment, use of physical punishment for aggression to adults in the home, and overall ratings of physical punishment. For measures of child aggression, the situation in which the behavior occurs is indicated as: at home in the presence of the mother, at school, and in doll play. (Only measures of child aggression are considered as the "consequent" behavior in these studies. This excludes a number of findings in the literature on conduct disorders, resistance to influence, and so on which have been interpreted in the punishment-aggression framework.) The tables also provide information on the number of subjects on which the results are based, and the findings for each sex (when reported by the original authors). The original data sources are indicated by page number and bibliographic identification. Correlations reaching at least the 5 per cent level of significance are marked with an asterisk.

A general hypothesis. Our first analysis is directed to the broad proposition that specifies only that punishment and frequency of aggression are positively related. Since this analysis strains the data through only the very coarse sieve of relations between *any* of the punishment measures and *any* of the aggression measures, the data reported in Tables 5, 6, and 7 are relevant. It should be apparent at the outset that such a hypothesized association between severity of punishment and amount of aggression is not strictly derived from the social learning hypotheses that have been described (pp. 56–58); it leaves out of consideration many of the theoretically relevant factors—for example, the possible inhibitory influences of the punitive agent. This perspective is taken only because it follows the kinds of summaries and generalizations found in the interpretative literature of this field. In taking this view we have adopted a most lenient attitude toward procedural variations; we have ignored them. After inspecting the evidence in this manner we shall re-view it with more careful regard both for the specific theory-derived hypotheses and for the procedural details of each study, with attention to the more nearly exact replications of measurement procedures.

In almost every investigation in our survey at least one statistically significant positive correlation appears between punishment and aggression. It must be added that these same studies generally report as many or more nonsignificant correlations between presumed equivalent measures of punishment and aggression. Sometimes the significant relationships are accounted for by the boys only, sometimes by the girls only. No significant negative relationships are reported, although just under a third of all correlations are negative in sign. The evidence in support of the general hypothesis with which we have begun is less than impressive; it can hardly be regarded as greatly convincing for *some* significant correlations to appear when *many* have been explored. In order to interpret the data as having established a link between high punishment and high aggression, it is necessary to select among the findings and to ignore many results that are not in line with the hypothesis.

Since much has been put into this one pot of correlations, consistencies of relations between more precisely defined conditions have, perhaps, been obscured. More specific hypotheses and stricter sorting of indices and designs may lead to clearer results, both empirically and theoretically.

In our reconsideration of findings on punishment and aggression, we shall refine our analyses in several ways: We shall want to note what specific indices have been used to measure the concepts of presumed antecedent and consequent variables, and what has been the consistency in results when nearly identical measures have been used. We shall ask what specific hypothesis is being tested, differentiating between hypotheses concerning aggressive behavior in the presence of the punishing mother, and in her absence; between expression of aggression toward other persons and in other settings than the one in which the punishment was given. We shall attempt to sort out findings of studies in which both the antecedent and the consequent data are obtained from a single source, and those in which the two data sets are obtained from independent sources.

Indices of punishment. Although punishment is the common "antecedent" in all of the studies, various indices of punishment have of course been used. There are two types of definitions. One refers to the *amount* of punishment, meaning frequency as well as severity; the other refers to the techniques of discipline—spanking, isolating, love withdrawal, power assertion, and so forth. Of the techniques, physical punishment has received most attention in relation to aggression and is sometimes regarded as a measure of severity. (On speculative grounds, it would seem that spanking is not necessarily more "severe" than ostracism or shame or isolation.) Cutting across severity and techniques is a further distinction, namely, whether the punishment is that given contingent on the child's aggressive acts or is the general punitive character of the mother's discipline. In the NIMH study we have included measures

Table 5

CORRELATIONS OF MATERNAL PUNISHMENT MEASURES WITH MEASURES OF CHILD'S AGGRESSION TO PARENTS

Punishment Scales	Correlations Between Punishment and Aggression			Study	Reference Information Page Reference	Variable Number	
	Total	Boys	Girls			Punishment	Aggression
Severity of punishment for aggression to parents	40*	42*	37*	NIMH		14	32
	23*	20	25	NIMH		14	42
	16*	11	18	Sears et al. 1957	259	III-31	III-29
		23	17	Sears 1961	476	III-31	III-29
		04	−15	Sears et al. 1965	138	60	W
		01	−28	Sears et al. 1965	138	60	Y
	−17			Burton unpublished		III-25	III-28
Punishment for aggression to adults and children	47*			Eron et al. 1961	466–7		
Severity of punishment: overall	08	−09	24	NIMH		20	32
	02	01	00	NIMH		20	42

72

				Source	N		
Physical punishment for aggression to parents							
	−01	−02	−01	NIMH	7	7	32
	12	15	10	NIMH	7	7	42
Physical punishment: overall							
	12	09	07	Burton unpublished		III-54	III-28
	10	−14	39*	Burton unpublished		III-55	III-28
	03	−07	17	NIMH		6	32
	08	−17	24	NIMH		6	42
	23*			Sears et al. 1957	262	III-46	III-29
		22	23*	Sears 1961	476	III-46	III-29
	43*	29	61*	Becker et al. 1962	522–3	MI 10	MI
	20	03	45*	Becker et al. 1962	522–3	MI 10	MR
		06	18	Sears et al. 1965	142	67	W
		27	−23	Sears et al. 1965	142	67	Y

Maximum sample sizes on which correlations are based: NIMH, 86 (43 boys, 43 girls); Sears et al. (1957), 379; Sears (1961), a subsample of the 1957 study (76 boys, 84 girls); Sears et al. (1965) (21 boys, 19 girls); Burton, 77 (40 boys, 37 girls); Eron et al. (1961), 59; Becker et al. (1962), 71 (36 boys, 35 girls).

Measures of aggression in the reported studies are those of antisocial aggression. In each instance the variables are identified by number and/or by page reference to the original data.

Table 6

CORRELATIONS OF MATERNAL PUNISHMENT MEASURES WITH MEASURES OF CHILD'S AGGRESSION IN SCHOOL

Punishment Scales	Correlations Between Punishment and Aggression			Reference Information			
	Total	Boys	Girls	Study	Page Reference	Variable Number Punishment	Aggression
Severity of punishment for aggression to parents	13	−05	29	NIMH		14	47
		15	02	Sears et al. 1965	138	60	194
		22	23	Sears et al. 1965	138	60	Z
		33	−12	Sears et al. 1965	138	60	214
Punishment for aggression to adults and children	03	analyses of variance[c]		Eron et al. 1961	466		
				Eron et al. 1963	854		
Severity of punishment: overall	09	−13	33	NIMH		20	47
General punitiveness		50*	−04	Sears et al. 1953	210	M 57	C 55
		60*	−41	Sears et al. 1953	210	M 57	C 173
Initial unqualified power assertion	−16			Hoffman 1960	136–7		to children[a]
	13			Hoffman 1960	136–7		to children[b]
	22			Hoffman 1960	136–7		to adults[a]
	29			Hoffman 1960	136–7		to adults[b]

Reactive unqualified power assertion	42			Hoffman 1960	136–7		to children[a]
	76*			Hoffman 1960	136–7		to adults[b]
	28			Hoffman 1960	136–7		to adults[a]
	11			Hoffman 1960	136–7		to adults[b]
Physical punishment for aggression to parents	−02	−01	−01	NIMH		7	47
Physical punishment: overall	−19	−16	−20	NIMH		6	47
		−09	14	Sears et al. 1965	142	67	194
		10	36	Sears et al. 1965	142	67	Z
		22	05	Sears et al. 1965	142	67	214
	25*	35*	12	Becker et al. 1962	522–3	MI 10	TR
	analyses of variance[d]			Lefkowitz et al. 1963	163		

Maximum sample sizes on which correlations are based: NIMH, 58 (30 boys, 28 girls); Sears et al. (1965), 40 (21 boys, 19 girls); Eron et al. (1961), 59; Eron et al. (1963), 451 (245 boys, 206 girls); Lefkowitz et al. (1963), 699 (366 boys, 333 girls); Sears et al. (1953), 40 (21 boys, 19 girls); Hoffman (1960), 22 (12 middle class, 10 working class children); Becker et al. (1962), 71 (36 boys, 35 girls).

[a] Middle-class children.

[b] Working-class children.

[c] A positive association between intensity of punishment for aggression and peer ratings of aggression: For total sample, $F = 8.85$, $p < .001$; for boys, $F = 4.21$, $p < .025$; for girls, $F = 6.24$, $p < .005$.

[d] A positive association between reported use of physical punishment and peer ratings of aggression: For total sample, $F = 5.30$, $p < .01$.

Table 7

CORRELATIONS OF MATERNAL PUNISHMENT MEASURES WITH MEASURES OF CHILD'S AGGRESSION IN DOLL PLAY

Punishment Scales	Correlations Between Punishment and Aggression			Reference Information		Variable Number	
	Total	Boys	Girls[a]	Study	Page Reference	Punishment	Aggression
Severity of punishment for aggression to parents	analyses of variance[a]			Levin and Sears 1956	145–7		
		−14	−13	Sears et al. 1965	138	60	290
		23	−05	Sears et al. 1965	138	60	291
General punitiveness	t-test[d]			Hollenberg and Sperry 1951	39	M 57	[b]
	t-test[e]			Hollenberg and Sperry 1951	39	M 57	[c]
		46[g]	41	Sears et al. 1953[f]	219	M 57	[b]
		23	46	Sears et al. 1953	219	M 57	
Physical punishment		−23	−15	Sears et al. 1965	142	67	290
		−01	00	Sears et al. 1965	142	67	291

Maximum sample sizes on which statistics are based: Hollenberg and Sperry (1951), 15 boys, 15 girls; Levin and Sears (1956), 126 boys, 115 girls; (same sample as Sears et al. (1957), 126 boys, 115 girls); Sears et al. (1965), 21 boys, 19 girls.

[a] Severity of punishment is unrelated to frequency of aggression. For girls, interaction between severity of punishment and mother as agent approaches significance, F's = 3.42, $p < .07$ and 2.64, $p < .10$ for first and second sessions respectively. Interaction between identification and punishment is significant in one out of two doll play sessions, F's = .71 and 4.37 ($p < .05$).

[b] Frequency of aggressive acts.

[c] Intensity of aggressive acts.

[d] The difference between the means on frequency of aggression approaches the 5 per cent level of confidence ($t = 1.9$).

[e] The difference between means on intensity of aggression is in the predicted direction but is not statistically significant.

[f] Data from Hollenberg and Sperry reported in Sears et al. (1953).

[g] Coefficient of .51 is required for the .05 level of confidence.

of severity, both contingent on the child's aggression and general, and measures of techniques, both contingent and general. (We have limited discussion here to physical punishment techniques.) Coder reliabilities on these indices (V's 6, 7, 14, 20) range from .70 to .83.

In the broad-sweep analysis of punishment and aggression just presented, the various indicators of maternal behavior have been treated as conceptual equivalents. An exploration of the intercorrelations among alternative indices was carried out to determine the reasonableness of such an interpretation. The intercorrelations among the four NIMH measures make it seem questionable. The "contingent" measures of severity (V 14) and physical punishment (V 7) are correlated +.26 in the NIMH data; the overall measures of each (V's 6, 20) are correlated +.29. When the overall rating of one and the contingent measure of the other are correlated, the associations are lower, +.14 and +.15. When a contingent measure is correlated with its own overall measure, the associations are +.54 for physical punishment and +.46 for severity of punishment. Sears, Maccoby, and Levin report a correlation of +.44 between their measure of severity of punishment for aggression to adults in the home and extent of use of physical punishment (p. 262) but, as the authors point out (p. 248), an overlap is built in by the definitions of their rating scales (physical punishment is a defining element for the "severe" end of the severity scale). In this sample of alternative indices one has evidence of enough variation in overlap of different ratings to suggest with some degree of confidence that ratings of severe punishment, for example, and codings of use of physical punishment are often not representing the same conditions of discipline, and, therefore, should not be regarded as interchangeable in assessing replications of findings. How each index is associated with child aggression is indicated in the tables and will be discussed in relation to the specific hypotheses being studied. (Uniquenesses in the aggression indices add further, similar complications in adding up the evidence.)

Punishment and aggression in mother's presence. If severe punishment from the mother is viewed as contributing to the amount of painful frustration that is imposed on the child (Sears et al., 1957, p. 26), then high child aggression should be its predicted accompaniment. If, on the other hand, one takes the point of view of a displacement model, an opposite prediction would be made for aggression in the mother's presence: High punitiveness should lead to an inhibition of aggression in the mother's presence, with increased aggression in other settings. From still another point of view, a highly punitive (aggressive) mother could be seen as providing the child with a model of aggressive behavior, thereby increasing the likelihood of aggressive expression by the child.

The findings relevant to these hypotheses are in Table 5. Ratings of severe punishment *contingent* on the child's expression of aggression toward adults in the family produce the most consistent positive and statistically significant associations across the several studies (Sears et al., 1957; NIMH; Eron et al., 1961). The evidence is not unambiguous, however. Two other studies using identical measures fail to find these associations (Burton; and Sears et al., 1965). Instead, both positive and negative correlations appear in the latter two studies, none of them statistically significant. Ratings of physical punishment *contingent* on the child's aggression show no significant associations, and no consistent direction of associations (NIMH). *General* severity of maternal punishment (NIMH, V 20) is unrelated to aggression in the NIMH data (V's 32, 42). With the overall ratings of physical punishment, the seesaw results continue: significant positive correlations are reported by Sears et al. (1957), Becker et al. (1962) for girls, and Burton for one of two measures for girls; no significant relations appear in the NIMH and Sears et al. (1965) investigations.

Thus, from six studies of very similar design, and all using the contaminated design, all measuring aggression in the presence of the punishing agent, there is relatively little replication of findings regarding the hypothesized positive link between punishment and aggression. Amount of aggression is sometimes related to severity of punishment for aggression, sometimes to general use of physical punishment, but just as often it is not related to either. Furthermore, when measures of severity of punishment and physical punishment are included in the same study, one measure may show a significant positive relation, while the other may not. It seems reasonable to conclude that the hypothesis that severe punishment *inhibits* aggression in the presence of the mother has little support in these studies;

the hypotheses that severe punishment *increases* aggression in the presence of the mother find only tentative support.

Punishment and aggression not in presence of punishing agent. It has been hypothesized that child aggression in other settings, *not* in the presence of the mother, varies positively with severity of punishment (Sears et al., 1965, pp. 139–40). The research evidence on this proposition has the methodological merit of having independent sources of ratings for the hypothesized antecedent and consequent conditions. How consistent are these results, keeping in mind the specific indices used?

When maternal behavior is defined as punishment given *contingent* on the child's aggression in the home, three out of four studies find no significant associations of this punishment with aggression expressed in school (Eron et al., 1961; Sears et al., 1965; NIMH). In Eron et al. (1963), one finds a positive relation with peer ratings of child's aggression in school (see Table 6). When general punitiveness is the punishment measure (it is impossible to distinguish clearly between severity and physical punishment because of the varied indices used by different authors), there is a thread of significant positive associations with antisocial aggression in school, but with qualifications: Lefkowitz et al. (1963) and Becker et al. (1962) report generally significant positive findings; Hoffman (1960) reports one significant correlation out of eight; Sears et al. (1953) have significant positive associations for boys, but nonsignificant negative correlations for girls; Sears et al. (1965) and NIMH find no significant associations at all.

The doll play studies carried out on the same subjects as those in the preceding analyses give no further statistically significant support to the hypothesis linking punishment and aggression (see Table 7). At best, some of the associations approach statistical significance (and then always in a positive direction), but both negative and positive signs appear among the nonsignificant coefficients.

In the 1953 study by Sears, Whiting, Nowlis, and Sears, findings were suggestive of sex differences in response to maternal punishment (pp. 213–220). A scanning of findings in Tables 6 and 7 for each sex does not reveal any general tendency for the directional differences reported in the Iowa study. The correlations for each sex often differ within a study, but a pattern for these differences is not discernible for either the direct aggression (Table 5) or the displaced or projected aggression (Tables 6 and 7).

Punishment and aggression: A summing up. In summary, the bivariate analyses of punishment and aggression in the research reviewed here leave most questions unsettled. Consistencies of significant positive associations are more likely to come in designs using the mother as the sole source of data than from designs using independent measures. But since the contaminated designs have provided the data on aggression in mother's presence, and the noncontaminated designs have produced the data on aggression in the mother's absence, one cannot disentangle a possible methodological bias from what might be a theoretical explanation. We are inclined to feel that the methodological contribution may be a significant one. Eron et al. (1961, pp. 468–469), who have given attention to this factor, furnish evidence that clearly points to the single source of data as a potent contributor to the size of correlations. They compared relations between punishment and aggression based on one parent's ratings of both variables with associations based on punishment scores from one parent and aggression scores from the other parent. There was a consistent shrinkage in going from the single source to the independent sources. In the Becker et al. (1962) study there are similar analyses, with similar results: correlations between physical punishment and aggression at home are +.43 and +.38 for data obtained from a single informant; +.18 and +.33 when the mother is the source of one set of ratings and the father the source of the other (p. 522). Eron et al.'s (1961, p. 469) conclusions are appropriate to all of these findings:

> This consistent drop, when going from correlations between predictor and criterion obtained from the same individual to correlations between predictor and criterion each independently obtained, reinforces suspicions of contamination in those studies which use only the mother as informant about both childrearing practices and child behavior.

How, then, has the image of firmly established research evidence regarding maternal punitiveness as an antecedent of child ag-

gression evolved? If the data in the tables are reasonably representative, and if the yardstick of statistical significance is applied, it would
seem that theoretical persuasiveness has led to a kind of selectivity
of evidence. Many nonconforming findings have been tolerated. If
direction of associations is taken as a more lenient criterion, is the
evidence perhaps more unambiguously in support of the generally
stated conclusion? Only slightly. Although none of the reviewed
studies reports significant negative associations between punitiveness
and aggression, just under a third of all the correlations (Tables 5,
6, and 7) are negative in sign; and the number of negative ones increases in the noncontaminated designs. One must conclude that
this body of research does not permit firm conclusions.

PERMISSIVENESS OF AGGRESSION

Companion to the hypothesis on punishment is the hypothesis
concerning the facilitating effects of permitting and rewarding aggression. Permissiveness has received far less attention than punishment in the interview studies. The mother who is tolerant of aggression in the home, it is hypothesized, is facilitating aggression in the
child. At the same time, by not interfering with the child's aggressive
expression, she is reducing the amount of frustration and thereby reducing the instigations to aggression. A mother may also directly encourage her child to be aggressive toward other children and reward
such behavior. The theoretical expectations of consequences of these
conditions of childrearing are stated by Sears et al. (1965, p. 144):

> . . . children whose parents permit aggression should
> behave more aggressively at home and in the parents' pres-
> ence than children whose parents are not permissive.
> We should also expect the amount of aggression ex-
> pressed outside the home to be less. Since permissively
> treated children do not suffer the added frustration of hav-
> ing their aggressive acts interfered with, they have less
> strength of response available for stimulus generalization.
> Furthermore, since severity of punishment is negatively re-
> lated to permissiveness, such children tend to suffer less
> punishment, and hence have less conflict drive to facilitate
> outside aggressions.

As in the preceding analyses, we shall look to evidence on these predictions that has accumulated across a number of studies. The findings are presented in Table 8 on mother's permissiveness of aggression in three situations (toward adults in home, toward siblings, or toward other children) and the associated aggression. (For questions on permissiveness see variables 13, 16, 17, and 18 in Appendix A.) In *Patterns of Child Rearing* and Sears (1961), permissiveness of aggression and frequency of aggression in the home are significantly positively related, +.23 for total sample, +.27 for boys and +.19 for girls (Variables III-29 and III-30). Comparisons identical to these were made in the Sears et al. (1965) study, but the relationship was not replicated. The correlation for boys, which was +.40 (Variables 58 and W), might be considered partial replication, although on the small sample this does not reach the 5 per cent level of significance; the relationship for girls was .00. The only other significant positive association in the 1965 study is between mother's demands for aggression to other children and boys' aggression to adults in the home, +.54 (Variables 55 and W). In the NIMH data only one out of 36 correlations relevant to this hypothesis reaches significance (permissiveness of aggression to siblings and frequency of aggression in the home, $r = +.21$ [V's 16, 42]); the nonsignificant associations are equally often negative and positive. In Burton, the direction of associations is positive but not significant. For data on the prediction of lower aggression outside the home with permissiveness of aggression in the home, we look to the correlations in the lower half of Table 8. None of these reaches statistical significance; somewhat more than half of the correlations are negative in sign.

Thus, considering the total evidence from these four studies, the hypotheses on permissiveness and aggression are not upheld by consistent or significant findings. Only if the entire table is appraised in terms of the signs of the correlations might one see tendencies in the predicted directions. Associations tend to be positive for permissiveness and child aggression at home, negative for permissiveness and child aggression outside the home. With such slight indications, however, the picture on permissiveness of aggression as a contributor to aggression remains unclear.

MULTIVARIATE ANALYSES

Three dimensions of child rearing—frustrations, punishments, permissiveness of aggression—have been studied singly in relation to child aggression. Relatively few of the relations explored in these analyses reach a criterion of statistical significance; furthermore, the amount of variance controlled in any of the significant associations is exceedingly small. Without a theory, it is difficult to find a compelling order in the findings, and even with a theory a good deal of faith is required to interpret the data as providing a tight network of evidence. If little has been definitely established in these bivariate analyses, might one not expect (certainly on theoretical grounds) to fare somewhat better if greater consideration were given to multiple conditions relating to aggressive responses in children? Only a very few analyses of this kind have been done in the interview studies of child rearing.

One such line of investigation has taken into account the hypothesized interactive effects of permissiveness and punishment of aggression. Conflict in the child deriving from instigation and inhibition of aggression should, theoretically, result in increased aggression. Mothers who encourage or permit aggression and who also punish it severely when it occurs should, according to this hypothesis, produce highly aggressive children. Exploration of this hypothesis is possible in data from three studies—Sears et al. (1957); Burton; and NIMH. In each study mothers were classified as providing one of four conditions of combined permissiveness and punitiveness (high or low on each dimension). When both dimensions are high in the mother's practices, high aggression is predicted. When both dimensions are low, low aggression is predicted. Data from Sears et al. (1957) conform to this ordering (reproduced in Table 9): The largest percentage of "highly" aggressive children was found with reported rearing conditions in which mothers were most permissive but also most punitive; the smallest percentage of "highly" aggressive children was found with nonpermissive and nonpunitive mothers. These findings have only very limited replication in the other two studies, however. There is no stable ordering in the NIMH study in which several alternative indices of punishment were used.

Table 8

CORRELATIONS OF MATERNAL PERMISSIVENESS AND ENCOURAGEMENT OF AGGRESSION
MEASURES WITH MEASURES OF CHILD'S AGGRESSION

	Correlations Between Permissiveness or Encouragement and Aggression			Reference Information		Variable Number	
	Total	Boys	Girls	Study	Page Reference	Permissiveness	Aggression
Child's aggression in mother's presence:							
Permissiveness of aggression to parents	−05	−07	−03	NIMH		13	32
	−05	00	−08	NIMH		13	42
	02	06	−01	NIMH		13	32A
	23*	27*	19	Sears et al. 1957	527	III-30	III-29
		40	00	Sears 1961	476	III-30	III-29
		01	20	Sears et al. 1965	146	58	W
				Sears et al. 1965	146	58	Y
	19	15	29	Burton unpublished	162	III-24	III-28
Permissiveness of aggression to siblings	12	16	06	NIMH		16	32
	21*	26	23	NIMH		16	42
	00	−05	03	NIMH		16	32A
	09			Sears et al. 1957	527	III-22	III-29
Permissiveness of aggression to other children	−20	−26	−15	NIMH		17	32
	10	−02	16	NIMH		17	42
	−13	−12	−14	NIMH		17	32A

Variable	(1)	(2)	(3)	Source	N	Code 1	Code 2
Encouragement of aggression to other children	03	−10	26	NIMH		18	32
	01	−13	22	NIMH		18	42
	08	−16	18	NIMH		18	32A
	04			Sears et al. 1957	527	III-26	III-29
		54*	41	Sears et al. 1965	146	55	W
		−09	−13	Sears et al. 1965	146	55	Y
Child's aggression not in mother's presence:							
Permissiveness of aggression to parents	15	24	03	NIMH		13	47
	−10	−10	−20	Sears et al. 1965	146	58	194
	−10	−10	−35	Sears et al. 1965	146	58	Z
	−09	−09	−05	Sears et al. 1965	146	58	214
	14	14	26	Sears et al. 1965	146	58	290
	−04	−04	16	Sears et al. 1965	146	58	291
Permissiveness of aggression to other children	−16	−07	−27	NIMH		17	47
Encouragement of aggression to other children	04	08	−14	NIMH		18	47
		−01	13	Sears et al. 1965	146	55	194
		06	14	Sears et al. 1965	146	55	Z
		−05	−16	Sears et al. 1965	146	55	214
		01	−07	Sears et al. 1965	146	55	290
		−01	−17	Sears et al. 1965	146	55	291

Maximum sample size on which correlations are based: NIMH, 86 (43 boys, 43 girls) for school data; 58 (30 boys, 28 girls) for home data; Sears et al. (1957), 379; Sears (1961), 160 (76 boys, 84 girls); Sears et al. (1965), 40 (21 boys, 19 girls); Burton, 77 (40 boys, 37 girls).

85

Table 9

PERCENTAGE OF CHILDREN RATED HIGH ON AGGRESSION IN RELATION TO
MATERNAL PERMISSIVENESS AND SEVERITY OF PUNISHMENT

Permissiveness of aggression to parents:	Severity of punishment for aggression to parents:	Sears et al. 1957[a]		NIMH Mother Interview	NIMH Mother Questionnaire	Burton
		High Aggression Boys	High Aggression Girls	High Aggression Total Sample	High Aggression Total Sample	High Aggression Total Sample
Low	Low	3.7% (27)	13.3% (30)	18% (11)	30% (10)	0% (3)
Low	High	20.4% (51)	19.1% (47)	48% (29)	48% (29)	35% (20)
High	Low	25.3% (81)	20.6% (63)	28% (32)	31% (32)	26% (23)
High	High	41.7% (36)	38.1% (22)	43% (7)	67% (6)	46% (26)

Permissiveness of aggression to parents:	Physical punishment for aggression to parents:		
Low	Not used	43% (21)	38% (21)
Low	Used	35% (20)	47% (19)
High	Not used	38% (21)	20% (20)
High	Used	22% (18)	56% (18)

Permissiveness of aggression to parents:	Severity of punishment: overall:		
Low	Low	41% (17)	50% (16)
Low	High	37% (27)	37% (27)
High	Low	32% (25)	33% (24)
High	High	25% (16)	38% (16)

Numbers within parentheses indicate the total n of children in each subgroup of maternal measures.
[a] Page 260.

To find so little support for a theoretically appealing hypothesis, and one which seems to move in the direction of the kind of analyses desired, is disappointing. The data, however, are poor for the purpose, for the methodological reasons already discussed. The conclusions must remain in doubt, and wait better multivariate approaches.

Only one other attempt to include a second interacting antecedent variable appears in the group of investigations reviewed. Sears et al. (1953) introduced the concept of identification as a hypothesized influence accounting for sex differences in their findings relating punishment to aggression. Severity of punishment and frequency of aggression in nursery school were associated positively and significantly for boys in their sample. Correlations for girls were negative. The scatter diagrams suggested a tendency to curvilinearity in the girls' data, with low aggression at both extremes of punitiveness. The authors' interpretation was that, "Because of their greater tendency to identify with their mothers, girls actually suffer more severe punishment than boys do from a given rated amount of maternal punitiveness, and hence show more indication of generalized inhibition" (p. 220).

This explanation, offered tentatively for the 1953 data, has not held up well in later studies. Levin and Sears' (1956) attempt to find confirmation of this interpretation yielded only ambiguous support for an explanation involving identification. They used the child's superego formation or conscience as an index of identification with parents (see their p. 142 for definition of index). Aggression in doll play was the dependent variable. Girls, they found, who "identified" highly and whose mothers reported severe punishment expressed more aggressive acts in doll play than girls in the other three combinations of high and low identification and high and low severity of punishment (p. 147). This trend appeared in one of two doll play sessions. No simliar association was found for boys in relation to the mother (although other congruent associations appear for boys in relation to the father).

Sex differences in the previously reviewed results on punishment and aggression are not consistent with the identification hypothesis. If greater identification is assumed in girls, then one should anticipate finding inhibition of aggression by girls in the mother's presence (Table 5). This has not been the case. Also, sex differences like those in the 1953 report should be found in other studies measuring aggression in school (Table 6). Again, the picture does not conform to the theoretical expectation. Becker et al. (1962) is the one study in this group in which a curvilinear relation appears; in this instance it is between reported use of physical punishment and girls' "Conduct Problems" in preschool. (The latter measure includes a number of dimensions in addition to aggression.) Although these authors consider identification as a possible explanatory principle, they also point out an important incongruity between this interpretation and the rest of their findings on girls; namely, that the girls' aggression at home, like boys,' is positively related to mothers' severity. Before further search in this direction is likely to lead to reliable findings, some of the conceptual ambiguities and measurement confusions relating to identification will have to be remedied.

Childrearing interview research has not gone far in attempting multivariate analyses, and what has been done has not altered the general status of findings. Whether the hypotheses or the techniques or both account for the inconclusive findings will have to be unraveled in further research.

▣ *THE LABEL AND THE MEASURE* ▣

The data on aggression, from what we regard as a reasonable sample of studies, have been interpreted variously in the literature of child rearing and in the analyses we have imposed on them. A number of factors, methodological in nature, contribute to a state of affairs that fosters this ambiguity. Prominent among these is the idiosyncratic nature of much of measurement, a lack of standard vocabulary, and a lack of standard defining behavior for the concepts being investigated. Different measured elements bearing the same conceptual labels are used by the same authors in different studies and by different authors. This is understandable, for many investigators are deeply concerned about the pressing need to find better indicators than now exist of the phenomena they wish to study. But the dilemma of equivalence thereby arises: When are the same relationships really being investigated? The substantiation of results by exact repetition of measures rarely occurs. At the same time, findings with little or no overlap in the measured behavior from one investigation to the next, but bearing identical concept labels, become the grounds for assuming that a consistent body of evidence exists, without the equivalence of the alternative measures ever having been established. When one is attempting to interpret similar but not the same measures, there are few ground rules for judging evidence as consistent or not. All too readily, theoretically attractive results with some semblance of measurement equivalence can be seized upon and knitted into one fabric of evidence. The findings and interpretations on punishment and aggression are an illustration. We found that problems of interpretation became acute when results from *similar* and presumably equivalent measures on the same mothers and children did not always replicate, and when the *same* measures on different samples did not always produce the same findings. The relationships regarding aggression were doubly vulnerable, for in both the dependent and independent variables various measures were subsumed under the same labels. When identical conceptual labels are attached to responses of many differing sorts and conditions, theoretical clarity is lost.

A labeling problem arises at another point in the machinery of research—in the coding process. Here the coder is sometimes instructed to feed into one categorizing label a variety of distinct dimensions of behavior. An illustration of such blending is provided in one of the maternal variables just reviewed, severity of punishment. "Severity," by definition, has absorbed form, frequency, and intensity of punishment. Differences in the provocation of punishment are not considered. In the data-gathering procedures that have been used, information on each of these several dimensions is likely to be provided very unevenly, and differently by different mothers. This leaves the coder with a difficult and ambiguous task: How shall he weight these various elements in arriving at an abstraction of severity, and how shall he deal with the unevennesses of information on the elements from different respondents? He may often place the same unifying label, "severe," on different types of actions that have little relation to one another on a single conceptual dimension. The investigator, also, is left with puzzles of interpretation: Which of the aspects of severity account for his findings?

Because it has not been possible to study directly many of the natural occurrences of child development, or to manipulate experiences in the model of experimental methodology, a wider gap than we readily admit has developed between the hypotheses that we wish to investigate and the array of data that we gather for these purposes. Labels, measures, and theories, as we know, must remain in close touch if inappropriate generalizations are to be avoided. The peculiar qualities of the research field we have been analyzing carry the potentials of a special kind of inappropriate generalization, which again makes us consider carefully the conceptual labels with which we are working. The data on aggression supply the illustrations.

"Severe" punishment and "highly" aggressive children have been important dimensions. In the theoretical writing on aggression, "hostility" and "rejection" by the parent are also involved. To test hypotheses concerning antecedents of aggression, the researchers have composed scales to reflect the "highs" and the "lows" in these relevant dimensions. The coders, armed with such scales, have had then to fit them to the data by evolving relative scales that distribute their samples of subjects. We have noted the homogeneity of samples that have represented the core of childrearing studies. The most likely mother-candidates for inclusion in these, we would hazard the guess, have not been those who viciously attack their children or subject them to extremes of neglect. "Severe" punishment from these mothers is likely to mean banishing the child to his bedroom, not speaking to him all day, or giving him "a sound spanking"—in other words, quite moderate punishments on an absolute scale. And the "highly" aggressive child in these studies is probably still a quite manageable child with momentary outbursts of angry kicks and bites and cries. The clinical picture of "high aggression," of vicious, intense, unjustified, generalized attack (Redl, 1951), similarly extends the aggression scale beyond the range of the children studied.

The rating scales have, therefore, been adjusted to a restricted range that may not really touch the "severe," "hostile," "rejecting," and similar categories.

We should, perhaps, ask ourselves the relevance of these contrasts for the theories we are attempting to build from the data we have used. Are there not problems in allowing the conceptual labels to be as freely elastic as we have tended to make them? Do we gain some different perspective on the information from the research of this field by recognizing that, because the subjects have been highly selected, the data from them provide us with variability within limited ranges on the dimensions of maternal rearing practices and child behavior? This limited variability can certainly be a factor in the paucity of results and instability of findings so characteristic of the data we have reviewed. Because of the limited ranges we may wonder, too: Can we extend interpretations of these childrearing data to the high keys in which theories of "aggression," "punitiveness," "rejection" and the like are expressed? If we have some misgivings about such interpretations, we pose another set of questions for ourselves: How shall these lower keys with which we have been dealing be interpreted?

◘ *CONCLUSIONS* ◘

We have remained uncommitted to particular theories and hypotheses concerning aggression; we have required the raw observations to speak strongly and unambiguously of a pattern in themselves. Our basic query has been concerned with the extent of stability of the relations obtained as this stability is intermeshed with issues of measurement, design, and analysis procedures. We have come to the rather severe conclusion that many of the hypotheses that have been advanced relating the child's aggression to frustrations and punishments and rewards in the rearing practices of the mother have not been substantially supported by consistent findings in the interview studies. The methodological factors that have posed the most serious questions have been the unknowns and inadequacies in instrument reliabilities, and the nonstandard, uncertainly equivalent, and uncertainly suitable conceptual labels in the data. For reasons to be found in such problems, it has been possible from the present work and from other reports and reviews in the literature about essentially the same body of research to come to quite different conclusions concerning the status of replicating support for hypotheses of maternal punishment antecedents of aggression. Interpretations of consistency, we feel, have slighted a great deal of evidence and have given theoretical expectations too compelling an influence.

CHAPTER 4

Conscience and
Its Correlates

Research design plays a part in shaping the nature of any research results. As the preceding chapters have indicated, the impact of design manifests itself at several levels—from the minutiae of measurement to issues of conceptualization of variables, and to broad levels concerned with general strategy for examining hypotheses. When one inspects the evidence on the development of conscience, the substantive focus of our discussion in this chapter, the guiding influence of design is apparent at every level, and its impact on issues of research strategy is especially obvious. In the pages that follow, we examine measures of the concept of conscience and its presumed antecedents in the mother's behavior, and assess the degree of replication achieved in research using these measures. Our own data and those of others permit us to raise questions concerning ways in which method may lead to spurious consistency in results. Further, these data enable us to raise a fundamental issue concerning the validity of measures of conscience and to appraise the adequacy of mother's reports in testing theories of the child's conscience formation.

One of man's age-old questions about man concerns the nature of what is morally "good" and "bad." With the development of social science, interest was directed to the empirical investigation of morality, and to the study of processes involved in its development. Researchers invested much energy in this area of questioning from the early 1900's up to the 1930's, the work of Hartshorne and May in 1928–1930 and Piaget in 1932 being the outstanding classics of the period. In the next two decades, however, little empirical work dealing directly with conscience and moral development followed up these studies. Then, beginning with Sears, Maccoby, and Levin's basic work (1957), the area of conscience development again became an active field of investigation. Sears' conceptualization and measurement of conscience have been influential in much of the childrearing research that has followed.

For our own exploration in this area, in addition to the data collected for this study, we have drawn on the data reported in Sears et al. (1957), Sears et al. (1965), and Burton (1959), plus additional analyses based on unpublished data collected as a part of that latter research. In this body of research, conscience is generally defined as an internalized control in which the child comes to punish or reward himself as though he has made the parent's standards his own. When he is tempted to deviate, the child whose conscience has developed appropriately exercises self-control without the need for external restraint; when he does commit a deviation from his standards, he experiences guilt or unpleasant feelings of remorse.

There are clearly two aspects of the construct "conscience" as defined here: the degree to which a person resists the temptation to deviate, and if he has deviated, the nature of his subsequent reactions. Does he experience guilt, confess his deviation, try to atone for his deed through making reparation, punish himself, hide, deny, blame others? In our current study, as in *Patterns of Child Rearing* and in a number of other studies of conscience development, the child's self-control when tempted is not measured; only the second aspect of conscience is measured—the child's reactions after he has deviated.

◘ *MEASURES OF CONSCIENCE* ◘

The research that we are examining has assessed conscience development through questions asked the mother about the child's behavior in a situation involving deviation. The interview questions in the NIMH study which closely parallel the questions used in the other studies are:

> How does X act when he has done something he knows you don't want him to do when your back is turned?
>
> Have you ever had the feeling that he has done something wrong that you don't know about? What indications did you have?
>
> Has he ever come to you and told you about it before you discovered it?
>
> When you ask him about something he has done that he knows he was not supposed to do, does he usually admit or deny it?
>
> How severe are you if he denies something you are pretty sure he has done?

Based on responses to this set of questions, the mother's descriptions of the child's reactions after deviation were rated on five-point scales on the following behavioral indicators: child grows silent, becomes very quiet (V 33b); looks or acts guilty, looks sheepish, sneaks around (V 33c); tells mother about deviation, blaming himself (V 33d); tells mother about deviation, blaming someone else (V 33e); no noticeable change in behavior (V 33a).[1] Coding reliability for these ratings ranged from $r = .73$ to $.84$. Responses to the questions

---

[1] Four additional indicators were dropped from analyses because almost no mother reported these behaviors. They were: child becomes more active and boisterous, asks mother for punishment, acts "nervous," and cries and whimpers.

concerned with the child's voluntary report of misdeeds (V 33) and his admitting wrongdoing when questioned (V 34) were also rated on five-point scales for the child's confession and admission of deviation. Coding reliabilities on these scales were .86 and .93, respectively. Finally, coders, considering all the information in response to this set of questions, made an overall conscience rating on a seven-interval scale (V 35). This scale from the Sears et al. (1957) codebook (III-34) is described as:

> Confession of deviation, acting guilty and feeling badly over deviations, admitting rather than denying. Hiding and other evidence of fear should be taken as evidence of *low* super-ego. Reparations are evidence of high super-ego. If any of the evidence of high super-ego explicitly occurs because of fear, however, it should be discounted. For example, if child admits rather than denies because he has been severely punished for denying, admitting is less direct evidence of super-ego.

This global rating has been generally used in investigating hypothesized antecedent-consequent relations. Coder reliabilities on this scale are .75 in the NIMH study, .63 in Sears et al. (1957), .83 in Burton (1959), and 94 per cent in Sears et al. (1965).[2] These reliabilities, of course, assess only the correspondence of judgments of the single interview report.[3] There is some evidence that correspondence is rather low when different persons provide independent reports of child behavior relating to conscience development. Eron, Banta, Walder, and Laulicht (1961), using the measure of confession, found a correlation between mother's and father's interview ratings of only +.25 (based on 50 parent pairs). Similar evidence appears in the NIMH study when ratings of confession and admission were made independently by the two teachers in each class. The

---

[2] See discussion of the method for computing percentage reliabilities in Sears et al. (1965) on pp. 282–283. The overall rating of conscience in that volume is a pooled rating from the interviews of both the mother and father.

[3] See pp. 62–64 of Chapter 3 for other types of reliability that might be considered.

interrater correlations were +.19 for ratings of confession and +.12 for ratings of admission. (Because of this very low correspondence, teacher ratings of conscience were dropped from our analyses.) Such evidence of disagreement between independent reporters raises serious doubts as to the adequacy of these indices. Are the behaviors observable by mothers? Are they so ambiguous in expression that they are not likely to be interpreted uniformly? The analyses we proceed on, therefore, will harbor doubts concerning the basic observations from which the conscience indices are derived.

INTERCORRELATIONS OF CONSCIENCE MEASURES

For a better understanding of the overall conscience rating, the intercorrelations of the component measures were examined: As is apparent in Table 10, confession and admission are strong contributors to the general measure. This is to be expected since they figure prominently in the definition of the concept used by the coders. Also, in the interview there were *specific* questions concerning the child's confession and admission after deviation. In contrast, ratings of the other specific behaviors entering the matrix depended on the mother's spontaneous reports of them. They were, therefore, much more subject to the vagaries of mothers' particular inclinations during the interview. In addition, skewness of the distributions of scores for these behavioral items probably acts to depress these correlations as compared with those of the more nearly normal distributions of the other conscience indices.

It is interesting that reports of the child's going silent, his looking or acting guilty, and his spontaneously blaming others tend to show negative associations with the overall conscience measure. What accounts for this? Coders may interpret these reported actions as evidence of hiding or fear and, according to coding instructions, would then consider them as evidence of *low* conscience development. The adequacy of the definitional set imposed for coding would seem to raise certain methodological difficulties. We shall return to this problem later in the discussion of findings on correlates of conscience development.

Table 10

INTERCORRELATION OF CONSCIENCE MEASURES
(TOTAL SAMPLE, MALES, AND FEMALES)

Variable Number	Conscience Measures	33a	33b	33c	33d	33e	33	34	35
33a	No noticeable change	—	-06 / -03	-34* / -12	-13 / 03	-08 / -01	-11 / -28	01 / -31*	-32* / -34*
33b	Goes silent	-05	—	14 / -08	08 / -08	-13 / -01	20 / 02	18 / -23	20 / -23
33c	Looks and acts guilty, sheepish, sneaks around	-23*	05	—	03 / -20	-04 / 12	-24 / -28	-09 / -10	05 / -30
33d	Tells mother about deviation, blames *self*	-06	00	-10	—	-23 / -16	64* / 67*	41* / 60*	53* / 31*
33e	Tells mother about deviation, blames *others*	-05	-08	04	-19	—	-08 / 05	-44* / -35*	-22 / -25
33	Confesses after deviation	-19	12	-27*	66*	-01	—	38* / 77*	60* / 70*
34	Admission after deviation	-13	02	-08	46*	-40*	50*	—	75* / 75*
35	Conscience	-33	-01	-14	41*	-23*	65*	74*	—

Maximum sample size on which correlations are based: 86 (43 boys, 43 girls). Data on total sample are below the diagonal. In each cell above the diagonal correlations for girls are indicated immediately beneath those for boys.

◘ *SOME HYPOTHESIZED ANTECEDENTS* ◘
OF CONSCIENCE

A generally accepted theoretical scheme for investigating conscience development has been delineated by Sears, Maccoby, and
Levin (pp. 363–393). According to their presentation, the optimum
condition for the development of conscience in the child is one in
which there is a warm mother-child relationship in combination with
the mother's use of disciplinary techniques that keep the child oriented toward restoring his mother's love following discipline. Given
such circumstances, the child should identify strongly with the parent
and incorporate the parent's values and standards as his own. With
this accomplished, the child should take over the rewarding and
punishing functions formerly only performed by the parents and
apply them to himself. This internalization of what were previously
externally administered sanctions leads to desired self-control and
conscience. In contrast, a parent who is rejecting and uses techniques
of punishment that tend to make the child want to avoid or hide
from him will inhibit the process of identification. A relatively low
level of conscience development should result.

This conceptualization has directed many of the childrearing
studies to the investigation of affectional relations and techniques of
parental control as possible contributors to conscience development.
In this body of literature the conclusion, which has become quite
firmly fixed, is that the relation between conscience and warmth
and love-oriented techniques of parental control has been well established. Sears has been quite consistent in his interpretation originally
stated in *Patterns of Child Rearing* (p. 389) that:

> We can say with some degree of conviction that
> mothers who love and accept their children, and who use
> love-oriented techniques of discipline rather than material
> or physical techniques, produce relatively more children
> with high conscience.

This view is repeated again in his summary of the growth of conscience:

> . . . the mothers of the children with strong consciences were the ones who were the "accepting" mothers, . . . who liked their children, who appear to have never had any reluctance to accept them as members of the family . . . (Sears, 1960, p. 104).

And Sears, Rau, and Alpert (1965, p. 225) state that "The *Patterns* findings are fairly well replicated for both sexes. Warmth, permissiveness, and the use of praise all appear prominently in both lists [of significant correlations for boys and girls between the parent-interview rating of conscience and ratings of childrearing practices]."

Reviews of research on conscience development have come to the same conclusions: "In summary, these various studies suggest that internalized reactions to transgression in the form of guilt or acceptance of self-responsibility for misdeed are more likely to occur when the parent is warm and uses techniques of discipline which utilize the love relations to the parent for their effects" (Becker, 1964, p. 185). "We may tentatively conclude that an internalized moral orientation is fostered by an affectionate relationship between the parent and child, in combination with the use of discipline techniques which utilize this relationship by appealing to the child's personal and social motives" (Hoffman, 1963(a), p. 305). "It seems clear from the research review that an internalized moral orientation is . . . fostered . . . by the combination of affection and inductive discipline, especially other-oriented induction, and the relative absence of power assertions" (Hoffman, 1963(b), p. 109). Kohlberg (1963, p. 298) also concludes that his review "suggests a relationship between both maternal and paternal nurturance and conscience." But that all is not completely consistent in this regard is indicated by Bronfenbrenner (1962) who, after quoting Hoffman's (1962) conclusion, states, "But as is readily apparent from a reading of Hoffman's painstaking survey, the preceding generalization, valid as it probably is, nevertheless conceals under its very generality a multitude of major lacunae, qualifications, ambiguities, and even contradictions" (p. S-11).[4]

[4] In his brief review, Bronfenbrenner did not have the opportunity to deal with many of the factors limiting the nature of the generalization one

Important sources of such qualifications concerning the antecedents of conscience may be traced to problems in research designs and techniques. Although research workers and reviewers of research have now and again indicated that there are problems in the work that has been done, in spite of such recognitions, some of the generally accepted conclusions regarding the development of conscience are based on data in which there are serious methodological weaknesses.

In the pages that follow, we consider interview studies of conscience to examine the extent to which the findings are consistent and convincing in the light of two major kinds of methodological difficulties. One of these concerns the nonindependence of data sources for the theoretically antecedent and consequent variables. The second concerns the difficulties in attempting to develop indices through verbal reports of complex processes such as conscience formation and affectional relations between mother and child.

CONSCIENCE AND THE AFFECTIONAL BOND

Measures of mother-child affectional relations that have served in the interview studies of conscience have been of two kinds: global ratings that take into consideration many different kinds of behavior on the part of the mother, and ratings based on answers to specific questions about affectional demonstrativeness, enjoying the child, playing with him, doing things to please him, and so on. Measures labeled "warmth" are generally the global ratings; the entire interview is the source of such appraisals. This warmth measure was used by Sears et al. (1957), and was followed in the studies by Burton (1959), Sears et al. (1965), and NIMH. Sears et al. (1957) used an additional global rating of rejection. On this (as they noted, p. 170) they encountered difficulties. Of 379 mothers in their study, 58 could not be scored, 220 mothers were rated as showing no rejection, and 101 were grouped together as showing *some*

---

may make about the relation between parental functioning and the child's conscience development. He did, however, sketch in illustratively the manner in which sex (both of the child and the parent) and family socioeconomic status played an important part in tempering the effect of the parent's behavior on the moral development of the child.

rejection, by allowing even the slightest indication to place them in the "rejection" category. To try to avoid similar difficulties, specific questions were used in the Burton and NIMH studies to attempt to assess rejection and acceptance. Thus, the studies in our analyses provide very nearly identical procedures for assessing warmth and affectional demonstrativeness, and different procedures for apprais-ing acceptance and rejection. The associations of these measures with conscience development appear in Tables 11 and 12.

Correlations on the *total samples* in the NIMH, Sears et al. (1957), and Burton[5] studies are consistent in showing a positive and statistically significant association between the warmth measure and the child's conscience. The measures of "acceptance" (number of things listed by mother that she likes about the child) also produced significant positive correlations for the total samples in both the NIMH and Burton studies. Associations between conscience and demonstrativeness are positive but not statistically significant in the studies reporting this measure. These findings, based on combined data for boys and girls, show clearly the basis for the conclusion that ratings of maternal warmth and ratings of conscience are positively related. This consistency is rather convincing replication.

For indices of "rejection," however, there is little evidence of association with a measure of conscience. For the total samples, "rejection" and conscience are unrelated in the NIMH and Burton studies[6] ($r = +.05$ and $+.01$, respectively [Table 11]), and very little related in Sears et al. (1957) when one compares proportions of high conscience children for mothers rated as more or as less "re-jecting" (Table 12). The percentage differences in the NIMH data do not follow the trend reported in *Patterns of Child Rearing*, which couples more conscience development with "acceptance." Burton's percentages are in the same direction as those of Sears et al., but it

---

[5] The NIMH procedure for summing scores was applied to the Bur-ton data. This differs from the procedures used in Burton, Maccoby, and Allinsmith (1961).

[6] The correlations between "number of things enjoyed" and "number of annoying things," hovering near zero in both Burton (1959) and the NIMH study, cast doubt either on the unitary nature of the concept, acceptance-rejection, or on the adequacy of these indices as measures of this concept.

Table 11

CORRELATIONS OF CONSCIENCE MEASURES WITH MEASURES OF AFFECTIONAL RELATIONS

Affectional Scales	Correlations			Reference Information		Variable Number	
	Total	Boys	Girls	Study	Page Reference	Affectional Rating	Conscience
Global rating of warmth	21*	24	19	NIMH		23	35
	10*	15*	04	Sears et al. 1957[a]	382	III-15	III-34
		15	−09	Sears 1961	476	III-15	III-34
		47*	−06	Sears et al. 1965[a]	226	118	89[b]
Summated warmth score	23*	32*	18	Burton unpublished		$\Sigma 12$[c]	4-31
Factor score of warmth		53*	13	Sears et al. 1965[a]	226	174[d]	89
Affectional demonstrativeness	12	20	04	NIMH		24	35
	10	03	14	Burton unpublished		4-10	4-31
		47*	06	Sears et al. 1965[a]	226	120	89
Things enjoyed in child	22*	30*	17	NIMH		26	35
	24*	13	36*	Burton unpublished		4-5	4-31
Annoying things about child	05	−16	19	NIMH		25	35
	01	−20	24	Burton unpublished		4-6	4-31

Maximum sample size in each study: NIMH, 86 (43 boys, 43 girls); Sears et al. (1957), 379; Sears (1961), 160 (76 boys, 84 girls); Burton, 77 (40 boys, 37 girls); Sears et al. (1965), 40 (21 boys, 19 girls). The Sears (1961) report is based on a subsample of the Sears et al. (1957) study.

[a] Additional information providing correlations on boys and girls separately was given by Robert R. Sears in personal communication.

[b] Conscience is a pooled rating from mother and father interviews.

[c] A mean of the standardized scores of eight scales measuring some aspects of the mother-child affectional relationship.

[d] Derived from weighting the five scales found in Sears et al. (1957) to load on the factor labeled "Warmth."

is of course obvious from the correlation of +.01 in Burton that there is no strong support for a proposition associating "rejection" with low conscience.

The picture of relationships between affectional measures and conscience becomes slightly more complicated (and possibly more clarified) when the data are analyzed for each sex separately. The correlations of Table 11 show that the associations between warmth and the other indicators of acceptance (or nonrejection) and high conscience are closer in the data for boys than for girls. (For 11 of 13 comparisons this directional pattern is stronger for the boys; and six of the correlations tabled reach significance for boys; for girls, only one.) Further, while the boys show *no* departure from directional consistency in associations between measures of conscience and affectional relations, four of 13 correlations for girls (warmth in Sears, 1961, and Sears et al., 1965; and number of annoying things about child in NIMH and Burton) depart, though not significantly, from the predominant directional pattern.

These analyses assessing the replicability of various aspects of the warmth-conscience relationship point out a necessary qualification of what has been considered a well-established finding. Conscience's tie both to measures of maternal acceptance and rejection cannot be satisfactorily appraised if sex of child is ignored in data analyses.

AFFECTIONAL RELATIONS AND DEPENDENCY IN RELATION TO CONSCIENCE

In the theoretical portrayal of the identification process (Sears et al., 1957; Sears et al., 1965), the child's dependency is considered to be a necessary but not a sufficient condition for identification and, in turn, for the development of conscience. A clearer relationship between conscience and its antecedent affectional conditions is predicted when both rejection and dependency are considered simultaneously as antecedents of the child's conscience development. The reasoning is based on the expectation of a positive relation between rejection and dependency, a positive association between dependency and conscience development, and a negative association between rejection and conscience. (Cf. discussion in Sears

Table 12

PERCENTAGE OF CHILDREN RATED HIGH IN CONSCIENCE IN RELATION TO HIGH
AND LOW RATINGS OF MATERNAL REJECTION

Rejection Measures	High Conscience	Reference Information		Variable Number	
		Study		Rejection	Conscience
Annoying things about child:					
Many	33% (33)	NIMH		25	35
Few	28% (53)				
Many	23% (13)	Burton unpublished		4-6	4-31
Few	31% (64)				
Rejection:					
Rejected	18% (99)	Sears et al. 1957, p. 382		IV-29	III-34
Accepted	31% (218)				

Numbers within parentheses indicate the total *n* in each subgroup of maternal measures.

et al., 1957, pp. 382–383.) Data from the Sears et al. and NIMH studies permit tests of this prediction:

(1) A slight positive association ($r = +.12$) between rejection and dependency was obtained in the Sears et al. study (p. 171). Associations between the NIMH rejection measure and dependency (V's 25, 28) are +.04 for the total sample, −.04 for boys, and +.10 for girls.

(2) A positive relation between dependency and conscience is reported in *Patterns of Child Rearing,* but only for boys and then only as a slight, statistically nonsignificant relation which goes in the theoretically expected direction. These findings are presented in percentage terms: Judged to have high conscience were 26 per cent of the more dependent boys, while only 16 per cent of the less dependent ones were so rated (p. 383). A subsequent report (Sears, 1961) indicates that dependency was correlated +.06 for a sample of boys and +.02 for girls from the 1957 sample. On comparable measures of dependency and conscience in the NIMH study, the correlations are .00 in the total sample, +.04 for boys, and −.05 for girls.

(3) A slight negative relation between rejection and conscience (percentage analysis) was reported by Sears et al. The NIMH measures of rejection and conscience produced correlations of +.05 for the total sample, −.16 for boys and +.19 for girls. The data from Sears et al. conform to the prediction that the inclusion of rejection and dependency would help to clarify the relation between conscience and the affectional measures. In the analyses of NIMH data the same pattern of relationships is not in evidence (Table 13).

TECHNIQUES OF CHILDREARING IN RELATION TO CONSCIENCE

Along with maternal warmth, the "love-oriented" techniques of discipline are considered to be positively associated with conscience development and the "materialistic" techniques to be negatively related to conscience. These classes of techniques have been variously labeled. "Love-oriented," "psychological," or "induction" techniques generally include praise, isolation, withdrawal of love, and reasoning. "Materialistic" techniques are similar to those

Table 13

PERCENTAGE OF CHILDREN RATED HIGH ON CONSCIENCE IN RELATION TO

RATINGS OF CHILD'S DEPENDENCY AND MATERNAL RATINGS OF REJECTION

Rejection Measures	Low Dependency High Conscience		High Dependency High Conscience	
	Boys	Girls	Boys	Girls
Annoying things about child (NIMH) :				
Many	29% (7)	83% (6)	22% (9)	18% (11)
Few	21% (14)	31% (13)	33% (12)	27% (11)
Rejection (Sears et al, 1957, p. 383) :				
Rejected	10% (30)	18% (17)	15% (26)	31% (27)
Accepted	21% (58)	36% (60)	33% (55)	37% (46)

Numbers within parentheses indicate the total *n* in each subgroup of maternal measures.

that have been labeled "object-oriented," "sensitization," "direct," or "power assertion" techniques; these include tangible rewards, deprivation of privileges, and especially use of physical punishment. The conclusion regarding an association between conscience and these two classes of techniques is considered well verified as evidenced by its being cited in Berelson and Steiner's (1964, p. 77) inventory: "The more the control of the child is love-oriented, rather than based on physical punishment, the more effective is the parents' control over desired behavior and the stronger the development of the child's guilt feelings for improper behavior." Before committing oneself to accepting this proposition, one should look at the generality with which it is supported by empirical data.

Maternal disciplinary and control practices have been studied in relation to conscience with similar procedures in the four studies used in our analyses. Evidence from these investigations is presented in Table 14. Not a single one of the disciplinary and control measures consistently shows statistically significant correlations with conscience across the four studies. Only if one considers the directions of the correlations, whether significant or not, can one find some consistencies in patterns of relations.

Of the love-oriented techniques, only the mother's reported use of praise and reasoning gives a consistent picture in the direction of positive associations. Findings on the role of isolation are quite inconsistent. Sears, Maccoby, and Levin reported that 29 per cent of the cases rated high in use of isolation were rated high conscience, while only 17 per cent of those rated low in use of isolation were similarly classed as high conscience (p. 386). In contrast, the NIMH study shows negative relations for both boys and girls. The Burton data show both positive and negative relations. Similarly, there are no consistent associations between the reported use of love withdrawal and conscience; the evidence does not support the generally familiar conclusion.

Among the *object-oriented* types of discipline, tangible rewards, use of physical punishment, and general severity of punishment tend to show the hypothesized negative relations with conscience; data on deprivation of privileges, however, fail to conform to the pattern. As is apparent in Table 14, the strongest support for

Table 14

CORRELATIONS OF DISCIPLINARY TECHNIQUES WITH MEASURES OF CONSCIENCE

Disciplinary Measures	Correlations Between Techniques and Conscience			Reference Information		Variable Number	
	Total	Boys	Girls	Study	Page Reference	Technique	Conscience
Love-oriented techniques:							
Praise	18*	19*	16*	Sears et al. 1957[a]	386	III-37	III-34
		19	19	Sears 1961	476	III-37	III-34
	15	13	16	Burton unpublished		3-36	4-31
	21	12	27			Σ17	4-31
		50*	23	Sears et al. 1965[a]	226	94	89
Isolation	—15	—23	—10	NIMH		1	35
	00	11		Sears et al. 1957	386	III-52	III-34
	—01	00	—12	Burton unpublished		3-43	4-31
	—02	02	—05			Σ18	4-31
			24	Sears et al. 1965[a]	226	66	89
Love withdrawal	—02	—06	02	NIMH		2	35
	09	03	11	Sears et al. 1957	386	III-53	III-34
			10	Sears 1961	476	III-53	III-34
	—04	—18	—02	Burton unpublished		3-41	4-31
	—17	—34*	03			Σ16	4-31
		08		Sears et al. 1965[a]	226	98	89
Reasoning	11	16	08	NIMH		3	35
	18*			Sears et al. 1957	386	III-57	III-34
	19	10	28	Burton unpublished		3-62	4-31
	23	24	22			Σ22	4-31
		32	11	Sears et al. 1965[a]	226	64	89

Object-oriented techniques:

Tangible rewards	NIMH	−19	−27	−11		4	35
	Sears et al. 1957[a]	−04	−06	01	386	III-36	III-34
	Sears 1961		−17	−04	476	III-36	III-34
	Burton unpublished	−03	11	−15		3-31	4-31
		−02	−09	07		Σ19	4-31
	Sears et al. 1965[a]		21	25	226	96	89
Deprivation of privileges	NIMH	11	02	24		5	35
	Sears et al. 1957[a]	−07	−07	−08	386	III-47	III-34
	Sears 1961		−14	11	476	III-47	III-34
	Burton unpublished	18	14	18		3-52	4-31
	Sears et al. 1965[a]		16	−03	226	69	89
Physical punishment	NIMH	−01	07	−07		6	35
	Sears et al. 1957[a]	−20*	−23*	−18*	386	III-46	III-34
	Sears 1961		−25*	−25*	476	III-46	III-34
	Burton unpublished	−18	−24	−17		3-54	4-31
		−15	−26	−05		Σ23	4-31
	Sears et al. 1965[a]		−14	−51*	226	67	89
Severity of punishment	NIMH	−06	03	−14		20	35
	Burton unpublished	−05	−10	−03		3-55	4-31
Severity of punishment for denial	NIMH	05	−01	10		14a	35

[a] Additional information providing correlations on boys and girls separately was given by Robert R. Sears in personal communication.

the view that object-oriented or power-assertion techniques are productive of low, rather than high, conscience comes from data on
physical punishment, where correlations are, with one exception,
negative, and in several instances significantly so.

Our survey of discipline and conscience formation has thus
far only inspected data in which the reported techniques were considered singly. The possibility remains that more clarification of the
manner in which such practices influence the development of conscience might result if one viewed the *combined* impact of techniques. Sears, Maccoby, and Levin have taken such an approach.
They reasoned that love withdrawal should have little effect on the
child's behavior if the relation between mother and child was one
in which little love existed. They considered, therefore, the combined
influence of the warmth of the relationship and the use of love withdrawal. A hypothesis was formulated that "The pattern most calculated to produce 'high conscience' should be that of mothers who
are usually warm and loving and then, as a method of control,
threaten this affectionate relationship" (p. 388).

This hypothesis, which sounds most reasonable, was explored
with their data. A percentage analysis was used in which mothers
high in both warmth and love withdrawal were compared with
mothers showing the other patterns of warmth and love withdrawal.
They found that high conscience ratings were most frequent among
children whose mothers were rated high on warmth and love withdrawal. Identical analyses were carried out in the NIMH and Burton
data (Table 15). In neither of these studies is there support for the
hypothesized interaction effect of warmth and love withdrawal on
conscience.

In general, then, the disciplinary techniques have shown
neither strong nor consistent associations across studies. The theoretical prediction for the class of love-oriented techniques to be positively related is not well supported, for both negative and positive
associations appear. The prediction for the class of object-oriented
techniques to be negatively related to perceived conscience development receives some support. We have also seen that the Burton and
NIMH data on the combination of warmth and love withdrawal

Table 15

PERCENTAGE OF CHILDREN RATED HIGH ON CONSCIENCE

IN RELATION TO

MATERNAL RATING OF WARMTH AND USE OF LOVE WITHDRAWAL

Ratings of Warmth and Use of Love Withdrawal	*NIMH* *High* *Conscience*	*Sears et al.* *1957, p. 388* *High* *Conscience*	*Burton* *High* *Conscience*
Low warmth:			
High love withdrawal	23% (13)	18%	23% (13)
Low love withdrawal	25% (12)	25%	13% (24)
High warmth:			
High love withdrawal	30% (30)	42%	31% (16)
Low love withdrawal	36% (28)	24%	50% (24)

Numbers within parentheses indicate the total *n* in each subgroup of combined maternal measures.

have not provided a replication of a major conclusion for conscience development.

▣ *METHODOLOGICAL ISSUES WITHIN THE INTERVIEW DESIGN* ▣

In reviewing the data on conscience and its correlates in childrearing conditions, we have appraised the consistency of results and the tenability of the interpretations that have been made of the findings. We have not questioned the data themselves in methodological terms, except to bring up the reminder that one often is dealing only with directions of associations, that statistical significance even at the 5 per cent level has not often been attained. We shall now reassess the data from the viewpoint of the particular hazards which derive from the verbal report designs that have been used. Among these factors, unreliability, nonindependence of the measures, and lack of validational evidence are especially relevant for these studies of conscience.

CODING RELIABILITY

Questions of unreliability of the data pertaining to conscience parallel those that have been examined in the discussion of aggression. Achieving adequate coding reliabilities has been difficult for some of the measures. For the dimension of maternal warmth that is of key importance in the hypotheses of conscience development, coefficients of reliabilities are .65 in NIMH and .53 in Sears et al. (1957); for love withdrawal, .68 in NIMH and .50 in Sears et al. (1957). A count of the mother's descriptions of annoying aspects of the child in NIMH presents fewer coding problems (.93). An overall rating of rejection was very difficult to make (.57, Sears et al., 1957). Interview ratings of conscience, too, suffer from coder disagreements (.75 and .63, NIMH and Sears et al., 1957, respectively). Even with the Spearman-Brown correction, many of these reliabilities account for less than 50 per cent of the variance. With such low reliabilities, it is to be expected that any relations found with these measures are only suggestive, and may be gross underestimates of the "true" relations between variables.

NONINDEPENDENCE

It is well known that independence of measures is necessary to obviate spurious relations within a study. The nonindependence with which we have been concerned in earlier discussions has been one in which both the "cause" and the "effect" are in the words of the mother-reporter. Under such circumstances, contaminations or built-in associations are quite likely possibilities. There are, in addition, other types of nonindependence that color the picture of consistencies and the interpretation of results. The measures of hypothesized antecedents of conscience illustrate this kind of nonindependence. For example, warmth, acceptance, and affectional demonstrativeness are scales and labels that have all been used for the same general domain of positive mother-child relations. Each is related positively to conscience (Table 11). All too easily these findings may become seen as consistency of evidence for the warmth-conscience hypothesis. It is here that the intercorrelations among these measures point out the fact that the several correlations cannot be considered independent tests of the hypothesis. In the NIMH data, warmth and demonstrativeness are correlated +.67, warmth and acceptance +.38, acceptance and demonstrativeness +.32. Similar overlap occurs in other studies. A return to the data-gathering and coding procedures reveals quickly the sources of overlap. The mother has been asked several questions, each of which draws upon the same or similar aspects of her responses. Next, the coder has been instructed to use some of the same responses for variously labeled ratings. Nonindependence of these kinds can produce a spurious notion of independently substantiated relationships.

Nonindependence of measures may enter at the point of coding procedures to influence in another way the relations between presumed antecedent and consequent dimensions. Findings for physical punishment seem to merit some special discussion in this regard. Summaries of findings on conscience development have concluded that there is a negative relationship between parental use of physical punishment and conscience, and one sees a basis for this conclusion in the generally negative signs of the correlations in Table 14. However, if one looks closely at the framework that guides the coders, one becomes aware of a possible contribution to this negative association within the coding instructions. Many of the studies have employed the measure developed by Sears, Maccoby, and Levin. One notes in the general description of the conscience measure (see p. 97) that any evidence of reactions after deviation based on fear or due to the child's having been severely punished is to be discounted as an indicator of conscience development. Such interpretive directions may have led to some conceptual ambiguity between investigator and coder. If, after reading that the parent has used corporal punishment to try to enforce his standards, the coder considers the reactions of the child to be based on fear of physical punishment, he may discount material that might otherwise have been weighted in the direction of high conscience. For example, a hypothetical mother might state, when asked whether her child ever denies a deviation, that "he never denies." But she continues:

> He once did, and I gave him a really good spanking for it. He almost always comes to me right away now to tell me if he's done something wrong. If he doesn't confess, I can always tell because he just looks so guilty.

Though it is clear that the child has internalized the parental standards, he will not be rated "high" on conscience if the coder observes the directions in the code to discount behavior that is due to fear or having been severely punished. The negative signs of the correlations between the rating of conscience and the ratings of the child's behavior of "going silent" and of "looking guilty" may be attributable to these instructions. That there is a generally negative association between punishment and conscience as measured in the interview cannot be gainsaid, but there is the possibility that the association has, to some degree, a methodological source.

VALIDITY

The preceding analyses and discussions may be considered by some students of conscience development to be premature. Until it has been established that the measures are appropriate for the concepts in which one is interested, considerations of consistency, reliability, statistical significance, and nonindependence may seem irrelevant. Researchers (and reviewers) have mainly followed two strategies to validate conscience measures used in the interview studies. The most common procedure for assessing validity has been to consider consistency in direction of relations in various studies using different measures and research designs (construct validity, Cronbach and Meehl, 1955), in this way assessing the justification of using the same rubric to encompass all the findings. A second strategy is to correlate interview ratings with behavioral data presumably measuring the same concept.

Only studies that were closely comparable in interview design, measures, and age of subjects have been included for comparison in our analyses of conscience development so far; the larger body of research on conscience will serve as a better basis for evidences of validity. In evaluating evidence on construct validity, these studies may be divided into those in which antecedent and consequent measures are obtained from a single source, and those in which the antecedent and consequent measures are obtained from independent sources. Interpretations of the findings from the *nonindependent* designs have generally been that warmth and psychological or love-oriented techniques of control are positively related to conscience, whereas use of physical punishment is negatively related to conscience (see reviews by Becker, 1964; Hoffman, 1963(a); Kohlberg, 1963). Quite different measures, bearing the same labels, have been used in the various studies. The consistency of results deriving from these varied sources supports an interpretation that the diverse measures have construct validity, but the nonindependence of data sources in these studies detracts from the persuasibility of the consistencies for validational purposes.

A number of studies permit validity assessments from *independent* designs in which comparisons are made of interview measures of conscience (essentially guilt) and behavioral measures of the child's resistance to temptation in a controlled experimental situation (Burton et al., 1961; Grinder, 1962; Sears et al., 1965). A complicating factor is at once apparent, for although guilt and resistance to temptation are by definition components of conscience, they *may* be quite distinct theoretically. These studies show no consistency in direction of relation between the *rating* of mother's description of the child's conscience and the child's conscience-relevant behavior in the experimental situations. For the two studies in which these were contemporaneous measures, one (Burton et al., 1961, p. 701) shows a slight though nonsignificant negative relation for both boys and girls; the other (Sears et al., 1965, p. 216) shows a nonsignificant positive association for boys and a nonsignificant negative association for the girls. Grinder (1962, p. 816) compared the interview measures of conscience with a measure of children's cheating in a game, *six years* later. He found no relation for boys, but a positive association for girls ($\chi^2 = 9.03$, $p < .05$). From these three studies, then, we do not accumulate support for a unitary construct of conscience.

Of cogency here, too, are comparisons of relations found between rearing practices and conscience when both sets of measures are from the interview with those obtained when rearing measures are from the interview and conscience measures are observed responses to temptation in a laboratory setting. The rearing correlates of resistance to temptation reported in three studies (Grinder, 1962; Burton et al., 1961; and Sears et al., 1965) are not consistent with the rearing correlates of interview ratings of conscience.

Overall, then, the evidence in support of construct validity is ambiguous: Where considerable consistency across studies is found, the nonindependence of data sources places limitations on the interpretations. Where observations of resistance to temptation and interview ratings of conscience (guilt) are involved, there are many discrepant findings. But since these are *different* conceptual aspects of conscience it is doubtful whether the discrepancies are relevant to questions of construct validity.

We turn now to data provided by a more direct approach to validation, one which compares verbal and behavioral measures of the same aspects of conscience. Sears et al. (1960 and 1965) provide such data. In this study mother-interview ratings of confession were correlated with confession measured in an experimental situation. The association was −.31 for both boys and girls. In this study, too, behavioral measures of emotional upset, confession following deviation, resistance to temptation, and fixing or making reparation for deviation were correlated with the interview measure of conscience (1965, p. 216). These analyses showed no significant relations for boys between the interview rating and the observed behaviors; there are actually mainly negative signs for the correlations. For the girls, there is one association, between observed emotional upset and interview rating, of +.45, which approaches significance. Further, when the childrearing correlates of the interview measure of conscience and the childrearing correlates of the behavioral measures of conscience are compared, the interview and behavioral indices are related to completely different rearing variables (1965, pp. 226, 234, and 236). Were these data from two independent samples of subjects, the conflicting results would be attributable to any number of things that invariably distinguish different studies. But the fact that the measures were obtained at nearly the same point in time and on the same subjects, and that confession and emotional upset following deviation are so very much the ingredients of the interview rating of conscience, implores serious students of conscience development to ask, as do Sears et al. (p. 236), whether the same terms should be applied to the measures derived from the interview and from the experimental assessment situation. These findings clearly challenge any assumption that parents' reports validly reflect internalization of moral norms as appraised through behavioral indicators, at least those in experimental situations. These findings also highlight the dangers involved in relying on consistency of relations within a nonindependent set of data to establish construct validity. The researcher must establish the validity of his measure through relations with independent sets of data, in ways such as have been delineated by Campbell and Fiske (1959). Just what has been measured in the mother interviews under the label of conscience development in the child seems unclear at this time. On the other hand, the evidence now available does indicate that there is little support for interpreting the measure as reflection of child behaviors in test situations that attempt directly to assess moral choices.

As has been stressed in this and preceding chapters, some methodological factors contribute to increasing the likelihood of finding certain "false" relations and others tend to erase "true" relations. To these precautions we must now add the sobering finding that validational evidence, as far as it exists, presents a serious challenge to interpretations that treat interview evidence as equivalent to behavior. Much more research is needed on the correspondence between verbal report measures of child and mother's behavior and observed behavior. The scarcity of such research is undoubtedly related to difficulties in measuring social interaction. From those studies that have attempted to measure parent-child interactions through both interviews and observations (Smith, 1953, 1958; Zunich, 1962; Brody, 1965; Sears et al., 1965), however, there is little comfort for assuming that ratings *labeled* the same in a parental interview and in direct observations are calibrating the same aspects of behavior.

In drawing conclusions from all these disparate results, from studies avowedly concerned with the same phenomena, one might best follow the guides for newspaper reporting and return to the actual measures to examine exactly *what* was measured and *when, where,* and *how* it was done. Such a guide may help in arriving at a reasonable appraisal of the theoretical significance of the findings.

These issues of validity of the individual measures of conscience lead to further considerations of their suitability for investigating theories of conscience formation.

◘ *METHODOLOGY AND THE TESTING OF*
THEORIES OF CONSCIENCE FORMATION ◘

General theoretical models of conscience formation are typically framed in a *developmental* context. Although psychoanalytically based theories of identification and behaviorally oriented theories of conscience formation may differ in emphases and in particulars, they share a common focus on the role played by parental handling of the child's deviations (especially parental punishment). These parental actions are viewed as precursors to feelings of guilt or remorse after transgression of rules and to the ability to resist temptation.

The following hypothetical example may enable us to portray how relevant theoretical orientations might interpret a sequence of events in a child's learning to comply with parental rules:

> Jennifer, at eighteen months, likes to climb up into her mother's new velvet chairs and bounce on the cushions. Her parents may try to "explain" to her at this age that the chairs will be "hurt" and her shoes will make the pretty velvet "ugly." But Jennifer's language development does not allow her to understand these reasons for not bouncing on the chair. Even if she might "understand" that her parents are not pleased when she bounces, it is such great fun that she does not care much about paying attention to what they are saying. But when her mother takes her by the arm and says, "No, no, Jennifer! You have to sit in this chair because that was naughty to bounce on the velvet chair," and physically takes her to a chair that isolates her from the other persons in the home, Jennifer does experience something she doesn't like and cannot ignore. Most parents will add enough direct physical control of the child with their actions so that the child will find the situation aversive. Sometimes in the months that follow the parent may take Jennifer quite roughly from the velvet chair and place her in the isolation chair, another time she may shake her, the next time she may raise her voice, and another occasion may elicit a spanking from the parent. The parent may also try to anticipate Jennifer's behavior and to stop her from climbing into the chair before she places her foot on the velvet.

The parent may also think that Jennifer is about to climb into the velvet chair but then she turns away. The mother may then say, "Good girl, Jennifer, not to climb into the velvet chairs. You know you are not to climb into *those* chairs." One day the parent may observe Jennifer saying to herself, "No, no, Jennifer, naughty!" when Jennifer has one knee on the velvet seat and is about to climb into the chair. The mother may then say, "Good girl, Jennifer," and watch her turn to something else. Another time, she may find Jennifer, of her own volition, sitting in the isolated chair and then discover that the spring has come through the cushion of the velvet chair.

As the months go by, Jennifer's linguistic ability increases so that she does comprehend many parental attempts to explain or reason with her about not breaking a rule. The parents also find that the verbal reprimands, which have accompanied the direct techniques and which were originally ineffective because Jennifer ignored them, are eventually sufficient to terminate or to prevent her undesired behavior. Even certain facial expressions from the parent now seem effective as punishment. Increasingly the parents rely on these less direct forms of control since they can be applied at a distance and with greater immediacy than the direct physical types of control. Occasionally it may be necessary for the mother to employ some direct control when it seems Jennifer does not react to the indirect forms. Gradually, such occasions diminish in frequency.

Theories of identification would interpret this series of events to be a portrayal of the child's internalizing the parent's standards as well as the parent's rewarding and punishing functions. The child's desire to recapture the nurturant parent when the child is alone (a motive brought about through the infant's initial dependency on the parents to satisfy all his needs), and the child's need to reduce anxiety about a punishing parent by adopting the parent's standards are hypothesized to be the major determinants in this process. The anxiety aroused by the helplessness of the infant when he needs something and the parent is not around to take care of it for him, results in the child's trying to take on some aspects of the parent through imitating him. The anxiety associated with actual or threatened punishment from the parent is the motive for the child's incorporating the parent's standards and finally for applying the punishment to himself. (Cf. Sears et al., 1957, pp. 363–382, for a more complete description.)

A learning (or behavior) theory interpretation, by comparison, would view the ineffectiveness of the parents' initial attempts to explain and reason with Jennifer as due to the absence of necessary associations between the verbal area and aversive experiences. In the account above, one sees a learning history in which the verbal and visual techniques acquire some anxiety-arousing qualities that can then effectively deter Jennifer from responding in certain ways. The effectiveness of these indirect techniques—those labeled psychological, love withdrawal, or induction—is then seen to derive from their having been associated with more intrinsically rewarding and punishing situations. Jennifer's resisting the temptation to bounce in the chair is interpreted as avoidance of anxiety aroused when she puts her knee on the seat preparing to climb up, anxiety that has become associated with these proprioceptive events through the direct punishment by the parents. Also, the positive reinforcement of Jennifer's turning away and then imitating the parental "No, no" provides differential reinforcement for desired and undesired behavior, conditions considered to be most effective for learning a difficult discrimination. Her self-punishment, sitting in the isolated chair before the mother discovers she has damaged the velvet cushion, indicates feelings of guilt. The interpretation for this behavior would be that, since punishment *followed* her bouncing on the chair, anxiety becomes associated with the stimulus situation *after* she has broken the rule. Having been warned that she might hurt the chair, she now has much anxiety aroused when she sees the spring come through the material. Since direct punishment was usually associated with the termination of such anxiety, she punishes herself in order to "get it over with" and to make her "feel better inside." (For fuller presentations of behavior theory relevant to conscience development, see Aronfreed, 1966; Burton, 1963; Burton, Maccoby, and Allinsmith, 1961; Solomon and Brush, 1956.)

For such theoretical interpretations as these, a central feature is that this process must be characterized as extending over a period of time, yet it is evident that the studies we have analyzed present relations between parent and child behavior which refer only to the present point in time. It is thus clear that the developmental characteristics of personality cannot be directly tested from correlations such as these. If Jennifer's parents are interviewed at the end of the process we have described, they will report that she sometimes punishes herself, resists temptation, and confesses. As a result, she will be rated high on conscience development. If the techniques of Jennifer's parents described in this episode are a reflection of their general disciplinary practices (a necessary assumption in most of these studies), they will report that they currently use reasoning and explanations with some love withdrawal and little or no physical punishment. The developmental character of the sequence in Jennifer's history is lost. The early use of direct punishment techniques by the parents has dropped out. Even if the investigator employs a retrospective interview to assess the historical aspects of childrearing techniques, it seems unlikely that the parents will be able to relate the important temporal links in this concatenation of parent-child interaction.[7]

◘ *CONCLUSIONS* ◘

The path provided by our own and similar research data on the development of conscience has led essentially to the same end point reached in our appraisals of the areas of dependency and aggression: The commonly held hypotheses concerning determining factors in conscience formation are not with any certainty supported by the available evidence. Presumably well-established findings now appear more dubious; one is hard pressed to find consistencies through the different studies. Even the apparently solid conclusion that "warmth" is related to "conscience" must be tempered by an acknowledgment that it is based on studies in which antecedent and consequent measures are based on materials from the same

[7] Research that we have reported elsewhere indicates that ratings of events based on information from mother's recall may have little correspondence with measures obtained contemporaneously with the occurrence of these events (see Yarrow, Campbell, and Burton, 1964).

respondent. The appearance of solidity of results in this area is still further limited by the fact that the association between conscience and parental acceptance seems, in a number of instances, to be related to the sex of the child in ways that are not always readily interpretable.

Several of the measurement problems alluded to in the preceding chapters remain a matter of concern (for example, low coder reliability as a factor that might obscure the "true" relations between variables, nonindependence of measures). One of the most critical issues relating to dependency and aggression, the extent to which measurement procedures provide an adequate index of the concept, is perhaps even more problematic for conscience, an aspect of the individual less readily accessible to view. Not at all reassuring is the available evidence comparing mothers' reports with experimentally obtained data relevant to children's conscience behavior. Such information suggests that the two types of measures are far from interchangeable. Even if we assume the validity of the verbal measures, they are often inadequate to test the hypotheses in which we are interested. From "here and now" childrearing correlates of complex kinds of behavior such as guilt, an investigator has little evidence that permits him to discuss the *origins* of such behavior. A design that assesses changes over time is necessary before one can draw firm conclusions about developmental sequences.

CHAPTER 5

Toward Continuity
in Developmental
Research

□▭□▭□▭□▭□▭□▭□▭□▭□

The premise that the responses of the individual are an outgrowth of his current circumstances and earlier experiences is a conceptual keystone to theory and research in the field of personality development, but precise knowledge of the controlling variables and their effects on the course of child development remains an unattained goal. If the research that we have examined is in principal respects typical, we must probably conclude that we are still searching for the specific conditions in the child's cumulative experience with his parents that evoke, strengthen, or modify his behavior. The questions of child rearing have not yielded easily to scientific study.

125

Though the problems confronting research seem to extend beyond current capacities of the science to deal with them adequately, issues of human development are not easily set aside for a later date. Therefore, research pursued with admittedly inadequate tools has been the major source of information on rearing influences on personality. With astonishing frequency, findings have been quickly and widely "established" and have been made the bases for extending and interpreting further research and directing practices in child care. But have our tools been adequate for the task?

Our study has concentrated on the problematics of method of this area. We have principally directed our attention to the research approach that depends on the interview for data on child rearing, and on interviews or ratings for assessments of child behavior. The data are summaries of general response tendencies of mother and child. Although the framework of interpretation is one that views the mother's behavior as "cause" and the child's behavior as "effect," the information used is the concomitant variation in the two sets of data.

Our analyses of this approach have been concerned with its vulnerabilities, which we have attempted to document with data from our own and other studies concerned with dependency, aggression, and conscience formation in young children. The studies have been selected on a theme of maximum replication in conceptualizations and procedures—that is, the maximum available in the existing research literature. Very nearly identical procedures have been used in some of the investigations. Other studies are near-replications. From such an assemblage, we wished to inspect at close range not only the reported data, but also all phases of the research process. In this summary discussion we shall look at the problems that have emerged most clearly as methodological hazards, generalize beyond the immediate content fields, and consider some strategies of research that may help to advance knowledge of personality development.

◫ THE INTERPRETATION OF RESEARCH FINDINGS ◫

Let us begin with the reported relationships between mother and child behavior and examine the uses and interpretations of these data. The picture of unstable associations is a discouraging one. Each of the content areas studied is similarly inconclusive. Convincingly consistent and statistically significant patterns have been hard to come by, regardless of whether we are summarizing the findings from repetitions of identical measures in different studies, from similar measures in different studies, or from different measures of the same subjects. In reaching this conclusion we have at times made different interpretations of data from those presented by the original investigators or from those arrived at in reviews or other secondary sources. Where many interpretations are much more optimistic and positive than ours have been, our approach has been one of caution, given the known methodological pitfalls in the research.

Raw data, as we know, do not entirely speak for themselves. The researcher needs to, wants to, and ideally should bring theoretical, or at least understandable empirical order out of his data. He wants to organize, to integrate, to summarize succinctly, plausibly, and convincingly the results of his research, and to weave his findings into comprehensive interpretations that encompass conclusions from previous research. But promise and hazard are inherent in this process. Though admirable in the long run, this motivation to find order in data may induce the researcher and synthesizer to interpret small inklings of support as sufficient reason to accept an explanatory line in the face of quite overwhelming ambiguities of data.

Such may very well be the case in areas of child rearing considered here. It would seem from the data we have examined that too much "order" has been imposed on the evidence. It has been well said by Sir George Thompson (1961, p. 15) that in science, "It is the observations that are closest to reality. The more one abstracts from them the more exciting indeed are the conclusions one draws and the more suggestive for further advances, but the less one can be certain that some widely different viewpoint would not do as well."

What, then, are guidelines for ordering and explaining data? For one help in steering a reasonably secure course between the mere recitation of raw observations and the free abstraction from them, the researcher, in interpreting his research, turns to a particular set of rules that are essentially statistical in nature. In so doing, he commits himself to the notion that whether a given hypothesis wins out over another is in part, and indeed in large part, a function of the extent to which the results of a test of that hypothesis cannot readily be attributable to chance occurrence. Having chosen to accept such a code, he cannot lightly abandon it. Thus, if he hypothesizes that a given conceptual entity, X, is related to a second such entity, Y, and if he posits that x_1, x_2, . . . , x_n are each representative of some key facet of the domain embraced by X, and he develops measures presumed to represent these pertinent aspects and uses them to measure X in a presumed suitable sample, he is then faced with the necessity of evaluating the hypothesized relationship in the light of the total array of findings from his measurements. If only x_1 is significantly related to his measure of Y, and the other measures presumably concerned with the same relationship do not yield the same results, he should excite neither himself nor his readers to such an extent as would be the case if each of the measures of X showed an association with Y. Further, if, for a given sample, x_1 through x_n are consistently related to Y, but only in a very modest fashion, he should not be too greatly misled by evidence of congruence in the absence of statistical significance. To the extent that x_1 through x_n are *not* independent of one another, there can be slight justification for considering these tenuously consistent results as additive. With the correlation explosion made possible by high-speed computers, investigations using many conceptually different variables and many alternative and nonindependent indices of each variable are almost guaranteed to provide the investigator with some findings which, on grounds of direction or sporadic significance of coefficients, can be plausibly ordered according to some theory. The net becomes exceedingly coarse, with an increasing possibility of catching artifactually produced associations.

Consistency among statistically significant findings should not, of course, be the sole criterion to determine the fate of a proposed interpretation of data. Correlation size as well as correlation significance is important to consider in interpreting childrearing findings. A statistically significant association may be a very small assocation, since significance is related to sample size, among other things. With 100 cases a product-moment correlation of just under .20 is significant at the 5 per cent level. But such a relationship accounts for slightly less than 4 per cent of the variance in one measure that is shared by another. With 1000 cases, a correlation of just over .06 reaches the 5 per cent level of significance. The extent to which such a relationship "explains" anything is minute indeed.

Bivariate relationships in childrearing studies are characteristically small. Indeed, on theoretical grounds, a single "antecedent" dimension in the history of mother-to-child responses would not be expected, in most instances, to control a very large amount of variance. How, then, should such slender relationships be interpreted? If one assumes that the contribution of single variables is "truly" small, one would want, of course, to determine such contributions but one would want also to be exceedingly careful in making interpretations of them which might be construed as simple cause-effect relationships. Further, if the magnitude of correlational associations is low, one must, it seems to us, insist that the associations be robust, that is, convincingly stable from one investigation to another in manifesting the same relationships. In relying on statistical significance, directionality of findings, or magnitude of association, the investigator may discern a pattern in his data that can be woven into a suitable theory line. But in the weaving how many threads have to be discarded? The behavioral scientist simply cannot afford to discard, ignore, or fail to discuss those relationships relevant to his theoretical formulations that do not demonstrate associations in the predicted direction. The number of such discarded relationships can accumulate to such an extent that even a casual perusal will reveal that much more is often swept under the rug than the rug can accommodate.

If, as investigators, we explain away inconsistencies or justify clinging to nonsignificant trends on the grounds of measurement problems, we should recognize that our consistent results and our sporadically significant findings may also be nothing more than a reflection of other types of measurement problems. We are open to the criticism of having concentrated on the cases that prove our point of view and of having ignored those that go against our beliefs. We should be unwilling to permit ourselves this luxury in the appraisal of research data. We should, then, keep in mind Bacon's dictum:

> In general let every student of nature take this as a rule—
> that whatever his mind seizes and dwells on with peculiar
> satisfaction is to be held with suspicion; and that so much
> the more care is to be taken, in dealing with such questions,
> to keep the understanding even and clear.
>
> (*Novum Organum*)

REPORTING THE RESEARCH PROCESS

Thus, the bridge (or gap) between the raw data and their final interpretative disposition and communication to the scientific and lay communities presents dangers worthy of more explicit recognition. Is there any strategy that might provide an intervening safeguard in interpretation, that would keep the stages in the evolution of a research conclusion more distinct and separable, permitting each to be evaluated?

The culture of the research community, it would seem, becomes a factor, a guardian of strategy at this point, for it determines, in large part, the kind of communication of research operations that is expected and is practiced. What does this culture require the investigator to communicate? What does it reward? In some respects, current expectations and practices may contribute to confusion. For example, some of the problems of research continuity might be eased if the investigator were obligated to report the procedures of his research more fully, and to indicate in more detail the steps by which he arrived at his conclusions.

The investigator is in the position to be most aware of the coherence of his data and the strength and clarity with which they suggest a particular kind of ordering. He knows also their limitations. He knows how much in the data is unexplained or how much does not fit the interpretive conclusion he has tentatively drawn. He is probably most in conflict when the data are somewhat ambiguous —when they may, but again may not, give support to an appealing hypothesis. He should be expected and encouraged to present, prominently, the problems in his data, the relevant cautions to be taken, the reasons why some interpretations are unwarranted. For the investigator who is dedicated to a particular explanatory principle and, thereby, apt to slight the contraevidences in his result, fuller communication of his procedures and his reasoning may be clarifying for himself as well as for other investigators. When reporting does not provide sufficient information about methods and measurements and analytic procedures to permit others to assess their adequacy, it falls short.

This is a proposition that both the scientist as author and the scientist as editor should bear in mind. Quite clearly, with the mounting pressure for journal space, there is rightful concern for brevity. Yet it should be equally clear that if brevity can only be achieved at the cost of adequate communication, then the cost must be viewed as excessive. Behavioral scientists in the area we have been discussing are not yet in a position to follow the style of the physical or biological scientist in communicating his experiment or study. Where the latter can, in many instances, convey his procedures adequately in shorthand fashion, we cannot because of the nonstandard measures we use. Further, a most difficult part of the struggles of this field is in finding good indices to represent the dimensions of developmental and behavioral theory. A single question in an interview, a response to a game, a manipulation of a toy as part of an experiment, a brief observation of the interchange of mother and child in a laboratory setting, are our procedural stand-ins for conceptually complicated psychological entities and processes. Measures such as these require a great deal of extrapolation from very special, unique, and sometimes doubtfully meaningful episodes, to the theoretical domains. A vivid image of these observations should, therefore, be kept in the minds of the interpreters and readers of research. Description of the steps in the research process that have led to given interpretations would help, and would provide for a more nearly complete dialogue in the scientific community. So long as many different measures are used for behavioral concepts, and so long as the technology of any given procedure is unstandardized, full communication of the research process seems exceedingly important.

INTERPRETATIONS OF RESEARCH IN SECONDARY SOURCES

Our principal concern has been with communications between the original investigator and the scientific community. By implication, the same problems exist in subsequent use of findings. Interpretations of results are out of the hands of the original investigator once his work is published. Reviews and summaries of a field impose further interpretations, as do other investigators who build upon preceding reports. The enhancement that often takes place in the secondary reports is of several kinds.[1] "Establishment" of findings is made firmer and easier as the original investigators' cautions and qualifications are lost. After an attractive, theoretically plausible result has been stated and restated in the literature, it is ever simpler to view it as established and to order other data in line with it. In this way a compelling structure of beliefs may be built.

This frequent "clarification" of relationships in secondary sources is illustrated concretely in the following comparisons of an original, disguised research report with the report of the same work in a secondary source:

Original

For girls, but not boys, consistent positive relations are found between Y measures and fathers' scores on X_1 and X_2. Two of these are significant. [I.e., one of five different Y measures is significantly related to X_1 and also to X_2.] These relations suggest that girls are more Y when fathers express attitudes of X. . . . Similar relations were not indicated for these X scores of mothers. These relations are in line with the hypothesis, then, but cannot be described as strong support for it.

Secondary Source

Some additional evidence supports the hypothesis that X [is] associated with the frequency of Y behavior. . . . [The investigator] found that parental X_1 and X_2 . . . were positively related to number of Y_1 [acts] made by girls in a nursery school.

---

[1] The processes of leveling, sharpening, and assimilation of information described by Allport and Postman in their *Psychology of Rumor* (1947) may very well characterize the factors at work in some interpretive summaries of research.

The reviewer has stayed reasonably close to the original, perhaps, but the original "for fathers only" finding has now assimilated the more general label, *parental*. That only one of five different indices of Y was related to X_1 and X_2 is lost. And the fact that the data for boys do not fit the same picture presented for the girls has dropped by the wayside.

A second comparison of original and secondary reporting illustrates other interpretive changes. In this instance, several strongly and clearly enunciated qualifications by the original authors are given a new look in a secondary use of the findings. The original study (Sears, Maccoby, and Levin, 1957) attempts to assess mothers' rejecting attitudes. The authors describe (p. 170) their difficulty in obtaining evidence on this dimension in the mother interviews: the protocols of only 2 per cent of the sample received ratings of high rejection ("4" or "5" on a five-point scale). Therefore, the sample was only dichotomized with respect to this trait: those mothers giving *any* indication of rejection, and those giving *no* indication. When a comparison was made of frequencies of high conscience ratings in children in these two groups, a difference appeared that was regarded by the authors as not large: 18 per cent of the children whose mothers showed *some* rejection and 31 per cent whose mothers showed no rejection were rated high in conscience. In translation by other writers, however, and out of the context of the original qualifications, this finding has been reported in substantiation of experimental findings as "children of highly rejecting parents show very poor conscience." The explicit communications of the original report regarding the highly inferential judgments of rejection, the difficulty in achieving any reliable distinction regarding rejection, the nearly complete absence of high rejection, and the emergence of a modest difference with respect to conscience (all qualifications on the relationship), have not been preserved in the later use. The finding appears there as unqualified evidence of a relation of rejection and conscience, and as such is absorbed as consistent with theoretical predictions.

It seems clear that incautious interpretations can quickly elevate indications to evidence and speculations to findings. Findings can assume a hardness not intended by the original authors; tentativeness of concept indicators may go unrecognized; and original hypothesis formation can be suddenly transformed into hypothesis testing. Especially at the present primitive state of the art of behavioral research, we would be well advised to keep a closer, more responsible tie between the raw observations of research and the conclusions about them.

▣ CHILDREARING INTERVIEWS ▣

Let us turn now from interpretation of data to an earlier phase in research—to the tools used to generate the data. The discussions of research on dependency, aggression, and conscience have concentrated on methodological problems in the interview. Some of these were anticipated to *increase* the probabilities of finding relationships and consistencies in the data, some to *obscure* possible "true" relations, and others to produce data only obliquely or doubtfully relevant to the hypotheses being tested. While it is recognized that no technique or method is immune to factors that distort or shape the data to some degree, that the scientist must be ever on the alert to minimize distorting factors or to identify their influences, it is also clear that the interview technique as it has often been employed in childrearing research is an especially loose method for the performance of a difficult task. Investigators continuing to work in this field must face up to the shortcomings in this approach.

If an investigator wishes to pursue issues of behavior with an interview in the style in which it has often been used, he cannot ignore the necessity of first establishing firm evidence on the validity and reliability of the data it yields before seeking further substantive findings. If his faith in the traditional interview has been irreparably shaken, he must choose alternative techniques: He may decide to attempt to develop a better tool, but still an interview tool, suited to testing the hypotheses in which he is interested, or he may decide to abandon the interview altogether and to rely only on direct observations of mother and child for the data of child rearing. No matter which choice, pure methodological research is needed of a kind that has not generally been done.

The first alternative—*to understand the traditional interview in childrearing research*—calls for basic methodological research comparing interview responses and observed behavior. If we assume that the mother's interview descriptions are approximations of response rates in the child's behavior ("How much attention does X want from you?"), or approximations of the nature of reinforcements and reinforcement schedules she uses ("What do you do when X asks you to help him? What do you do when X asks and you are busy?"), we should determine the correspondence between such reports and trained observers' direct observations of the same behaviors. (This begs the question, for the moment, of the technology of observation!) Evaluations of such correspondence, with uncompromising criteria, should provide the basic perspective on the *validity* of interview data as they have been obtained historically in this field. This will require extensive study. If, as one might assume, such comparisons of behavior and verbal reports of behavior will reveal *degrees* of correspondence or *differential* correspondence for different areas of information, then finer methodological pursuits could be summoned. These would pin down the specific kinds of information that are more or less validly given by the mother in a childrearing interview, and identify specific distorting factors entering into her interview that might be corrected for or minimized. Explorations in the data of the present study suggest a few factors that might affect how much the verbal report is a veridical reflection of the behavior it is intended to index.

ACCESSIBILITY TO OBSERVATION

To report behavior accurately, the mother will have had to observe it. Among the kinds of information that have been reviewed on dependency and conscience, two items may serve as examples of apparent differences in accessibility. One piece of information that seems reasonably observable is the young child's reactions to his mother's leaving him. To a considerable extent, such behaviors can be seen and heard, and they occur at specific critical points in time when attention is most likely to be focused on them. One might anticipate, therefore, that they can be faithfully reported in an interview. In contrast, evidence of conscience in a child would appear to be much less easily observable behavior. A child's conscience is generally called into play in circumstances when the child has an opportunity to transgress with some degree of impunity (that is, out of sight of the adult); moreover, the pangs of conscience after a transgression are likely to be a more private affair. Often the adult has only ambiguous cues on which to rely. In observing and reporting on conscience, a mother (as well as a trained observer) might encounter difficulties.

Evidence on the relative accessibility of the separation and conscience variables is found in comparing the amount of consensus in the interview reports of pairs of nursery school teachers. The correlation between teachers' ratings of child's reactions to his mother's leaving him (V 46), an item of apparent high accessibility, is +.67. On items of conscience, with low accessibility—child's confession (V 49) and admission (V 49a) of deviance—interteacher correlations are +.19 and +.12, respectively. Theoretically, the pairs of interviewees were drawing upon very similar experiences with the children; each had been given similar behavioral definitions of the phenomena to be observed. Therefore, from their high agreement on separation reactions and their lack of agreement on conscience, it might be concluded that the visibility of what is to be observed is not insignificantly affecting the nature of the interview datum.

CULTURAL SENSITIZATION

Undoubtedly many other dimensions influence the suitability of an interview measure. Similar to accessibility of the behavior to observation seems to be a matter of how much the mother has been "trained" by the culture or the childrearing specialist to be aware of the behavior and to "size it up" in the particular terms of interest to the researcher. Again, we can take clues from the present study. Mothers' reports of use of praise (V 4a) gave us no useful differentiation among mothers. When asked about their use of praise, virtually all the mothers in our study indicated that of course they praised their child, but their responses were such that coders could not reliably distinguish differences in shades of "much" to "little" praise. We are not ready to conclude that these mothers did not differ in this respect.

We might speculate about how mothers have been trained

to think of praise. Traditional childrearing education has generally approved of praise, but has not particularly distinguished types and frequencies and contingent uses. These mothers probably take for granted that they will praise their child in obvious circumstances of praiseworthy behavior. Whether they are equally attuned to the kind of praise that is given in very low key is less certain. For example, a mother tries to get her five-year-old to brush his teeth more efficiently. She remembers her careful demonstrations of "up and down" and her pleasure and her praise of him when he has "caught on." Is she likely to observe her own little exclamations of "fine," "good," "um hum," in this process? Yet this is the stuff that much of praise is made of, and probably the aspect in which mothers differ. This behavior is not dramatic or isolated in occurrence and, unlike a temper tantrum, it does not interrupt the ongoing business; it is part of the course of events and may not register as special in her behavior, especially if the professional childrearing literature has not highlighted it. Hence, our groups of mothers may not have been reporting on such behavior at all, but instead they may have had in mind only the "extreme" conditions. In contrast to mothers' reports on praise, punitive techniques are described at length and with variety. Over the years, mothers have probably had much more education in the popular literature about punishment techniques than about positive reinforcements. This difference in emphasis may help to make punishment techniques more differentiable by the mothers and more readily discussed in an interview.

SOCIAL DESIRABILITY

The popular literature and most certainly social norms give meanings to behaviors that mothers are asked to reveal in the interview. These meanings do more than make mothers differentially aware of these actions. Some behaviors have strong social endorsement, others are equally strongly disapproved. The possibility of such value-biasing factors has concerned users of interview and test responses (see Edwards, 1957; Crowne and Marlow, 1964). In the context of appraising the childrearing interview, it may be well to consider the influence of social standards. Is there a tendency for mothers to attribute to themselves and their children characteristics that have socially desirable value and to reject those with undesirable value? Since middle-class mothers are especially likely to be aware of what is acceptable behavior in the realms of child rearing and child behavior, a social-desirability dimension is not out of the question.

We attempted a small exploration of this factor in our own data. In examining the data, we reasoned that if a social-desirability bias were influencing the relationships between ratings of mother and child behaviors, we should find socially valued behaviors consistently associated with other socially valued ones. We examined our data with this hypothesis in mind. The variables used were those with a minimum of procedural overlap. These were six "consequent" variables and 25 "antecedent" ones.[2] We set the directions of rating scales on these variables so as to be consistent with what we judged to be socially valued characteristics:[3] low scores on the scales were assigned to the assumed valued characteristics. We then inspected the signs of the correlations among variables. Given the probability of .5 for either a plus or minus sign if the correlations

[2] The child variables included in this analysis were: independence (V 26), summed dependency (V 28), aggression to parents (V 32), quarreling with siblings (V 32a), overall compliance (V 32b), and conscience (V 35). The maternal variables were: isolation (V 1), love withdrawal (V 2), reasoning (V 3), tangible rewards (V 4), deprivation of privileges (V 5), physical punishment (V 6), scolding (V 8), diverting attention (V 9), commanding (V 10), response to dependency (V 11), response to independency (V 12), permissiveness of aggression to parents (V 13), severity of punishment for denial (V 14a), comfort after punishment for aggression (V 15), permissiveness of aggression to siblings (V 16), permissiveness of aggression to other children (V 17), encouragement of aggression in self-defense (V 18), overall restrictiveness (V 19), overall severity of punishment (V 20), negative emotional expression (V 21), labeling of child behavior (V 22), warmth (V 23), affectional demonstrativeness (V 24), annoying things about child (V 25), and things enjoyed in child (V 26).

[3] It must be emphasized that we do not have an independent SD measure. The consensus of judgments by the authors and, on questionable variables, the additional judgments of colleagues have been the criterion. The reader will want to inspect the assignments of direction in Appendix A. For our analysis it is necessary to hypothesize that mothers will be relatively consistent on the social-desirability tendency in all of their responses; some will be consistently low on the SD dimension across all items in contrast to some who will be consistently high.

for the entire matrix were completely random, the theoretical mean number of positive (and of negative) correlations for each antecedent measure with the six consequent measures is three. The theoretical mean number of positive (and of negative) correlations for each consequent measure with the 25 antecedent measures is 12.5.

The results of these inspections are as expected if there were a value-biasing dimension operating within these measures: There is a predominance of positive correlations. Eighteen of the 25 antecedent measures produce more positive signs than the theoretically expected mean. In contrast, five of the antecedent measures produce more negative correlations than the expected mean. This ratio is 18:4 for girls, and 14:6 for boys. For the six consequent measures, five in the total sample show more than the expected number of positive correlations. Five measures for girls and four for boys show slightly more than the expected mean number.

With such consistency in direction of relationships and with chance variations in magnitude of correlations, one would expect an occasional correlation to reach significance; the likelihood of such occurrence should be greater the more highly loaded are the two items on the common dimension of social desirability. To explore this possibility, antecedent measures were grouped on amount of consistency in signs (those *more than* one standard deviation from the expected mean in number of either positive or negative correlations, and those *within* one standard deviation. When measures falling into these two groups were compared on the number of *significant* correlations they produced with other variables, measures with the most consistency in signs tended to produce the greatest number of significant correlations. Thus, of the 14 antecedent measures showing the greater sign consistency, 11 produced more than the median number of significant correlations. Of the 11 antecedent measures showing less sign consistency, only four produced more than the median number of significant correlations. The data are similar for each sex.

While this is by no means a full-fledged test of a social-desirability hypothesis, the results are consistent with a hypothesis that this is a "hidden" dimension that affects both the patterns of relations and the probability that relations will be significant. They suggest the reasonableness of testing such a possibility in other data in child rearing. It must be pointed out that our data showing that judged "good" things go with other "good" things might also be interpreted as reflecting relations in the "real world." Such relationships are strongly consonant with the beliefs of most of us. Isn't this the simplest and most parsimonious explanation for the findings? It is with just this kind of intuitively appealing confirmation of the researcher's values, beliefs, and/or theoretical expectations that "so much the more care is to be taken" (Bacon, *Novum Organum*).

GENERAL QUESTIONS AND SPECIFIC BEHAVIOR

Our critique of the childrearing interview has by implication placed considerable responsibility for problems on the mother as respondent, but our earlier discussions of dependency, aggression, and conscience have pointed to other potential sources of error stemming from the nature of the interview questions themselves and difficulties inherent in the analysis processes. Interview responses are the captives of the questions used to obtain them, and frequently the data of child rearing are captives of a particular kind of question. As noted earlier, questions in the interview typically approach behavior of mother and child from a "trait" point of view, and ask for general descriptive accounts. The situations in which behavior has occurred are not differentiated except in a very gross sense (such as behavior at home or at school). Both the open-ended nature of the accounts and the situationally nonspecific descriptions tend to create a number of analytic problems.

Consider, first, problems arising from an approach in which the situation of behavior is not specified. The investigator does not know the sampling of behavior that is the basis of a mother's responses. He proceeds, therefore, with unknown and probably different samples from each respondent. For example, when mothers describe their reactions to their children's demands for attention, or their attempts to control child behavior, are they smoothing a curve of responses in many different situations, are they recalling the most vivid or recent ones, or are they describing situations in which they have had the most satisfactory experiences? Which specific rearing circumstances are in the sampling of events from which they abstract descriptions of themselves and their children? Are different mothers sampling differently? It seems likely that they are. Is a given mother consistent with herself in different parts of an interview or on different occasions? She may very well not be. How, then, do these idiosyncrasies permitted by these questions affect the researcher's purposes? Certainly one anticipated effect is an instability in responses from the same mother from one measurement to the next. If a mother's reference points vary on different occasions of questioning, the kinds of interaction she reports about herself and her child may also vary. Such variability is suggested in the comparisons reported earlier (p. 63) of mothers' questionnaire replies and their responses later in an interview. Yet this variability may not reflect any change in the mother's usual functioning with regard to specific circumstances and child responses.

Without knowledge of, or control over, the particular conditions about which mothers are reporting, the researcher runs into other difficulties—difficulties in testing specific hypotheses of antecedent-consequent associations. A hypothetical case may be illustrative of the basic problem: Suppose an investigator is interested in the disciplinary antecedents of aggression and conscience, and for this purpose he inquires into the frequency with which spanking and love withdrawal are used as techniques of control. Responses from our hypothetical mother put both techniques into her repertoire of punishment practices. Her responses, along with those of other mothers, are interpreted by the researcher in antecedent-consequent terms with respect to aggression and conscience. Let us suppose, however, that we know more about this particular mother. We know that her points of reference for describing physical punishment and withdrawal of love are several recent traumatic situations with her child in which a baby sibling's safety was at stake. We know, also, that she reacts to the child's aggression and other misdeeds by reasoning and isolation. What, then, has the investigator done in interpreting the mother's methods as antecedents of aggression and conscience? If our hypothetical mother represents reality, we as investigators may find ourselves fitting into statistical associations data that have no logical or functional relation to one another.

To some extent the case of our hypothetical mother is documented in data from the NIMH interview. We found, in a sample of questions concerning disciplinary practices, that ratings of behavior in one situation are not readily substitutable for ratings in another. It will be recalled that questions were asked about disciplinary techniques in specific types of situations of control (bedtime, mealtime, aggression) and separate ratings were made for each situation. Findings on physical punishment, isolation, love withdrawal, reasoning, and severity of punishment (dimensions most involved in antecedent-consequent hypotheses) were examined. Each pair of situations was compared on each of the techniques. For example, if physical punishment was used for management of bedtime requirements, was it used also for mealtime misbehaviors? If love withdrawal was not used for mealtime, was it then not used for aggression? Only for ratings of severity of punishment is there a statistically significant link across the situations. (Correlations between ratings of severity in pairs of settings are +.23, +.24, and +.40 for aggression and mealtime misbehavior, aggression and bedtime, and mealtime and bedtime, respectively.) But use or nonuse of a given disciplinary technique (physical punishment or other) in one situation is by no means predictive of its use in another. In the 12 comparisons of pairs of circumstances, only five show significant correspondence in χ^2 analyses. For example, mothers who reported using physical punishment to handle misbehavior at mealtime were, to a statistically significant degree, likely to report using such punishment for transgressions associated with bedtime, but use of physical punishment in these settings was not significantly linked to its use as a means for handling aggression toward parents. Similar examinations of the use of other techniques in these three situations yielded similar results. Thus, it appears more than likely that when measures do not take settings into account, good hypotheses may be inadequately tested and, perhaps, mistakenly discarded.

CODING AND ITS CONSEQUENCES

Not the least of the analytic problems with the childrearing interviews can be traced to the indiscriminate use of open-ended questions. Familiar coder biases, halo effects, and intercoder differences have all been mentioned in reviewing the substantive data. We might reexamine these issues from the point of view of a job analysis of the interview coder. The typical protocol the coder is given is a record of a kind of continuous dialogue between mother and interviewer, resulting in a case study of mother and child. Though steered by specific questions, the mother gives the information in a relatively nonregimented manner. A good deal of the individual mother's fluency, style, and openness is reflected. The coder is given a set of categories for a series of behavioral dimensions which he must impose on this information. As he proceeds in coding, he soon becomes familiar with the total protocol and, of necessity, he forms an impression of mother and child. His purpose—that of making ratings of specific behavioral dimensions—is at variance with the way in which the basic raw information comes to him. He has, in a sense, an almost impossible job. To assume that his *general* impression will *not* enter into his *specific* ratings is to fly in the face of much evidence on social perception. Theoretically, only by requiring the coding of each behavioral dimension independently, without knowledge of other dimensions, would the coder job be designed to rule out the possibilities of halo effects, of built-in internal consistencies.

If the coder job were redesigned so that separate assessments were made of each section of an interview by different coders, would the relationships among variables be materially different from those obtained by present coding procedures? Particularly, would antecedent-consequent relations be altered? The question is intriguing and one that we sampled for the variables of severity of punishment (V 14) and aggression (V 32). Child aggression to adults was rated by an analyst who was given only the interview material relating to this dimension. Another coder was given only the mother's responses about her punishment of the child for his aggression toward adults. (When the independent codings and the original adjudicated ratings on aggression were compared, the correlation for one coder was +.88 and for another coder, +.90. The correlations between the two sets of ratings of punishment were +.84 and +.70.) If nonindependence of coding has the effect of enhancing antecedent-consequent relationships, we should expect the correlation between punishment and aggression to be less on the independent coding than on the original nonindependent coding. Such change in the expected direction appears in the association between severity of punishment and aggression resulting from the new sets of ratings. When based on the original coding (with knowledge of the whole interview), punishment and aggression are related +.40; when based on the recoding (with knowledge of only a single variable) the association is +.24. The nonindependence of ratings might have an exactly opposite result from the one illustrated. If coder bias were operating, it could work to depress relationships between variables that coders expected *not* to be related. In either direction, then, the resulting relationships might be changed in magnitude, if coding appraisals of "antecedent" and "consequent" variables were made independently.

To continue with the coder job, the low reliabilities in coding responses to open-ended questions underscore the difficulties in dealing with replies to such items. Even careful training of coders has not eliminated different interpretations of interview information. Thus in the NIMH and the Sears, Maccoby, and Levin studies correlations between coders' ratings range from the 30's to the 90's, with the average in the 70's. The causes of this lack of agreement are undoubtedly many—some in the coders, some in the interview questions, and some in the mothers. The analytic consequences of concern here are, of course, how such unreliability affects the correlation between variables. McNemar's (1955) statements in this respect are particularly relevant and are offered as summaries of an unsolved problem with interview data: ". . . if the reliability coefficients are . . . less than unity . . . the correlation between obtained scores will be less than that between true scores; i.e., errors of measurement tend to reduce or attenuate the correlation between traits. . . . If the correlation between true scores is unity and if the reliability for 1 variable is perfect, the obtained correlation between the 2 cannot exceed the square root of the reliability coefficient for the other variable. If the correlation between the true scores is perfect and if each variable is subject to errors of measurement, then the obtained correlation cannot exceed the product of the square roots of the 2 reliability coefficients" (pp. 160–161).

IMPROVING RESEARCH TOOLS

Each of the preceding explorations thus seems to indicate that if a childrearing interview is to be used at all, it needs remodeling. What would constitute a better research tool? Can it be developed? These are matters for methodological research beyond the purposes of the present study, yet several promising possibilities might be mentioned. One such approach might be to look at the development of an interview schedule as a psychometric problem. Much of the interview-based research on child rearing has attempted to measure complex concepts by indices based on just one or a very limited number of questions—questions that have usually been developed on an ad hoc basis. Would the maternal interview be a psychometrically more sound and also a more successful instrument if stable measures based on many items were developed for each conceptual dimension?

A second approach might focus on the mother as an observer, since her powers of observation ultimately determine the value of interview data. An innovation worthy of some consideration is to train the mother to observe. Some of the techniques investigators have used in training research observers (providing a language as well as a procedure for observing), and certainly new methods for systematic observations, might well be adapted for mothers' use. Such training might help in moving away from trait or impressionistic descriptions of behavior to clearer, more specific designations of responses and the events surrounding them, descriptions that are more closely related to behavior theory.

When all is said and done, however, many investigators may choose to abandon the interview approach. They may choose instead to turn to direct observations where (theoretically) specific responses and conditions can be put under precise scientific surveillance. There is an indisputable advantage in recording behavior through trained eyes or mechanical means, provided, of course, that new methodological problems and other old ones do not accompany, or become magnified under, direct observation. Unfortunately, precision is not achieved easily. Direct observations, naturalistic or in laboratory settings, confront the investigator with the very same kinds of problems. He faces problems of construct validity, observer bias, observer and coding reliability, and sampling of behavior equal to those he has escaped in abandoning the interview. The observational approach to the measurement of social behavior is still often primitive and open to a great many sources of error, whether the design be a field study or a laboratory experiment (Rosenthal, 1967). There might well be an investment of ingenuity in the development of sound, new tools and procedures for observations as well as for interviews.

▣ TESTING HYPOTHESES OF ANTECEDENT-CONSEQUENT RELATIONS ▣

The sense of uncertainty that our sifting and questioning of the measures of child rearing and child behavior have produced carries over to the hypothesis-testing for which the measures are used. These hypotheses, in each instance, are concerned with the conditions under which given child behaviors are established, maintained, or modified, with relations between responses in a causal chain. By now, many of the reasons why the measures seem methodologically inadequate to the job are obvious.

One of the most critical doubts is in regard to the adequacy of correlational data as evidence of antecedent-consequent processes. The view that child behavior results from maternal causes is so commonly held that it firmly "fixes" the interpretation of interview data in such directional terms and makes reevaluations without prejudgment difficult. It cannot be stated too strongly that the correlational evidence is not evidence for cause-and-effect relationships, or for a one-way cause-effect process. Though theory suggests parental functioning as the antecedent and child behavior as the consequent response, contemporaneously obtained measures shed no light on the reasonability of this assumption. As Sears, Maccoby, and Levin (p. 175) have noted, ". . . just which way the cause-and-effect arrows point is impossible to say. . . . The whole relationship could be circular. An enormous amount of painstaking research will be required to untangle these phenomena." Steps toward such untangling will have to be made through techniques other than covariational measures of here-and-now behavior. Indeed, a great amount of ingenuity will be required to design such studies, but until they are done a significant portion of the issues concerning parent and child influences upon one another remains unexamined.

Not only are present data not interpretable as evidence for hypotheses in cause-effect terms, there is reason to object to their interpretation as support of hypotheses of *behavior*. By far the major share of information is impressionistic verbal report which has an unknown, and improbably close resemblance to behavior. Current findings should be regarded more appropriately as the offspring of self-impressions that mothers make public to an interviewer who they know is concerned with what makes "right" in a child's behavior. As temporary stand-ins for behavior such impressions may aid in the formulation of behavioral hypotheses; they do not constitute tests of such hypotheses, however. The pioneering research in child rearing was undertaken to test the applicability of theoretical propositions deriving from laboratory and clinical practice to the normal, developmental processes in socialization. Studies were carried out with the purpose of scanning the evidence for leads for the formulation of new hypotheses. Unfortunately, these tentative, formulative aspects were too quickly lost and the research became interpreted as the *test* of antecedent-consequent behavioral processes as the findings were handed on in succeeding investigations and in the general scientific literature.

If one returns to an interpretation of the literature as tentative evidence on behavioral processes, experience from the years of research on socialization gives direction to new hypothesis formation. In particular, the data suggest the need for reformulations in multivariate rather than bivariate terms. The very small amount of variance apparently controlled by any single variable so far explored might well be increased in a combination of relevant variables. In such multivariate hypotheses, child as well as adult responses should be considered as influences on the behavior of both participants. Further, since the treatment of behavior in trait terms has not contributed much to childrearing research, reformulations of theory and measurement might give more attention to a view of behavior as responsive to specific experiences in the immediate setting and in the history of settings. Such modifications would have the effect of bringing theory building, measurement, and theory testing into closer proximity with one another.

◘ REPLICATION AND CONTINUITY ◘

There has been a long intervening step between the questions with which we began—of how well the hypotheses of child rearing have been substantiated through replicated measurements—and our conclusions. To appraise accumulated research knowledge in methodological terms, we have dismantled instruments and analyses of this research field, and questioned their properties. In doing so, the present inquiry adds its evidence to that of other examinations of the technology of research and its products—assessments that have pointed to instrument effects, experimenter effects, and other aspects of methodology that contribute in problematic ways to data and interpretations of data. Research on child rearing attempts to establish reliable and valid propositions concerning causes and consequences of behavior. Yet our measurements are sufficiently imprecise and our hypotheses sufficiently primitive that we must generally content ourselves with statements concerning *likely,* rather than *invariant* relations between specified variables. In the light of this disquieting state of affairs, the difficulties of research have become increasingly clear. The conclusion is inescapable that built-in replication is essential for interpreting new data and for establishing continuity in findings.

Easier said than done, however. Although the generally understood procedures of replication provide the model for verifying findings, it is difficult to decide on what constitutes reasonable repetition. Conceptual continuity in successive studies often exists, but links based on theory alone are not enough. Is there a more effective strategy of replication, one that ensures procedural and empirical overlaps, as well as the continuity furnished by conceptual frameworks? For the researcher, such a strategy must be practical as well as ideal; it should *add* to knowledge as well as *reaffirm* a prior finding. This can be accomplished if each new study, as a matter of course, incorporates some aspects of previous research as a check on the foundations (measures, assumptions, hypotheses) upon which it rests or proposes to build. This does not call for total repetition; the key to a workable strategy that provides for both procedural and conceptual overlaps is to be found in selecting for replication crucial aspects of the particular research question, at the particular point in the development of a field. Wise selection rests much on the investigator's understanding of the preceding research structure and on what his proposed addition intends to clarify or extend. For each study, selection depends on what is least verified and most critical to the current inquiry.

For illustration, taking one of the conceptual areas that we have discussed, let us turn back the clock and follow through a possible research strategy. Consider a hypothetical program that has begun with a theory about conscience formation and, in an initial study, has found a relationship between parental behavior and children's conformity to moral standards: The independent variable, X_1, the parent's reports of general use of praise, was associated with observational data on the dependent variable, Y_1, the child's not breaking rules in a particular experimental game. A verbal report concerning one aspect of parental behavior now stands as the index of a broad conceptualization of parental control procedures; and, similarly, specific responses of the child in a unique experimental situation serve to represent a child's general conformity to moral standards.

To develop this research in a solid and productive fashion, can we call upon the strategy of replication that we have advocated? At the assumed initial stage in this field, interested investigators might first ask about the reliability of measures on which the finding is based, measures likely to appear and reappear in succeeding studies: Can investigators confidently proceed on the assumption that X_1 on Test 1 $= X_1$ on Test 2 and Y_1 on Test 1 $= Y_1$ on Test 2? Once praise and not-breaking-the-rules have been demonstrated to be reliable, there is less need to incorporate replications on this point as new studies are designed.

An investigator turns, then, to his objective of testing the generalization of the praise-conformity relationship, using new indices and subjects of a different subculture. In a first study, while extending the measures of the child's conformity to a variety of "moral" standards $(Y_2, \ldots, Y_n)$, he retains the initial measures of praise (X_1) and conformity (Y_1). He recognizes that he cannot automatically assume interchangeability of measures; equivalence of indices is just as much a testable proposition as are hypotheses concerning the relations between variables. Hence, he builds in this kind of overlap. Such a strategy accomplishes a number of things: the stability of the original association between X_1 and Y_1 is assessed; the equivalence of the indices of the dependent variable Y may be determined, and if the correlates of X_1 are extended to $Y_2, \ldots, Y_n$, the idea of a general X,Y relationship is supported. Our investigator also begins by this process to bridge the chasm between specific procedures and the general concepts for which they stand, thus guarding against the equation of a particularistic manipulation and a complex conceptual entity.

In this effort at extensional replication all may not proceed smoothly: The expected essential equivalence of alternative measures may not occur $(Y_1 \neq Y_2)$, or independent and dependent variables may not conform to the anticipated pattern relating X and Y. What then? With built-in procedural overlaps, the investigator is signaled specifically concerning points in method or theory where things are "going wrong," where he must begin again. Without measurement ties with the prior study, he would be at a loss to explain discrepancies: Are his indices at fault? Should new hypotheses be advanced to explain the behavior of the new sample? And so on.

Our hypothetical reseacher's procedures merely illustrate a general approach that could strengthen continuity. His choice of replication has been governed by an assessment of research requirements and a recognition of the necessity to maintain appropriate ties with prior research.

Given a working commitment to such a system of checks, provocative and theoretically significant findings that appear and seem destined to become "classics" or standards against which new evidence will be weighed can be quickly tested. If they are not reproducible, researchers, spared a false break-through, will return to the operations that produced the original findings to seek explanations for their occurrence. If the relation *is* repeated, it gains stature as an established one that can be used in evaluating succeeding research. Under such conditions, failure to reproduce such a confirmed result should force careful exploration of the procedures that led to the discordant data. Can they be repeated? If not, the apparently antithetical results can be dismissed. If discordance persists, it may be worth investigating *why* the "established" relation is not found. Such nonreplication could result in most significant advances regarding interpretations of the "established" finding itself.

If we are not dealing with pure variables, and our measures are approximations of the constructs we are trying to measure, and the propositions we wish to study involve multivariate analyses, then the results of replicated investigations, too, must be approximations; but, with care, they can be the nearest approximations possible.

◙ *A SUMMING UP* ◙

This investigation has had two interwoven goals. One has been to examine the degree of order in the empirical data on child-rearing influences, the second has been to inquire into the contribution to order or disorder deriving from measurement and analysis procedures. In general, we have had to conclude that studies of child rearing of the kind reviewed have not done very well in delivering up the secrets of socialization processes. Since consistency of results is not the rule, some, and perhaps many, of the conclusions regarding maternal determinants of the young child's behavior seem to have been relegated to the status of hypotheses. The reasons for this failure of findings to add up in convincing fashion seem to be many—many of which are methodological in nature.

This is not to conclude that research on behavioral development has not progressed over the years. From a historical perspective, a great deal has been learned since the 1940's when childrearing investigations first began to assume importance in the literature. With child development research so much in the current mainstream of psychological theory, it is taken for granted that this has always been so, but of course it has not. In a very important sense the programmatic, theoretically oriented research on childrearing questions in the 1940's and 1950's gave great impetus to this change. This research constituted a significant stage of hypothesis formulation in a field that was essentially atheoretical and outside the main currents of systematic research. With hindsight, one can say that it is unfortunate that the "classical" childrearing designs have relied on data so open to measurement error, and so vulnerable in interpretation as cause-effect evidence. Childrearing research is a curious combination of loose methodology that is tightly interwoven with provocative hypotheses of developmental processes and relationships. The compelling legend of maternal influences on child behavior that has evolved does not have its roots in solid data, and its decisive verification remains in many respects a subject for future research. The findings from the preceding analyses of data make it difficult to continue to be complacent about methodology, and difficult to continue to regard replication as a luxury. The child's day-to-day experiences contribute significantly to his behavior and development and are in many respects the essence of developmental theory. An exact understanding is important to science and society. In attempting to build on this knowledge, each researcher is a methodologist and as such has a responsibility for excellence.

As a result of our having undertaken this research, we as investigators have had what we view as a learning experience. Perhaps some of this learning may be better characterized as a process of rediscovery, one of more fully understanding aspects of methodology and principles of research that are already known but sometimes disregarded. We hope that others will find something of this same value in this research.

A

Identification of Variables

Description of Instruments in Replication Study

A description of the measures in the replication study is presented here. All of the NIMH measures and the corresponding items from *Patterns of Child Rearing* are included.

Column 1. *Variable Label.* The variable number and the descriptive title of each scale are given as they appear in the NIMH data files.

Column 2. *NIMH Questions and Scoring Procedures.* The specific questions of the mother interview, mother questionnaire, and teachers' ratings are listed by groupings of similar dimensions. The question or questions that are the bases for appraisals of the variables in column 1 are listed directly opposite the relevant number and label. Where the score for a variable is based on the entire interview or a summation of item scores, this is so indicated.

Column 3. *Scale Direction and Intervals, NIMH.* The direction of the scales is indicated by labels of the low and high categories. The possible number of intervals used in coding or used by the respondent in making ratings is indicated. In parentheses is the number of scale intervals actually used, when this is less than the possible range.

The scales do not run in the same direction for each of the dimensions. For all of the tables in the text, however, the name of the scale denotes a high score. When the direction of a scale in the text is the reverse of its direction in this appendix, an *r* appears in the column below the description of scale direction.

Column 4. *"Patterns of Child Rearing" Questions and Scoring Procedures.* The questions in *Patterns* corresponding to those used in the NIMH study are listed. If the two studies have identical questions, it is so indicated; if they differ, the original question is quoted. In some instances parallel questions do not exist. When the entire interview is the basis for ratings, this is indicated.

Column 5. *Scale Direction and Intervals, "Patterns."* The direction of the scale is indicated by labels of the low and high categories. The original scales used by the coders usually consisted of five intervals. Nine-interval scales were produced by an ordering of the averaged scores of the two coders when they differed by only one scale point. For example, ratings of "4" by one coder and "5" by a second coder are given an average rating of 4.5, which is then scored "8" on the final scale.

Column 6. *Coder Reliability.* Scores in both studies are the combinations of independent ratings made by two coders. In *Patterns*, the method of handling coders' differences of one point is described above. When coders differed by more than one scale point, they discussed their ratings and agreed on a final category. In the NIMH study, each coder used scales with the number of intervals indicated for each question in column 3 of this table. In cases of disagreement, the coders discussed the material and arrived at consensus. The final score on an item was an adjudicated rating by the two coders.

For variables 36 through 49 from Mother Questionnaire and Teacher Ratings, no coder reliability is reported since these scores derived from precoded responses.

Variable Label (1)	NIMH Questions and Scoring Procedures (2)	Scale Direction and Intervals NIMH (3)	Patterns of Child Rearing Questions and Scoring Procedures (4)	Scale Direction and Intervals Patterns (5)	Coder Reliability Patterns NIMH (6)
FROM MOTHER'S INTERVIEW Techniques of control:	Each technique of control is coded as used or not used in each situation: (mealtime, neatness, bedtime and noise, aggression to sibs, aggression to parents, safety). A summed standardized				

score is derived based on use of technique across situations. For each, mother is asked:

#	Variable	Description	Source	Scoring		
1.	Isolation	How do you go about getting X to act as you want him to? Describe in as much detail as you can the different things you do. Think of some extreme things X has done (at the table, etc.); how have you handled that? How upset were you? How did you show it? For safety: There are certain things that involve the total safety of a child, such as playing with matches, running in the street,—What would you do? Identical procedures were used for variables 1, 2, 3, 5, 6, 8, 9, 10, 10a, 10b.	Entire interview is source, III-52.	Summed standardized score Low score = little use	.65	.53
2.	Love withdrawal	See variable 1.	Entire interview is source, III-53.	Summed standardized score Low score = little use	.68	.50
3.	Reasoning	See variable 1.	Entire interview is source, III-57.	Summed standardized score Low score = much use	.70	.42

r

155

Variable Label (1)	NIMH Questions and Scoring Procedures (2)	Scale Direction and Intervals NIMH (3)	Patterns of Child Rearing Questions and Scoring Procedures (4)	Scale Direction and Intervals Patterns (5)	Coder Reliability NIMH (6)	Patterns (6)
4. Tangible rewards	Suppose X has just done something that you feel is very good, or suppose that he has been particularly good. What do you usually do at those times? Do you have any ways of praising or rewarding him? Do you have material tangible rewards such as candy, toys, money, or outings, or do you use intangible rewards?	Summed standardized score Low score = much use r	. . . how you go about correcting X and getting him to behave the way you want him to . . . Do you have any system of rewarding him for good behavior? Do you have any ways he can earn money? Can he earn points or gold stars or anything like that? Q. 45, 45a, 45b, III-36.	1 = never used 9 = regularly used	.85	.68
4a. Praise	See questions for variable 4.	1 = always 5 = not used (3) r	Some parents praise their children quite a bit when they are good, and others think that you ought to take good behavior for granted and that there's no point in praising a child for it. How do you feel about this? Q. 46 and entire interview, III-37.	1 = never used 9 = very often used	.34	.67
5. Deprivation of privileges	See variable 1.	Summed standardized score Low score = little use	Do you ever deprive X of something he wants as a way of disciplining him? How often? Q. 52 and entire interview, III-47.	1 = never used 9 = very often used	.63	.67

6.	Physical punishment	See variable 1.	Summed standardized score Low score = little use	How often do you spank X? How about your husband? How often does he spank him? For instance, how often has X been spanked in the last two weeks? How about when he was younger —say two or three years old? How often did you spank him then? Q 48, 48a and b, 49, and entire interview, III-46.	1 = never used 9 = very often used		.80	.74
7.	Physical punishment for aggression to parents	See variable 1.	1 = not used 2 = used	Score not obtained.	—		.83	—
7a.	Physical punishment for aggression to siblings	See variable 1.	1 = not used 2 = used	Score not obtained.	—		.84	—
8.	Scolding	See variable 1.	Summed standardized score Low score = little use	Score not obtained.	—		.54	—
9.	Diverting attention	See variable 1.	Summed standardized score Low score = much use r	Score not obtained.	—		.66	—
10.	Commanding	See variable 1.	Summed standardized score Low score = little use	Score not obtained.	—		.55	—

157

Variable Label (1)	NIMH Questions and Scoring Procedures (2)	Scale Direction and Intervals NIMH (3)	Patterns of Child Rearing Questions and Scoring Procedures (4)	Scale Direction and Intervals Patterns (5)	Coder Reliability NIMH (6)	Coder Reliability Patterns (6)
10a. Positive model	See variable 1.	Summed standardized score. Low score = much use r	Do you ever say, "Your mother and daddy do it this way"? Do you say that? Under what circumstances? Who else do you hold up as an example? Q 47, 47a, III-38.	1 = never, 8 = often	.34	.74
10b. Negative model	See variable 1.	Occured in only 13 cases.	Is there anyone you mention as an example of what not to do? Q 47b, III-39.	1 = never, 7 = often	—	.87
11. Response to dependency	How do you feel about it when X hangs on you and follows you around? How do you generally react if he demands attention when you're busy? If he asks you to help him with something you think he could probably do by himself?	1 = positive to dependency, 7 = negative to dependency	Identical question in Patterns and NIMH. Q 30c, d, e, and 31, III-11.	1 = rewards dependency, 9 = punishes dependency	.60	.57
12. Response to independency	Do you encourage his trying things even when he's not able, or his making decisions for himself, or doesn't it make any difference?	1 = positive to independency, 7 = negative to independency (6)	Question not asked.	—	.56	—

158

#	Variable	1957 interview question	1957 code	1951-52 interview question	1951-52 code	r	r
13.	Permissiveness of aggression to parents	Sometimes a child will get angry at his parents and hit or kick or shout angry things at them. How much of this do you allow? How have you handled it when he acts like this?	1 = permissive 7 = not at all permissive (6) r	Sometimes a child will get angry at his parents and hit or kick or shout angry things at them. How much of this sort of thing do you think parents ought to allow in a child of X's age? How do you handle it when X acts like this? Give me an example. Q 42, 42a, III-30.	1 = not at all permissive 9 = completely permissive	.68	.71
14.	Severity of punishment for aggression to parents	See variable 13.	1 = no punishment 6 = severe punishment (5)	How do you handle it when X acts like this? Give me an example. How did you teach him not to do this? Q 42, 42a and b, III-31.	1 = no punishment 8 = severe punishment	.70	.62
14a.	Severity of punishment for denial	How severe are you if he denies something you are pretty sure he has done?	1 = no punishment 5 = very severe (5)	What do you do about it if he denies something you are pretty sure he has done? Q 44c.	Not coded	.76	—
15.	Comfort after punishment for aggression	After a blowup and you've been pretty severe, what do you usually do? Is that the end of it?	1 = comfort given 2 = no comfort given r	Question not asked.	—	.85	—
16.	Permissiveness of aggression to siblings	How do X and his sisters (brothers) get along? How often do they quarrel? How much of this do you allow?	1 = permissive 7 = not at all permissive (5) r	How do you feel about it when they quarrel? How bad does it have to get before you do something about it? Q 37a, III-22.	1 = not at all permissive 9 = completely permissive	.74	.60

Variable Label (1)	NIMH Questions and Scoring Procedures (2)	Scale Direction and Intervals NIMH (3)	Patterns of Child Rearing Questions and Scoring Procedures (4)	Scale Direction and Intervals Patterns (5)	Coder Reliability NIMH (6)	Coder Reliability Patterns (6)
17. Permissiveness of aggression to other children	When X is playing with another child in the neighborhood (same sex) and there is a quarrel or fight and you can't determine who started it, how much do you allow?	1 = permissive 7 = not at all permissive (6) r	How about when X is playing with one of the other children in the neighborhood and there is a quarrel or a fight, how do you handle this? Q 40, III-28.	1 = not at all permissive 9 = completely permissive	.55	.54
18. Encouragement of aggression in self-defense	Have you ever encouraged him to fight back?	1 = never encourages 7 = strongly encourages (6)	Identical question in Patterns and NIMH. Q 41a, III-27.	1 = never 8 = strongly encourages	.72	.79
19. Restrictiveness: overall	A summed standardized score based on ratings (1 to 7) on level of demands concerning mealtime, modesty, neatness, care of furniture, bedtime, noise, watching TV, whereabouts of child, checking on child, permissiveness of dependency, of independency, of aggression to sibs, to other children, to parents.	Summed standardized score Low score = little restrictiveness	Score not obtained.	—	.72	—
Level of demands: 19a. At mealtime	What do you expect of X in the way of table manners? Do you expect him to stay at table	1 = low demands 7 = high demands	Identical question in Patterns and NIMH. Q 12a, II-40.	1 = no restrictions 8 = high restrictions	.80	.60

through meal, or is he allowed to leave the table?

	Is he allowed to use fingers?	1 = low demands 5 = high demands	Identical question in *Patterns* and NIMH. Q 12b, II-41.	1 = no restrictions 9 = high restrictions	.88	.74
	How about interrupting adult conversations? Is that allowed?	1 = low demands 7 = high demands (6)	Identical question in *Patterns* and NIMH. Q 12c, II-42.	1 = no restrictions 9 = high restrictions	.71	.64
	Entire set of questions on mealtime behavior used as basis for rating.	1 = low demands 7 = high demands (6)	Overall rating of demands for table manners made from all information on table manners. Q 12, 12a, II-43.	1 = no restrictions 9 = high restrictions	.81	.54
19b. For modesty	How do you feel about allowing him to run about without clothes on?	1 = low demands 7 = high demands	Identical question in *Patterns* and NIMH. Q 18, II-53.	1 = not at all permissive 9 = completely permissive	.84	.84
19c. For neatness	How about personal grooming and cleanliness? What do you insist on? What about keeping his room neat and orderly? What do you insist that he do or at least help to do?	1 = low demands 9 = high demands	The question of being neat and orderly and keeping things clean. What do you expect of X as far as neatness is concerned? Q 21, II-61.	1 = low standards 9 = high standards	.79	.46
19d. For care of furniture	What do you insist on about being careful about marking on walls and jumping on furniture and things like that?	1 = low demands 7 = high demands (6)	How important do you think it is for him to be careful about marking on walls and furniture and things like that? Q 22, II-62.	1 = few restrictions 9 = many restrictions	.57	.54

Variable Label (1)	NIMH Questions and Scoring Procedures (2)	Scale Direction and Intervals NIMH (3)	Patterns of Child Rearing Questions and Scoring Procedures (4)	Scale Direction and Intervals Patterns (5)	Coder Reliability NIMH	Coder Reliability Patterns (6)
19e. For bedtime routines	What about bedtime rules? What do you insist on?	1 = low demands 7 = high demands (6)	What are some of the rules? How about bedtime? Q 23a, II-65.	1 = not at all strict 9 = very strict	.64	.59
19f. For noise	How much noise do you allow?	1 = low demands 7 = high demands (6)	How about making noise in the house—how much of that do you allow? Q 23b, II-66.	1 = not at all strict 9 = very strict	.69	.66
19g. For watching TV, etc.	How about the amount of time he can spend listening to radio or record player or watching TV? Do you have rules on this?	1 = low demands 7 = high demands (6)	How about the amount of time he can spend listening to the radio or watching TV programs? Q 23c, II-67.	1 = no restrictions 9 = high restrictions	.65	.72
19h. For whereabouts outside home	Do you have rules about where he can play outside and where he cannot?	1 = low demands 7 = high demands	How far away is he allowed to go by himself? Q 23d, II-69.	1 = no restrictions 9 = high restrictions	.78	.59
19i. Checking on whereabouts	How often do you check on where he is?	1 = never 5 = constantly	Do you keep track of exactly where X is and what he is doing most of the time or can you let him watch out for himself quite a bit? How often do you check? Q 29, III-5.	1 = rarely 9 = constantly	.80	.75
19j. Insistence on obedience	Some parents insist that children obey immediately. Others don't think	1 = low demands 7 = high demands (6)	Some parents expect their children to obey immediately. Others	1 = does not expect obedience 9 = expects instant	.61	.59

Variable	Definition	Scoring	Source question		obedience		
19k. Consistency in "following through"	If he doesn't do what you ask, do you ever just drop the subject or do you always see to it that he does it?	1 = doesn't follow through / 7 = always follows through	it's terribly important for a child to obey right away. What do you insist on?	don't think it's terribly important for a child to obey right away. How do you feel about this? Q 26, II-73.	1 = does not follow through / 9 = always follows through	.77	.78
Severity of punishment: 20. Overall	A summed score based on the standardized scores of severity in each of the following situations: mealtime, modesty, neatness, bedtime and noise, aggression to siblings, physical danger, and aggression to parents.	Summed standardized score / Low score = low severity		Identical question in Patterns and NIMH. Q 28, II-78.	Score not obtained.	.70	—
20a. At mealtime	See questions for techniques of control.	1 = no punishment / 6 = severe punishment (5)		What do you do about it if he does some of the things you don't allow? Q 14, II-44.	1 = no pressure / 9 = high pressure	.43	.57
20b. For modesty	See questions for techniques of control.	1 = no punishment / 6 = severe punishment (3)		What have you done to teach X about this? Q 18a, II-54.	1 = no pressure / 8 = high pressure	.78	.76
20c. For neatness	See questions for techniques of control.	1 = no punishment / 6 = severe punishment (4)		How do you go about getting him to do this? Q 21a, II-63.	1 = no pressure / 9 = high pressure	.59	.52
20d. For bedtime and noise	See questions for techniques of control.	1 = no punishment / 6 = severe punishment		Score not obtained.	—	.60	—

163

Variable Label (1)	NIMH Questions and Scoring Procedures (2)	Scale Direction and Intervals NIMH (3)	Patterns of Child Rearing Questions and Scoring Procedures (4)	Scale Direction and Intervals Patterns (5)	Coder Reliability Pat-NIMH terns (6)
20e. For aggression to siblings	See questions for techniques of control.	1 = no punishment 6 = severe punishment (4)	Score not obtained.	—	.66 —
20f. For physical danger	See questions for techniques of control.	1 = no punishment 6 = severe punishment (5)	Score not obtained.	—	.57 —
Negative emotional expression: 21. Overall	A summed score based on the standardized scores of emotional component of mother's punishments in each of the following situations: mealtime, modesty, neatness, bedtime, noise, etc., aggression to siblings, aggression to parents.	Summed standardized score Low score = little expressiveness	Score not obtained.	—	.76 —
21a. At mealtime	See questions for techniques of control.	1 = not expressive 7 = very expressive (5)	Score not obtained.	—	.69 —
21b. For modesty	See questions for techniques of control.	1 = not expressive 7 = very expressive (3)	Score not obtained.	—	.59 —
21c. For neatness	See questions for techniques of control.	1 = not expressive 7 = very expressive (5)	Score not obtained.	—	.67 —
21d. For bedtime, noise, etc.	See questions for techniques of control.	1 = not expressive 7 = very expressive (5)	Score not obtained.	—	.65 —

No.	Variable	Description	Scale	Source	Scale (alt)		
	to siblings	niques of control.	7 = very expressive (4)	Score not obtained.	—	.63	—
21f.	For aggression to parents	See questions for techniques of control.	1 = not expressive 7 = very expressive (6)	Score not obtained.	—	.50	—
22.	Labeling of child's behavior	See questions for techniques of control.	1 = much labeling 5 = no labeling r	Score not obtained.	—	.54	—
23.	Maternal warmth	Entire interview rated for evidence of warmth and affection for child. Manifested by playing with child, enjoying him, doing things to please him, demonstrating affection in words and action.	1 = warm 7 = hostile (5) r	Entire interview is source. III-15.	1 = predominantly hostile 9 = very warm	.65	.53
24.	Affectional demonstrativeness	Some mothers are very demonstrative in their affection toward their children—hugging, kissing, cuddling; others are more reserved. How would you describe yourself?	1 = very demonstrative 7 = not demonstrative (6) r	Do you show your affection toward each other quite a bit, or are you fairly reserved people, you and X? Q 33b, III-13.	1 = none 9 = a great deal	.75	.62
25.	Annoying things about child	What kinds of things does X do that get on your nerves? Score is number of things reported.	1 = none 7 = many	Entire interview for evidences of not wanting the child, feelings of irritation, derogation. IV-29.	1 = no rejection 9 = complete rejection	.93	.57
26.	Things enjoyed in child	What sorts of things do you enjoy about him? Score is number of things reported.	1 = everything 8 = nothing (7) r	Score not obtained.	—	.70	—

Variable Label (1)	NIMH Questions and Scoring Procedures (2)	Scale Direction and Intervals NIMH (3)	Patterns of Child Rearing Questions and Scoring Procedures (4)	Scale Direction and Intervals Patterns (5)	Coder Reliability NIMH (6)	Coder Reliability Patterns (6)
27. Independence	What are some things X tries to do by himself even when he isn't quite able? How often? What are some decisions X tries to make for himself?	1 = independent 7 = dependent (5) r	Score not obtained.	—	.68	—
28. Summed dependency	A summed score based on standardized scores on attention wanted, closeness wanted, and separation anxiety.	Summed standardized score. Low score = little dependency	Q 30, 31, 32 and entire interview, III-10.	1 = none 9 = a great deal	.87	.53
29. Attention wanted	How much attention does X seem to want from you?	1 = none 7 = constantly (6)	Identical questions in Patterns and NIMH. Q 30, III-6.	1 = none 9 = a great deal	.82	.74
30. Closeness wanted	Does he follow you around and hang on to you?	1 = never 7 = constantly (6)	How about following you around and hanging on to your skirts? Q 30a, III-7.	1 = none 7 = a great deal	.79	.75
31. Separation anxiety	How does X react generally when you go out and leave him at home with someone else?	1 = no objection 7 = objects strongly (6)	How does X react generally when you go out of the house and leave him with someone else? Q 31, III-9.	1 = none 8 = a great deal	.72	.75
32. Aggression to parents	How much of a problem have you had with X about shows of temper, angry shouting and	1 = none 7 = a great deal	Identical question in Patterns and NIMH. Q 42c, III-29.	1 = none 9 = a great deal	.80	.52

Item	Description	Scale	Alternate question	Alternate scale		
32a. Quarreling with siblings	How do X and his brothers (sisters) get along together? How often do they quarrel? ...that sort of thing around the house? (Aggression toward siblings excluded.)	1 = none 7 = a great deal (6)	Would you tell me something about how X and his brother (sister) get along together? Q 37, III-21.	1 = none 8 = a great deal	.85	.67
Compliance: 32b. Overall	A summed score based on standardized scores on compliance at mealtime, for modesty, neatness, care of property, bedtime, noise, TV, aggression to parents.	Summed standardized score Low score = much compliance	How much do you have to keep after X to get him to do the things he is supposed to do? Q 25, II-77.	1 = no problem 5 = constant problem	.74	.49
32c. At mealtime	In general, considering all his behavior about table manners, how compliant is he?	1 = compliant 7 = constant problem (5)	Score not obtained.	—	.75	—
32d. For modesty	Is it easy or difficult for him to comply? How compliant is he?	1 = compliant 7 = constant problem (5)	Score not obtained.	—	.64	—
32e. For neatness, care of property	Question identical to 32d.	1 = compliant 7 = constant problem (6)	Score not obtained.	—	.72	—
32f. For bedtime, noise, TV	Question identical to 32d.	1 = compliant 7 = constant problem	Score not obtained.	—	.69	—
32g. For aggression to parents	Question identical to 32d.	1 = compliant 7 = constant problem (6)	Score not obtained.	—	.77	—

167

Variable Label (1)	NIMH Questions and Scoring Procedures (2)	Scale Direction and Intervals NIMH (3)	Patterns of Child Rearing Questions and Scoring Procedures (4)	Scale Direction and Intervals Patterns (5)	Coder Reliability NIMH (6)	Coder Reliability Patterns (6)
Evidence of conscience:						
33. Confession after deviation	How does X act when he has done something he knows you don't want him to do, when your back is turned? Have you ever had the feeling that he has done something wrong that you don't know about? What indications did you have? Has he ever come to you and told you about it before you discovered it? When you ask him, does he usually admit it or deny it?	1 = always 5 = never r	When he has deliberately done something he knows you don't want him to do, when your back is turned, how does he act? Does he ever come and tell you about it without your having to ask him? When you ask him about something he has done that he knows he's not supposed to do, does he usually admit it or deny it? What do you do about it if he denies something you are pretty sure he has done? Q 44, 44a, III-32.	1 = seldom 7 = always	.86	.33
33a. No noticeable change in behavior	See questions for variable 33.	1 = always 5 = never r	Score not obtained.	—	.77	—
33b. Grows silent, becomes very quiet	See questions for variable 33.	1 = always 5 = never r	Score not obtained.	—	.74	—

No.	Variable	Description	Scale	Description	Scale	r	r
33c.	Looks or acts guilty, looks sheepish, sneaks around	See questions for variable 33.	1 = always 5 = never r	Score not obtained.	—	.84	—
33d.	Tells mother about deviation, blaming himself	See questions for variable 33.	1 = always 5 = never r	Score not obtained.	—	.73	—
33e.	Tells mother about deviation, blaming someone else	See questions for variable 33.	1 = always 5 = never r	Score not obtained.	—	.75	—
34.	Admission of deviance	See questions for variable 33.	1 = always 5 = never r	See questions for variable 33. Q 44, 44b, III-33.	1 = admits 5 = denies	.93	.68
35.	Conscience	See questions for variable 33.	1 = high conscience 7 = low conscience (6) r	See questions for variable 33. Q 44, 44a-c, III-34.	1 = weak conscience 9 = strong conscience	.75	.63

FROM MOTHER'S QUESTIONNAIRE

No.	Variable	Description	Scale
36.	Child's compliance	Child complies without question to adults.	1 = definitely yes 5 = definitely no
36a.	Restrictiveness at mealtime	Age at which child is expected to eat with fork, spoon; not spill food, etc.	1 = low demands 9 = high demands
36b.	Restrictiveness for neatness	Age at which child is expected to pick up toys, etc.	1 = low demands 9 = high demands
37.	Independence	Child tries to do things on his own, doesn't ask help.	1 = definitely yes 5 = definitely no r

	Variable Label (1)	NIMH Questions and Scoring Procedures (2)	Scale Direction and Intervals NIMH (3)	Patterns of Child Rearing Questions and Scoring Procedures (4)	Scale Direction and Intervals Patterns (5)	Coder Reliability Pat- NIMH terns (6)
38.	Summed dependency	A summed score based on standardized scores on questions on attention wanted, closeness wanted, and separation anxiety.	Summed standardized score Low score = little dependency			
39.	Attention wanted	Is very demanding of adults' time and attention, wants a lot of help.	1 = definitely no 5 = definitely yes			
40.	Closeness wanted	Shy in a social situation, loses confidence on his own, stays close to adult.	1 = definitely no 5 = definitely yes			
41.	Separation anxiety	Gets upset when mother leaves, does not accept her departure readily.	1 = definitely no 5 = definitely yes			
42.	Aggression to parents	Shows a lot of temper, kicking, hitting, screaming, biting when thwarted.	1 = definitely no 5 = definitely yes			

FROM COMBINED TEACHER RATINGS

	Variable Label (1)	NIMH Questions and Scoring Procedures (2)	Scale Direction and Intervals NIMH (3)	Patterns of Child Rearing Questions and Scoring Procedures (4)	Scale Direction and Intervals Patterns (5)	Coder Reliability Pat- NIMH terns (6)
43.	Summed dependency	A summed score based on standardized scores on questions on attention wanted, closeness wanted, and separation anxiety.	Summed standardized score Low score = little dependency			

44.	Attention wanted	Is very demanding of adults' time and attention, wants a lot of help.	2 = definitely no 14 = definitely yes (11)
45.	Closeness wanted	Shy in a social situation, loses confidence on his own, stays close to adult.	2 = definitely no 14 = definitely yes (11)
46.	Separation anxiety	How did X react in the beginning when his mother left him at school?	2 = no objection 14 = strong objection (12)
47.	Aggression in nursery school	How much of a problem have you had with X about show of temper, angry shouting and that sort of thing? Include aggression toward teachers and other children.	2 = none 14 = great deal
48.	Annoying things about child	What kinds of things does X do that get on your nerves? Score is number of things reported.	0 = none mentioned 11 = 11
49.	Confession after deviation	How does X act when he has done something he knows you don't want him to do, when your back is turned? Have you ever had the feeling that he has done something wrong that you don't know about? What indications did	2 = always 14 = never (8)

Variable Label (1)	NIMH Questions and Scoring Procedures (2)	Scale Direction and Intervals NIMH (3)	Patterns of Child Rearing Questions and Scoring Procedures (4)	Scale Direction and Intervals Patterns (5)	Coder Reliability Pat-NIMH (6)
	you have? Has he ever come to you and told you about it before you discovered it? When you ask him, does he usually admit it or deny it?				
49a. Admission of deviance	See questions for variable 49.	2 = always 14 = never (7)			
49b. Conscience	See questions for variable 49.	2 = high conscience 14 = low conscience (11)			
50. Sex of child					

APPENDIX B

Intercorrelation of Variables

Three sets of data are presented: In each cell with two entries (all cells above the main diagonal), the top entry is the correlation for boys; that beneath it, the correlation for girls. Each single-entry cell gives the correlation for boys and girls combined. Total N = 86, 43 boys and 43 girls. Correlations significant at the 5% level for the total sample are .21; for each sex, .30.

Variables are identified by number only. For names of scales and direction of scoring, see corresponding variable numbers in Appendix A. Where direction of scale in the matrix is reversed from its use in the text, an r has been placed adjacent to the variable number in the matrix.

Var.	1	2	3(r)	4(r)	5	6	7	7a	8	9(r)	10	11	12	13(r)	14	14a	15(r)	16(r)	17(r)	18	19	19a	19b	19c	19d	19e	19f
1	—	08 / -22	22 / 02	-20 / -23	-02 / 27	-12 / 10	12 / -08	30 / 00	29 / 00	26 / -10	00 / -38	02 / 06	-25 / 09	16 / 11	13 / 19	00 / 30	-08 / -04	-13 / -29	-02 / 08	20 / -05	-10 / 17	14 / 08	-13 / 14	-17 / 05	-19 / 15	22 / 04	06 / 03
2	-07	—	02 / -34	-05 / 05	-09 / -04	13 / -38	-10 / -19	64 / 02	15 / 31	04 / 07	32 / 10	20 / -01	09 / -26	-21 / -05	-03 / -08	-11 / -13	-25 / -07	31 / -04	11 / -10	-19 / 20	08 / -14	-27 / 07	06 / -09	-06 / 00	24 / 00	-01 / -15	12 / 22
3(r)	12	-11	—	-13 / -22	-17 / 08	11 / 10	-07 / -04	09 / -02	-06 / -25	21 / 25	-06 / -26	11 / 08	00 / 15	23 / 00	39 / -10	03 / -22	21 / 13	12 / -11	16 / 10	-26 / -17	-03 / -02	-06 / 12	-27 / 44	-05 / -05	-21 / -20	19 / -12	02 / -25
4(r)	-22	-02	-16	—	-02 / -31	03 / 01	09 / -05	-69 / -05	01 / 04	-10 / -10	10 / 05	00 / -29	23 / 16	-01 / -24	-20 / -28	-29 / -18	20 / 14	15 / 06	06 / -14	-23 / -04	08 / -11	-03 / -07	06 / -18	00 / -10	31 / 03	-19 / 10	02 / 31
5	15	-08	-08	-17	—	31 / 16	07 / 23	21 / 17	08 / -06	23 / 19	-03 / -07	22 / 07	06 / -25	35 / -06	26 / 16	-06 / 23	-11 / -11	-01 / -12	-25 / -19	42 / -05	40 / 02	35 / 20	07 / 15	49 / 15	29 / 18	31 / 26	40 / -07
6	-01	-07	11	04	22	—	38 / 69	24 / 35	17 / -04	26 / -08	14 / -02	08 / -13	25 / -05	07 / -19	24 / 06	19 / -21	15 / -04	26 / 08	17 / 01	-20 / 18	21 / 03	-07 / 07	-18 / 05	28 / -12	13 / 15	18 / 19	20 / 01
7	00	-12	-03	03	13	54	—	-11 / 21	03 / 02	-32 / 02	08 / 00	08 / -13	-01 / -07	16 / -24	26 / 26	-17 / 00	03 / -06	-23 / 25	-07 / 11	-08 / -07	09 / -08	05 / 06	-19 / 04	25 / -14	22 / -15	10 / 05	04 / -11
7a	12	39	04	-34	20	30	08	—	27 / -07	20 / -28	22 / 31	21 / 09	-30 / -12	11 / -04	15 / 01	10 / 13	-28 / -05	20 / 28	05 / 17	26 / 41	19 / 09	08 / -07	-14 / 27	21 / -24	22 / -15	21 / 25	26 / -06
8	16	20	-15	01	03	07	03	12	—	12 / 09	-16 / 21	16 / -16	-04 / -19	02 / 14	09 / 11	10 / 13	22 / 01	05 / -02	06 / 09	05 / -09	-06 / 00	-05 / 04	-05 / -04	13 / 14	21 / 06	-03 / -26	-05 / 42
9(r)	06	05	23	-09	20	05	-13	-08	11	—	-14 / 10	07 / -05	-14 / -04	09 / 07	-02 / 07	16 / 04	-15 / -18	19 / -30	-08 / -11	23 / -16	04 / -11	26 / 31	-16 / 00	13 / 14	-06 / 00	11 / -11	12 / 07
10	-22	23	-17	05	-05	04	03	24	02	02	—	-04 / 02	14 / 03	-18 / 02	-13 / 30	19 / -06	-15 / -18	-05 / -03	02 / 05	-05 / 07	20 / 03	08 / -15	-06 / -10	09 / -10	22 / -13	06 / 34	27 / 19
11	03	14	11	-11	02	15	-01	18	03	-10	-04	—	09 / 10	27 / 14	26 / 01	06 / -30	-03 / 00	29 / -05	34 / -07	-17 / -23	31 / 31	00 / -14	-17 / -06	09 / 03	-03 / -06	32 / 22	38 / 03
12	-08	-04	08	20	-08	10	-04	-21	-10	-10	09	22	—	04 / 03	15 / 27	-09 / -26	-03 / 05	-15 / -04	-08 / -03	07 / 22	21 / 14	-25 / -10	11 / 09	-18 / -21	00 / -17	-07 / -05	18 / -04
13(r)	15	-16	13	-10	20	-05	-02	05	06	07	-10	22	03	—	65 / 45	-24 / 17	22 / 18	-15 / -04	-08 / -03	07 / 22	58 / 29	37 / 14	-05 / -01	48 / 12	20 / -03	35 / -40	41 / 04

			(r)	(r)						(r)				(r)			(r)	(r)	(r)								
14	18	–05	14	–24	22	14	26	08	10	02	09	15	21	56	—	–47 34	06 04	–32 –13	02 10	–09 –04	20 14	–13 02	–24 –03	40 –02	–08 –12	34 –04	09 –07
14a	16	–10	–11	–23	08	–03	–12	08	12	11	11	–12	–16	–05	–06	—	05 –16	29 07	27 –14	08 –10	09 03	33 19	05 –01	–03 29	12 09	25 –05	05 –04
15(r)	–05	–17	17	17	–11	05	–02	–29	–18	11	–18	–01	01	20	05	–09	—	–08 –14	–01 03	–21 32	19 23	21 18	–02 –11	26 19	00 23	27 05	–02 13
16(r)	–21	14	00	14	–08	17	05	26	02	–11	28	00	11	–09	–20	16	–09	—	59 70	–01 –06	48 18	03 –27	–10 –02	00 –18	44 –13	04 –11	49 11
17(r)	03	03	14	–04	–22	09	02	11	08	–11	03	07	16	–07	06	10	00	64	—	–30 –12	07 28	–33 –26	–09 04	–30 –17	05 –30	–18 –09	12 20
18	13	–07	–21	–18	24	–01	–07	29	02	07	03	05	–19	13	–04	02	02	–08	–22	—	24 35	47 33	16 08	06 43	13 18	23 10	34 07
19	05	00	–01	03	24	12	02	17	–04	–05	08	33	17	46	16	04	21	35	15	22	—	52 52	24 27	63 61	57 43	53 24	71 54
19a	12	–15	02	–04	29	00	05	02	–02	28	–03	–05	–19	28	–06	25	20	–10	–30	41	53	—	18 28	50 70	40 43	37 07	39 26
19b	03	–01	10	–03	13	–06	–07	07	–05	–08	–08	–11	10	–03	–12	–01	–06	–06	–04	09	27	23	—	09 02	21 –04	13 05	08 12
19c	–02	–05	–04	–04	28	04	03	–04	–20	12	–05	10	–20	29	15	11	22	–07	–24	19	62	59	07	—	40 46	41 18	32 21
19d	00	14	–19	19	22	14	09	03	13	–01	02	–03	–08	09	–10	09	12	14	–13	12	51	41	08	44	—	08 23	39 44
19e	14	–06	03	–05	28	19	07	24	–13	00	21	27	–06	01	14	11	16	–03	–14	19	40	23	09	27	16	—	31 21
19f	05	14	–10	16	17	10	–03	11	15	09	20	23	07	25	01	01	06	30	15	19	64	33	11	27	42	26	—
19g	13	–05	–03	00	11	–18	03	20	–11	–13	07	12	–04	28	08	08	01	04	–07	–03	37	19	07	20	–04	38	02

Var.	1	2	3 (r)	4 (r)	5	6	7	7a	8	9 (r)	10	11	2	13 (r)	14	14a	15 (r)	16 (r)	17 (r)	18	19	19a	19b	19c	19d	19e	19f
19h	-03	-03	-18	00	-22	-01	-08	03	03	-26	-05	-09	12	-02	-16	-12	09	24	15	05	26	-08	-05	-11	00	-20	07
19i	-06	04	-08	-03	01	-02	-01	03	05	-22	05	-07	05	08	-04	-23	07	13	01	11	21	-13	-04	-02	00	-26	01
19k	21	01	13	-17	07	-03	-11	10	-21	28	-07	18	-22	23	08	05	26	-18	00	11	20	33	01	32	14	21	11
20	28	03	-03	-23	32	29	15	30	18	04	23	19	-07	38	46	19	16	08	03	30	59	40	17	48	28	49	43
20b	04	-04	-03	-08	-01	04	00	09	06	10	13	05	06	-11	-10	18	03	-15	05	20	23	09	68	10	-01	06	19
20c	03	12	-12	-09	28	22	06	12	12	-01	00	22	00	26	17	-08	17	06	-09	32	60	46	16	52	46	33	34
20d	19	-07	00	-17	17	22	11	05	04	-07	21	21	-04	19	24	12	10	09	-06	09	44	22	03	37	13	60	31
20e	30	22	18	-19	18	19	05	55	36	-11	18	07	-19	24	22	17	-01	27	36	25	29	04	10	01	09	21	25
20f	07	03	-18	-13	03	07	14	08	03	15	25	-06	-33	02	-08	18	15	05	-07	12	09	30	02	14	19	21	26
21	17	01	08	-16	19	45	20	26	33	11	09	27	-03	15	20	-06	-08	12	-01	20	11	02	-13	03	18	13	14
22(r)	-22	-18	32	-08	-25	10	-09	-12	-07	14	-02	05	18	-10	02	-15	10	11	25	-15	-31	-41	-39	-27	-32	-23	-21
23(r)	16	-11	24	-14	08	-14	-18	10	06	23	-27	11	-05	27	08	09	06	-17	-08	22	06	15	00	06	03	05	-05
24(r)	17	00	19	00	02	-10	-04	12	06	13	-24	1~	11	32	10	04	10	04	05	14	16	13	00	-06	09	-03	05
25	27	03	12	-36	25	23	12	32	16	-01	08	~	05	10	09	18	07	0~	0~	0~	1~	1~	0~	0~	0~	07	02

176

Var.	1	2	3 (r)	4 (r)	5	6	7	7a	8	9 (r)	10	11	12	13 (r)	14	14a	15 (r)	16 (r)	17 (r)	18	19	19a	19b	19c	19d	19e	19f
26(r)	09	-09	33	-11	-08	-06	-27	-18	11	11	-25	02	15	12	-04	-04	11	-20	-12	-03	05	09	23	-08	09	-11	-02
27(r)	07	-18	16	-15	18	-04	-12	03	08	-08	-07	18	09	19	04	11	-10	07	-01	10	13	08	09	-08	-09	-05	12
28	11	14	-13	09	09	01	14	03	04	-19	14	08	20	-03	-05	-17	-20	-04	-01	17	16	09	23	-02	11	01	10
29	21	08	-19	09	09	-01	01	08	11	-14	14	13	08	-01	-05	01	-13	-02	-01	29	19	06	20	03	13	10	16
30	00	-02	01	-03	10	-02	08	03	-06	-11	06	-01	14	-04	-08	-13	-13	-04	-02	19	16	23	26	04	10	-01	00
31	05	27	-14	16	04	06	25	-04	04	-20	15	07	27	-02	00	-31	-21	-12	01	-05	04	-09	10	-11	05	-07	07
32	19	-12	25	-28	-06	03	-01	-01	-04	-16	00	10	18	05	40	04	-08	00	20	03	-02	-19	-04	-14	-27	04	-09
32a	25	-08	25	-05	05	17	-13	15	07	10	04	11	22	-02	12	05	04	-07	13	08	12	-08	19	-14	-03	18	16
32b	34	-03	27	-19	05	15	05	-05	21	-03	-10	18	15	08	23	00	-18	-07	26	-11	-07	-21	-06	-21	-17	-14	01
32c	07	04	09	02	05	18	01	09	18	00	-01	12	11	10	08	-05	-04	16	06	10	06	-04	-14	-06	-15	-08	18
32d	46	-04	11	-10	08	-08	09	-03	00	12	-26	13	02	-03	01	-12	-20	-24	-04	-21	-05	-09	27	-06	-04	-12	-28
32e	09	-03	21	-18	08	11	02	-04	13	-02	-07	07	01	10	12	10	-07	-11	15	07	03	-01	-07	-01	07	-01	09
32f	24	00	19	-21	-10	12	04	03	32	-02	-03	22	09	05	15	-01	-14	01	31	-01	-11	-20	-13	-31	-15	-17	-01
32g	24	-08	21	-09	08	06	02	-19	-01	-15	02	-01	23	-02	31	03	-13	-10	27	-38	-18	-30	-02	-18	-23	-06	-04

177

Var.	1	2	3 (r)	4 (r)	5	6	7	7a	8	9 (r)	10	11	12	13 (r)	14	14a	15 (r)	16 (r)	17 (r)	18	19	19a	19b	19c	19d	19e	19f
33(r)	12	-01	12	-01	-01	11	02	00	-03	14	-03	17	04	18	02	-13	10	-24	01	12	00	-03	05	-12	-17	06	-03
34(r)	17	-05	09	-01	00	08	-07	-07	07	11	-10	14	08	23	18	-19	22	-30	03	-11	02	-03	-17	06	-07	-13	02
35(r)	15	02	11	-19	-11	01	-15	-08	09	16	00	11	00	15	13	-05	22	-26	12	10	01	-08	-04	-05	-11	-03	04
36	13	11	10	-03	-22	-06	-02	-16	-04	-19	06	08	16	05	18	-01	-18	04	12	-41	-10	-33	-05	-15	-33	-08	-11
36a	16	11	-02	-08	-07	-08	04	24	08	-02	16	21	01	07	10	31	-10	01	03	15	06	13	-25	10	15	05	-02
36b	06	01	04	00	-06	00	07	09	-04	-06	02	06	09	10	00	35	07	00	03	01	11	22	03	15	17	-04	-03
37	02	-09	00	-10	-03	-09	-14	10	04	-13	08	08	00	-02	-04	25	-23	-05	07	-07	07	-07	05	02	-12	-02	-08
38	00	06	-16	-03	-14	-16	-12	-01	-13	-17	01	09	15	-04	00	-02	01	-09	05	10	00	-05	-03	-07	-23	-02	-03
39	10	10	01	-08	-02	-13	-13	04	-06	-12	-12	36	12	04	-01	13	-11	-12	07	13	13	06	-03	02	-14	03	-02
40	01	08	-08	04	-04	-01	-04	01	-09	-04	-03	-20	-04	-22	-13	-09	10	03	05	02	-14	-01	01	-09	-13	-08	-02
41	-13	-05	-27	-02	-23	-19	-09	-07	-12	-19	17	03	23	08	13	-08	04	-11	-03	09	00	-16	-04	-08	-21	09	-02
42	06	-07	-03	-14	-08	08	12	02	-07	-06	-01	00	10	05	23	-15	-13	-21	-10	01	-14	-11	-06	-06	-06	-10	-21
43	07	-31	07	-16	-02	26	22	12	-11	-13	-04	21	15	12	22	-22	14	02	-11	16	10	-08	-04	18	-10	13	01
44	-01	-28	12	-22	-05	13	13	10	-17	-08	07	20	08	02	28	-06	15	03	-07	12	12	-10	-09	22	-08	22	-02

178

Var.

Var.	1	2	3 (r)	4 (r)	5	6	7	7a	8	9 (r)	10	11	12	13 (r)	14	14a	15 (r)	16 (r)	17 (r)	18	19	19a	19b	19c	19d	19e	19f
45	03	-34	15	-12	05	22	09	-01	-23	10	-04	11	07	-03	02	-17	10	-20	-24	17	-05	-01	00	23	-14	17	-06
46	13	-07	-10	-02	-06	24	28	18	15	-31	-11	16	18	28	17	-29	06	19	08	08	16	-06	01	-05	00	-09	09
47	09	12	-14	-09	-19	-19	-02	-27	12	-23	28	06	06	-15	13	01	-15	15	16	04	04	-19	-02	-08	00	-02	03
48	44	-02	-01	-34	15	-17	05	-24	-03	-08	-16	-01	06	07	42	02	-08	-11	-04	11	-02	-12	01	08	-22	-02	-02
50	03	00	06	07	-01	01	00	14	-07	-07	-12	12	-02	05	01	-24	05	14	-07	-23	19	06	12	18	08	00	08

Var.

Var.	19g	19h	19i	19k	20	20b	20c	20d	20e	20f	21	22 (r)	23 (r)	24 (r)	25	26 (r)	27 (r)	28	29	30	31	32	32a	32b	32c	32d	32e
1	16 / 02	-19 / 11	-16 / 07	33 / 14	29 / 26	-06 / 11	-03 / 08	09 / 28	47 / 17	25 / -10	15 / 17	-34 / -15	16 / 13	13 / 22	23 / 27	-15 / 27	06 / 09	00 / 21	14 / 27	-13 / 10	-01 / 14	-04 / 42	-06 / 46	15 / 47	09 / 06	25 / 56	05 / 10
2	-01 / -15	00 / -10	11 / -08	01 / 00	11 / -01	08 / -24	18 / 11	-07 / -07	42 / -03	-05 / 18	17 / -21	-15 / -30	-16 / -01	00 / 00	-02 / 10	-11 / -10	-11 / -30	20 / 00	16 / -06	-05 / 01	38 / 05	-12 / -15	-06 / -09	-02 / 02	-02 / 15	13 / -19	-14 / 19
3 (r)	10 / -18	-24 / -14	-21 / 04	-07 / 31	11 / -14	-34 / 20	-22 / -06	24 / -24	50 / -05	-17 / -18	11 / 02	32 / 32	31 / 15	21 / 15	27 / -01	44 / 26	18 / 16	-33 / 05	-39 / -01	-26 / 26	-16 / -14	42 / 08	44 / 10	44 / 10	33 / -12	01 / 09	24 / 21
4 (r)	-03 / 03	-03 / 03	04 / -13	-22 / -11	-26 / -22	00 / -16	-10 / -11	-21 / -12	-24 / -13	-19 / -04	-01 / -30	-18 / 02	-13 / -16	-03 / 04	-37 / -40	-05 / -20	-01 / -31	18 / -06	09 / 07	01 / -12	33 / -11	-29 / -25	-15 / 05	-03 / -35	-06 / 12	25 / -32	-04 / -36
5	-02 / 19	-12 / -35	04 / -05	09 / 03	31 / 33	-23 / 17	39 / 21	22 / 12	-06 / 31	-05 / 12	17 / 20	-19 / -32	01 / 14	-04 / 08	-09 / 56	-13 / -08	20 / 07	16 / -01	23 / -08	06 / 12	11 / -07	-17 / 07	-02 / 09	-01 / 06	15 / -08	-26 / 24	-01 / 17
6	-07 / -29	-15 / 11	-15 / 09	-07 / 00	41 / 22	01 / 08	19 / 25	30 / 14	34 / 10	-10 / 23	35 / 50	20 / 04	-18 / -10	-12 / -08	16 / 29	-01 / -09	06 / -11	-04 / 05	06 / -07	-23 / 17	09 / 02	-07 / 17	18 / 18	15 / 14	25 / 12	-13 / -12	04 / 22
7	-20 / -17	-23 / 06	06 / -08	-07 / -14	17 / 14	-02 / 05	-02 / 13	20 / 00	03 / 08	06 / 22	07 / 29	-15 / -04	-26 / -08	-10 / 04	03 / 19	-32 / -23	-15 / -10	25 / 01	18 / -17	01 / 15	42 / 04	-02 / -01	-21 / -04	05 / 06	-01 / 03	13 / 04	-05 / 10
7a	19 / 20	-05 / 08	-08 / 12	21 / -02	44 / 19	-10 / 20	18 / 04	09 / 01	69 / 48	17 / 03	25 / 22	00 / -20	09 / 12	17 / 04	36 / 30	-14 / -20	06 / 06	08 / -07	18 / -08	12 / -09	-11 / 01	-07 / 08	01 / 31	-04 / -09	11 / 06	13 / 04	03 / -06

Var.	19g	19h	19i	19k	20	20b	20c	20d	20e	20f	21	22 (r)	23 (○)	24 (r)	25	26 (r)	27 (r)	28	29	30	31	32	32a	32b	32c	32d	32e
8	05 / -34	-12 / 21	-18 / 33	-19 / -27	24 / 17	06 / 15	30 / -02	10 / -05	39 / 32	-22 / 36	48 / 24	-09 / -06	-4 / -0	12 / -06	20 / 15	08 / 18	19 / -06	23 / -19	35 / -19	09 / -21	12 / -07	-12 / 09	10 / 02	26 / 22	10 / 29	36 / -20	10 / 15
9(r)	-04 / -25	-12 / -37	-20 / -23	21 / 31	11 / 03	-20 / 39	21 / -13	-06 / -09	15 / -28	00 / 26	00 / 18	10 / 18	36 / 09	24 / 01	06 / -04	11 / 12	22 / -29	-32 / -03	-22 / -06	-19 / 00	-39 / -01	-22 / -06	10 / 09	-08 / 03	17 / -11	-09 / 22	-13 / 09
10	-10 / 30	19 / -24	19 / -05	-07 / -07	18 / 31	11 / 21	-03 / 05	13 / 32	19 / 16	22 / 26	09 / 13	-07 / 01	-50 / -02	-27 / -20	-10 / -06	-33 / -20	-09 / -08	36 / -04	26 / 08	18 / -01	43 / -17	-13 / 15	-09 / 14	-09 / -08	-02 / 00	-08 / -29	-10 / -10
11	14 / 06	-14 / -05	-09 / -06	11 / 27	20 / 17	-06 / 11	20 / 22	23 / 17	10 / 07	-15 / 07	40 / 15	03 / 08	17 / 01	39 / -14	08 / 31	11 / -12	33 / 04	-06 / 24	-01 / 28	-20 / 20	06 / 08	14 / 02	06 / 19	34 / -04	36 / -16	18 / 06	22 / -11
12	-10 / 07	06 / 18	02 / 08	-27 / -17	-04 / -07	22 / -06	05 / -03	-06 / -01	-24 / -15	-34 / -33	15 / -19	18 / 18	-12 / 06	03 / 21	14 / -21	01 / 30	10 / 09	16 / 25	-04 / 21	09 / 20	33 / 20	10 / 32	00 / 44	19 / 11	11 / 12	-09 / 10	18 / -21
13(r)	33 / 20	-13 / 09	07 / 09	26 / 21	43 / 35	-43 / 31	39 / 15	30 / 02	17 / 33	04 / -01	08 / 24	-09 / -10	34 / 17	31 / 35	17 / 01	05 / 20	08 / 33	-06 / -02	-08 / 06	-02 / -09	-04 / -01	07 / 03	-06 / 01	14 / -02	15 / 04	-02 / -07	21 / -05
14	03 / 13	-38 / 04	-17 / 10	08 / 07	38 / 52	-37 / 15	05 / 27	25 / 24	34 / 13	-11 / -05	26 / 16	21 / -13	06 / 12	-03 / 24	11 / 08	-05 / -04	-10 / 16	-11 / -01	-12 / 02	-18 / 01	05 / -06	42 / 37	08 / 15	23 / 21	17 / 00	-16 / 05	25 / -01
14a	12 / 08	-07 / -10	-34 / 00	-17 / 21	25 / 23	18 / 23	-01 / -07	17 / 10	41 / -06	20 / 13	07 / -09	08 / -36	04 / 20	03 / 08	15 / 25	09 / -15	13 / 06	-05 / -29	07 / -03	14 / -36	-33 / -32	-02 / 18	31 / -21	-04 / 11	-11 / 01	-12 / 07	02 / 13
15(r)	-05 / 04	17 / 01	03 / 11	26 / 27	08 / 21	03 / 06	-01 / 30	11 / 09	-14 / 10	10 / 20	-14 / -01	?? / ??	05 / 09	07 / 13	-14 / -03	18 / 04	-15 / -05	-39 / -01	-35 / 07	-32 / 03	-28 / -13	-06 / -12	-03 / 10	-27 / -08	-05 / -03	-03 / -33	-19 / 07
16(r)	-14 / 19	35 / 15	34 / -08	-12 / -26	21 / -03	05 / -32	16 / -04	18 / 00	35 / 24	-18 / 27	16 / 05	?? / ??	-18 / -16	07 / -01	13 / 06	-24 / -15	25 / -05	22 / -35	13 / -25	22 / -33	21 / -27	-16 / -06	05 / -03	-12 / -06	15 / 16	-32 / -33	-15 / 00
17(r)	-19 / 13	-06 / 37	-01 / 03	05 / -06	00 / 06	06 / 01	-11 / -07	-12 / 02	31 / 41	-25 / 08	01 / -04	-0 / -0	07 / -27	14 / -09	22 / -02	02 / -25	00 / -03	04 / -05	02 / -03	09 / -12	00 / 02	26 / 15	12 / 14	31 / 21	25 / -10	-19 / 07	24 / 04
18	00 / 00	15 / 01	17 / 09	-02 / 21	20 / 43	12 / 41	24 / 47	-01 / 17	18 / 32	07 / 12	15 / 29	-19 / -14	20 / 22	08 / 18	06 / 18	-11 / 07	24 / -07	31 / 06	40 / 18	40 / 06	-03 / -07	-10 / 26	-16 / 18	-22 / 03	08 / 12	-29 / -12	-06 / 23
19	31 / 40	27 / 25	35 / 05	23 / 18	55 / 66	09 / 36	56 / 64	41 / 50	16 / 49	02 / 20	08 / 14	-36 / -27	11 / -03	28 / 00	10 / 18	-07 / 18	21 / 06	17 / 09	16 / 19	16 / 09	11 / -05	-09 / 09	09 / 19	-09 / -11	07 / 03	-09 / -15	05 / 07
19a	25 / 05	-03 / -14	-11 / -17	26 / 43	28 / 53	-27 / 49	34 / 59	19 / 27	-02 / 11	34 / 26	-03 / 09	-48 / -35	12 / 21	12 / 15	11 / 12	-02 / 22	24 / -10	18 / -05	19 / -13	32 / 11	-07 / -11	-24 / -11	-06 / -10	-27 / -15	-13 / 07	-15 / -10	-16 / 23

Var.	19g	19h	19i	19k	20	20b	20c	20d	20e	20f	21	22 (r)	23 (r)	24 (r)	25	26 (r)	27 (r)	28	29	30	31	32	32a	32b	32c	32d	32e
19b	02/06	-01/-10	-01/-09	17/-13	19/14	69/66	32/03	04/02	-29/38	32/-24	-28/-06	-46/-34	05/-05	-07/11	-01/05	19/26	-04/21	25/19	32/05	23/26	05/16	-24/19	23/17	-17/05	-33/04	37/20	-17/07
19c	16/17	-05/-16	09/-12	24/40	44/48	-19/27	34/61	34/41	04/02	14/16	-04/06	-30/-25	-02/17	-03/-07	-17/15	-27/05	-07/-07	-06/-03	-02/04	-08/08	-05/-18	-15/-16	-05/-18	-24/-25	-02/-11	-24/-08	-08/10
19d	-01/-09	05/-05	13/-12	08/20	21/35	-10/06	43/48	-05/32	30/-04	-01/39	07/28	-43/-25	00/08	05/15	-03/05	-11/28	-13/-04	23/-03	21/04	14/03	20/-14	-28/-27	-12/06	-16/-18	-22/-09	13/-17	-04/23
19e	23/54	00/-39	-07/-44	31/12	60/41	01/11	40/28	58/63	34/12	10/32	26/05	-20/-25	15/-07	17/-25	03/11	01/-23	21/-26	-08/09	-03/23	-14/11	-03/-13	01/07	11/25	-19/-09	00/-15	-09/-17	-11/10
19f	-02/02	10/05	17/-17	25/-02	50/38	09/27	38/29	37/24	28/28	14/41	19/11	-31/-13	05/-17	16/-07	07/-02	-13/08	46/-20	28/-13	32/-05	16/-20	19/-07	-15/-02	10/21	01/-01	15/20	-21/-38	05/18
19g	—	03/-11	-03/-37	03/05	17/37	-07/01	16/12	16/52	11/56	01/03	-01/-23	-06/-34	06/05	18/-04	09/-01	11/-22	19/-08	10/12	12/31	12/-02	01/-02	31/02	30/11	16/-30	11/-22	42/15	19/-24
19h	-04	—	68/59	-05/-33	-01/-11	46/-24	10/-01	04/-15	-16/22	-14/-21	-10/-03	-08/02	01/-29	13/-10	02/-09	05/12	-06/19	-09/12	-11/03	08/-01	-19/27	-11/18	03/00	-24/23	-08/29	-10/15	01/-05
19i	-17	64	—	-12/-23	-06/-12	27/-13	07/-02	09/-24	-19/16	-10/-25	-28/04	-04/22	-05/-06	10/-14	-04/24	-11/20	-15/32	11/04	02/06	13/04	12/-01	-05/29	-06/-06	-15/12	02/16	-13/00	-05/-12
19k	04	-19	-17	—	23/29	02/17	22/35	03/15	-05/-27	20/25	-16/04	-41/02	13/33	20/26	21/14	-16/-10	-02/-09	-17/-02	-07/08	-09/08	-26/-22	-17/-18	-15/13	-12/-24	-03/-43	-04/-10	-01/10
20	30	-06	-08	26	—	22/42	60/75	71/72	58/59	36/43	48/42	-29/-40	-03/16	-02/09	10/35	-12/01	06/-04	12/00	30/09	-05/10	04/-20	-09/24	19/30	07/12	29/12	05/-21	-06/28
20b	-01	16	09	12	34	—	-03/17	11/17	-24/16	06/-18	-23/08	-26/-22	-14/04	-14/18	-16/17	16/09	06/32	08/24	23/15	04/31	-08/13	-29/11	39/11	-14/-08	-10/-07	19/-04	-17/-04
20c	17	04	03	29	69	11	—	36/52	01/24	09/23	31/26	-39/-29	20/15	27/07	04/30	-07/03	09/02	22/-09	23/-13	13/18	17/-28	-26/-03	-04/09	01/-10	09/08	19/-40	-06/29
20d	31	-05	-06	09	70	13	43	—	32/21	10/29	36/25	-05/-31	-10/-07	-14/-16	-05/21	-02/-03	24/-23	04/12	14/29	-10/10	06/-11	04/16	14/27	15/08	34/00	-13/-11	-15/16
20e	36	06	00	-18	59	01	14	26	—	06/33	50/32	05/-35	17/05	13/04	32/33	-01/-01	05/08	01/04	14/11	-05/-06	-07/05	06/18	19/42	15/10	23/24	-12/-19	12/08

181

Var.	19g	19h	19i	19k	20	20b	20c	20d	20e	20f	21	22(r)	23(r)	24(r)	25	26(r)	27(r)	28	29	30	31	32	32a	32b	32c	32d	32e
20f	03	-17	-18	22	39	-09	15	18	21	—	-09 / 44	-32 / -14	-21 / 05	-27 / -04	-05 / 20	-12 / -07	-26 / -54	13 / -16	27 / 00	05 / -14	00 / -24	-14 / -04	03 / 27	-25 / 14	-18 / 10	25 / -34	-33 / 41
21	-10	-05	-09	-04	43	00	27	29	36	16	—	01 / 13	-03 / 34	04 / 05	14 / 17	-17 / 26	11 / 02	02 / -23	12 / -22	-22 / -17	15 / -15	01 / 23	-13 / 41	28 / 40	43 / 27	13 / 12	06 / 43
22(r)	-22	-02	10	-17	-35	-24	-33	-18	-18	-22	09	—	08 / 18	-05 / -03	10 / -18	28 / 15	10 / 13	-29 / -22	-37 / -16	-14 / -22	-19 / -15	45 / 08	12 / 03	21 / 12	24 / -02	-28 / 00	19 / -02
23(r)	05	-12	-06	22	05	-07	16	-09	11	-09	14	13	—	78 / 50	36 / 13	45 / 31	10 / 18	-44 / -13	-43 / -08	-16 / -09	-49 / -15	08 / 17	12 / 31	20 / 11	09 / 03	14 / 20	26 / 19
24(r)	08	03	-01	23	02	-02	15	-15	08	-16	04	-04	67	—	38 / -05	34 / 31	10 / 15	-25 / 07	-28 / 17	-04 / 02	-29 / -01	13 / 10	10 / 48	26 / 00	24 / -18	24 / 05	35 / -01
25	07	-04	11	16	27	06	21	08	33	08	18	-07	24	16	—	14 / -14	06 / -04	-04 / 10	-10 / 10	18 / 17	-19 / -04	15 / 23	19 / 09	28 / 13	04 / -01	-07 / 01	41 / 20
26(r)	-02	09	04	-14	-03	12	00	-02	-01	-10	07	21	38	32	00	—	21 / 23	-25 / 09	-19 / 09	-10 / 07	-32 / 06	35 / 33	60 / 20	28 / 24	11 / 17	30 / 19	14 / 21
27(r)	04	08	09	-05	01	21	04	01	07	-40	06	12	13	12	00	22	—	29 / 14	30 / -12	26 / 21	16 / 25	06 / -03	30 / -14	19 / -13	21 / -13	-22 / 16	19 / -18
28	12	01	08	-11	07	20	07	08	02	-01	-07	-25	-32	-12	04	-08	21	—	87 / 78	80 / 85	79 / 78	-06 / 05	-04 / 39	02 / -05	-03 / -31	-14 / 37	00 / -25
29	22	-03	04	-01	19	22	05	21	11	13	-04	-26	-28	-09	02	-05	08	83	—	58 / 54	56 / 35	-02 / 23	12 / 51	05 / -03	03 / -28	01 / 21	04 / -29
30	09	04	09	-01	05	23	18	-01	-06	-05	-15	-18	-13	-02	19	00	22	82	57	—	38 / 50	-05 / 00	02 / 22	-07 / -07	-09 / -23	-40 / 22	04 / -10
31	-01	02	07	-24	-08	02	-06	-01	00	-10	02	-17	-36	-18	-12	-15	20	78	46	42	—	-08 / -11	-28 / 21	08 / -02	-02 / -27	04 / 46	-09 / -23
32	19	02	09	-17	08	-09	-13	09	12	-10	12	27	11	11	19	34	02	-01	09	-02	-09	—	52 / 46	50 / 68	34 / 35	-06 / 28	47 / 29
32a	18	01	-06	00	26	25	03	20	31	16	19	07	21	28	13	38	07	17	31	12	-02	49	—	46 / 46	19 / 04	21 / 27	41 / 20

Var.	19g	19h	19i	19k	20	20b	20c	20d	20e	20f	21	22(r)	23(r)	24(r)	25	26(r)	27(r)	28	29	30	31	32	32a	32b	32c	32d	32e
32b	-03	00	-02	-19	10	-10	-06	12	12	-10	36	17	15	13	21	26	04	02	03	-03	04	59	44	—	68 60	35 39	65 57
32c	-04	11	09	-24	19	-09	09	18	23	-04	34	09	06	04	02	14	03	-16	-11	-15	-12	34	11	65	—	-05 03	26 27
32d	28	06	-04	-09	-09	13	-18	-09	-14	-21	19	-07	15	11	03	26	02	20	16	05	27	17	23	42	04	—	07 -14
32e	00	-02	-08	04	10	-14	10	-02	11	02	23	09	23	20	29	16	02	-12	-12	-04	-14	39	32	59	25	-07	—
32f	-09	-06	10	-09	06	03	-04	14	08	-04	25	32	14	15	27	21	05	11	14	09	05	40	36	65	30	09	19
32g	-14	-08	-14	-23	-01	-29	-20	10	06	-07	07	04	-11	-12	-01	06	-01	09	07	-01	15	47	34	68	26	10	29
33(r)	17	-08	04	26	07	00	03	-19	-07	01	-02	08	10	15	01	02	17	12	09	15	06	07	23	07	-06	-10	10
34(r)	05	-01	04	17	07	-15	04	-11	-05	19	11	18	02	00	00	19	-01	10	10	12	02	16	41	29	07	-03	22
35'(r)	01	05	10	24	06	03	03	-08	01	13	07	19	21	12	-05	22	16	00	01	02	-03	29	44	30	01	-12	32
36	17	08	00	-26	-08	-09	-12	02	-02	-21	-16	13	-20	-04	03	00	-09	05	-01	03	10	35	02	33	17	08	20
36a	15	-15	-22	08	13	-19	10	08	23	-05	08	-15	11	17	19	-14	-01	06	14	-01	01	06	-05	03	00	06	-07
36b	00	-13	-15	08	18	04	07	03	25	12	13	-15	21	25	23	05	-08	-08	-01	-07	-11	09	-03	-05	05	00	-02
37(r)	29	09	08	-15	-04	08	-06	04	06	-14	-14	05	03	12	08	15	21	13	18	11	04	35	15	19	12	08	06
38	08	17	07	-01	-07	02	02	-01	-02	-14	-29	-02	-10	10	-07	-12	13	39	28	37	28	10	12	05	04	-06	-06

Var.	19g	19h	19i	19k	20	20b	20c	20d	20e	20f	21	22 (r)	23 (r)	24 (r)	25	26 (r)	27 (r)	28	29	30	31	32	32a	32b	32c	32d	32e
39	18	09	04	01	-08	00	03	00	-03	-25	-14	03	13	29	00	02	17	27	21	23	20	23	11	24	15	17	21
40	-03	06	01	01	-05	-12	-03	-13	12	17	-18	-07	-16	-03	02	-08	-02	20	15	24	11	01	19	-04	-03	-09	-17
41	03	23	10	-03	-01	16	04	10	-14	-20	-28	01	-18	-05	-15	-19	12	35	25	34	28	-03	-04	-09	-05	-22	-17
42	-23	23	08	-08	02	04	01	04	-27	-14	19	18	-08	-08	08	06	-15	10	00	16	08	29	03	32	22	21	15
43	19	-18	-02	-12	17	-01	-08	24	10	00	02	22	-16	-11	15	14	04	29	35	23	10	32	25	14	13	01	11
44	27	-13	00	-08	20	02	-07	28	03	-04	-05	23	-05	-17	12	11	-01	06	19	16	-18	44	27	18	29	03	10
45	05	-29	-18	05	05	18	-10	11	-15	-06	02	21	-04	-06	08	19	02	08	20	08	-09	25	16	10	18	05	10
46	12	01	13	-24	12	-18	-01	15	31	10	07	06	-26	-02	12	01	08	50	40	28	50	02	14	04	-18	-07	04
47	04	15	15	-13	09	06	01	17	-09	-09	-12	-04	02	06	19	15	-15	-10	01	-11	-15	33	02	19	15	10	25
48	09	04	01	01	19	09	-07	25	-14	-16	-12	-09	06	08	18	17	-02	-12	03	-20	-11	44	15	29	07	24	24
50	18	03	02	-03	11	19	14	01	-07	-08	10	00	-03	-04	12	08	-04	12	13	18	-02	04	-05	09	03	24	-12

Var.	32f	32g	33 (r)	34 (r)	35 (r)	36	36a	36b	37 (r)	38	39	40	41	42	43	44	45	46	47	48
1	12	-01	22	01	23	03	34	08	-07	-09	-10	04	-13	-07	-08	-12	-01	-07	08	34
2	36	42	05	31	10	17	-01	07	10	06	26	01	-13	13	20	09	01	32	12	50
3	03	-04	10		06	08	09	03	02	-06	06	-02	-15	-24					01	-26

Var.	32f	32g	33 (r)	34 (r)	35 (r)	36	36a	36b	37 (r)	38	39	40	41	42	43	44	45	46	47	48
3 (r)	25 11	44 01	-01 25	10 07	16 08	28 -03	36 -36	22 -08	-02 02	-15 -15	-09 13	-02 -11	-18 -35	-11 01	20 -12	35 -20	19 08	-08 -14	11 -42	23 -25
4 (r)	-22 -22	07 -27	-05 03	-09 10	-27 -11	10 -19	-17 01	-02 01	-15 -03	-22 13	-02 -16	-18 25	-24 19	-25 -07	-33 09	-44 10	-30 11	-03 -02	-03 -16	-38 -30
5	-13 -10	14 -01	06 -10	08 -16	-02 -24	-33 -09	-06 -05	-15 06	-02 -03	-09 -21	03 -10	-18 09	-03 -44	-15 -02	03 -14	-04 -09	02 04	09 -24	-24 -07	18 11
6	09 15	14 00	02 18	14 05	-07 07	03 -12	07 -22	13 -10	-12 -05	-17 -14	-14 -11	00 -01	-20 -19	-17 24	42 07	32 -08	49 -09	16 30	-16 -20	18 -43
7	11 -04	-01 05	09 -07	-07 -07	-22 -09	10 -12	13 -03	15 01	-16 -11	-04 -19	-06 -19	-07 -02	05 -20	15 10	50 -16	25 -04	35 -28	55 -01	-01 -01	32 -23
7a	10 -07	-28 -14	02 -02	02 -22	12 -23	-13 -18	27 21	02 19	23 -03	21 -16	27 -15	11 -05	06 -17	-06 04	09 08	15 00	-02 -09	08 22	-29 -23	-18 -29
8	30 35	-03 01	-06 -02	04 14	02 15	01 -07	23 -08	-08 01	22 -22	00 -27	14 -31	-06 -10	-08 -17	04 -17	06 -32	-10 -25	-04 -46	28 04	-05 33	-14 11
9 (r)	-10 10	-09 -17	27 01	10 15	25 10	-16 -18	15 -19	-13 -02	-11 -13	-16 -17	-13 -11	03 -10	-22 -17	-49 24	-05 -16	06 -19	08 20	-27 -35	-16 -33	-02 -10
10	-10 08	03 02	-22 15	-13 -01	-23 17	33 -13	06 29	08 -05	11 04	12 -10	09 -37	00 -05	14 21	05 -01	-12 11	-08 26	-15 10	-04 -14	19 38	-25 -10
11	28 11	-03 01	15 22	18 06	18 07	01 13	27 13	03 12	23 -14	12 06	54 16	-20 -21	-13 18	-15 11	08 37	08 36	01 19	10 22	08 05	-03 01
12	04 17	28 17	-05 13	19 -02	09 -09	17 15	-09 11	10 08	00 -01	12 17	06 19	00 -08	19 26	-05 23	-03 38	-13 35	-04 21	11 26	00 12	-05 17
13 (r)	-01 13	07 -13	19 19	30 12	16 14	00 10	04 10	-12 37	-06 04	-07 -02	04 04	-20 -24	03 13	00 08	21 -01	14 -17	06 -13	28 29	-24 -03	-03 18
14	05 26	32 31	01 04	30 02	10 15	22 15	18 03	03 -03	-18 11	-07 05	-05 03	-13 -12	03 19	20 25	52 -14	51 01	37 -36	29 05	-05 29	32 52
14a	11 -03	-13 22	-10 -21	-18 -17	01 -10	-13 12	55 13	44 26	26 21	06 -13	33 -11	-05 -16	-11 -02	05 -19	-09 -36	04 -16	-08 -24	-19 -36	-17 15	-40 40

185

Var.	32f	32g	33(r)	34(r)	35(r)	36	36a	36b	37(r)	38	39	40	41	42	43	44	45	46	47	48
15(r)	-45 20	-05 -21	05 16	10 33	05 37	-04 -31	-08 -12	11 03	-35 -11	-26 22	-29 06	-07 23	-16 20	-19 -10	04 27	12 21	14 06	-17 31	-06 -27	05 -21
16(r)	05 -07	-21 -03	-34 -18	-39 -21	-23 -28	12 -02	12 -10	04 -02	04 -14	27 -33	26 -44	19 -07	12 -27	-26 -23	-07 04	-05 12	-19 -32	07 27	-03 35	-32 09
17(r)	30 33	21 33	-13 15	-08 18	04 19	-01 26	15 -10	24 -23	05 09	-04 11	12 02	-09 16	-12 05	02 -16	-09 -13	03 -17	-03 -47	-20 40	07 27	-32 22
18	-05 04	-46 -28	13 06	-15 07	-06 30	-55 -23	10 24	-11 14	13 03	05 13	16 03	-16 20	13 08	-13 22	-01 66	04 44	04 59	-10 46	08 -14	13 01
19	-09 -22	-31 -11	07 -04	05 -09	03 01	-16 -06	-04 16	-11 42	10 03	05 -04	32 -05	-25 -03	03 -01	-23 -10	00 25	05 23	-10 -02	05 31	-07 22	-08 07
19a	-15 -30	-25 -37	15 -27	-02 -08	-07 -08	-41 -27	26 -03	04 42	-04 -11	04 -13	09 04	04 -05	-04 -28	-18 -08	00 -19	-03 -22	00 -01	03 -18	-22 -17	-08 -17
19b	-09 -22	-16 09	20 -08	-01 -41	09 -13	-23 07	-26 -26	-05 12	-01 10	02 -04	-07 02	01 03	10 -15	-16 -02	-19 15	-22 07	-14 14	-07 11	09 -13	-05 08
19c	-30 -39	-13 -25	08 -26	10 -04	-03 -04	-22 -14	01 16	-01 30	02 02	-06 -05	67 02	-12 -06	-07 -08	-09 -09	30 05	35 08	24 20	09 -17	-20 03	09 08
19d	-05 -29	-25 -24	-25 -08	-20 04	-27 03	-37 -32	12 17	02 32	02 -28	-23 -24	07 -31	-27 -02	-24 -19	-13 -03	-28 11	-24 12	-31 02	-09 09	-06 08	-38 -11
19e	-17 -18	-20 06	13 -02	-16 -09	-05 -01	-05 -10	12 -01	-04 -04	02 15	-04 -01	13 -07	-23 03	00 02	-08 -12	05 25	08 39	13 24	-10 -09	-04 -01	20 -21
19f	01 -07	-05 -05	-17 12	-05 06	-07 15	-34 07	00 -04	-13 09	04 -23	03 -09	21 -25	-11 06	-05 00	-51 00	-06 08	-06 04	-06 -10	-02 23	-19 37	-10 08
19g	07 -37	-25 -08	41 -07	14 -13	19 -17	31 -01	05 25	-21 23	28 32	08 08	30 08	-16 08	03 04	00 -52	16 24	21 38	-03 12	21 01	02 12	15 01
19h	-21 10	-40 21	-12 -05	-01 -02	03 06	11 05	-49 15	-28 03	-03 23	10 23	05 12	-11 19	25 21	08 09	-24 -15	-09 -18	-22 -40	-24 27	19 11	10 -01
19i	-06 30	-28 -02	-04 15	03 04	05 14	13 -12	-54 09	-28 -03	04 12	08 06	10 -01	-13 12	19 03	12 06	-05 -03	00 -03	-21 -19	10 17	24 05	06 -05

Var.	32f	32g	33(r)	34(r)	35(r)	36	36a	36b	37(r)	38	39	40	41	42	43	44	45	46	47	48
19k	-14 / -02	-15 / -31	29 / 22	04 / 33	18 / 29	-28 / -24	01 / 15	-14 / 30	-15 / -16	-01 / 01	-11 / 13	06 / -03	03 / -08	-18 / -01	-08 / -15	03 / -22	12 / 03	-34 / -12	-04 / -28	11 / -09
20	04 / 06	-11 / 04	03 / -09	05 / 04	-03 / 14	-06 / -11	19 / 07	05 / 28	-04 / -04	-07 / -06	-05 / -09	-10 / -01	01 / -03	01 / 00	26 / 02	27 / 10	27 / -22	06 / 16	-13 / 33	15 / 23
20b	02 / 01	-40 / -25	-02 / 04	-02 / -34	18 / -08	-06 / -12	-47 / 04	-31 / 36	10 / 08	05 / -02	00 / -02	-07 / -16	17 / 13	-11 / 10	-03 / -02	06 / -07	16 / 15	-25 / -10	23 / -02	26 / -03
20c	05 / -15	-24 / -20	24 / -10	04 / 00	04 / 04	-18 / -10	06 / 11	-18 / 27	00 / -11	01 / 04	06 / 03	-20 / 08	14 / -02	-05 / 02	-11 / -07	-15 / 01	-10 / -13	-01 / -02	-23 / 26	-17 / 01
20d	20 / 04	12 / 08	-07 / -33	-13 / -10	-13 / -04	11 / -07	11 / 06	-02 / 08	09 / -02	00 / -02	01 / -01	-13 / -13	12 / 10	09 / -01	29 / 21	29 / 30	21 / 01	16 / 14	-01 / 40	26 / 25
20e	17 / 01	-02 / 12	-17 / 01	-22 / 13	-10 / 08	05 / -06	44 / 08	30 / 20	01 / 11	-09 / 00	09 / -13	-08 / 24	-18 / -11	-06 / -38	02 / 20	07 / -02	-07 / -24	04 / 57	-13 / -06	-15 / -13
20f	-18 / 14	-17 / 04	-08 / 08	06 / 37	-10 / 31	-18 / -23	-04 / -04	13 / 11	-05 / -25	-02 / -24	-22 / -30	30 / 06	-10 / -29	-06 / -18	-09 / 06	-13 / -01	00 / -09	02 / 20	-10 / -02	-06 / -27
21	18 / 28	02 / 08	-13 / 08	-15 / 30	-32 / 33	-08 / -23	45 / -17	22 / 09	-02 / -25	-13 / -40	06 / -32	-09 / -22	-21 / -33	06 / 23	43 / 00	47 / -02	33 / 09	20 / -07	11 / -17	-08 / -18
22(r)	19 / 47	19 / -07	-16 / 29	07 / 30	04 / 30	37 / -05	-10 / -20	03 / -30	15 / -05	08 / -07	05 / 01	04 / -15	06 / -02	23 / 15	-17 / -11	-06 / -02	-05 / 03	-28 / -24	08 / -09	03 / 09
23(r)	20 / 05	-12 / -12	21 / -04	-06 / 14	24 / 19	-22 / -19	12 / 10	12 / 32	16 / -16	-14 / -07	14 / 11	-25 / -08	-17 / -19	-13 / -01	-12 / -08	-08 / -28	-02 / -08	-19 / 19	20 / -14	00 / 17
24′(r)	14 / 17	-20 / -03	26 / 03	-03 / 08	20 / 04	01 / -10	19 / 15	16 / 36	27 / -07	10 / 08	41 / 15	-17 / 09	-03 / -07	-18 / 01	25 / -02	20 / 01	20 / -12	18 / 06	15 / 26	15 / 21
25	32 / 21	03 / -06	19 / -13	20 / -25	16 / -19	-05 / 07	19 / 18	24 / 24	00 / -16	10 / -15	-01 / 02	18 / -08	03 / -27	08 / 04	03 / 25	10 / 13	14 / 26	-17 / 15	25 / 05	17 / 19
26(r,)	22 / 19	12 / 01	03 / 02	25 / 09	30 / 17	09 / -08	-12 / -18	07 / 04	24 / 04	-03 / -18	07 / -02	02 / -15	-15 / -23	-08 / 15	26 / -23	12 / -17	22 / -21	27 / -10	-33 / 04	-01 / -03
27(r)	19 / -08	10 / -09	09 / 25	14 / -15	25 / 09	-09 / -09	-03 / 01	-30 / 11	25 / 17	34 / -03	38 / -03	15 / -14	14 / 11	-38 / 02						

187

Var.	48	47	46	45	44	43	42	41	40	39	38	37(r)	36b	36a	36	35(r)	34(r)	33(r)	32g	32f
28	-31/11	-25/14	50/52	-03/17	-07/26	17/45	00/15	37/36	18/25	26/31	40/42	08/21	-11/-04	-07/18	09/-02	-04/05	14/02	08/19	09/08	12/06
29	-11/19	-07/14	35/47	06/36	-02/48	17/62	-12/06	15/34	12/20	24/21	26/33	12/26	-07/07	-03/29	-03/-02	-04/06	09/08	05/16	01/13	07/19
30	-35/-05	-33/20	35/19	00/08	10/20	20/22	11/15	54/19	23/27	27/24	51/32	08/14	-15/03	-13/10	05/-03	05/02	17/01	11/24	-01/-02	14/-02
31	-27/11	-22/-03	50/53	-12/-05	-22/-10	06/18	01/16	22/35	10/13	12/31	22/36	-01/10	-04/-19	-02/05	19/00	-09/04	09/-05	04/07	23/07	09/-01
32	47/41	39/25	-03/09	29/19	54/27	35/26	22/35	-01/-05	-01/04	34/12	15/05	37/31	23/-06	14/-05	37/33	28/31	21/07	00/18	37/59	32/50
32a	27/11	13/-07	-14/37	15/24	37/22	13/41	-25/21	-11/00	04/27	16/05	05/15	36/-07	-19/07	-19/05	24/-15	46/42	40/47	15/30	32/36	24/50
32b	16/42	27/19	-01/10	11/-03	19/05	12/06	17/38	-04/-14	-13/01	30/21	06/04	32/06	14/-24	30/-21	29/37	36/28	33/22	21/-02	57/75	70/62
32c	09/05	16/13	-18/-19	23/09	33/21	17/06	05/33	-02/-07	-10/03	27/06	07/01	28/-06	04/07	16/-16	10/22	14/-08	20/-07	15/-24	24/27	44/13
32d	09/30	48/-05	02/-16	-18/05	-28/12	-22/00	-11/28	-23/-23	-26/-02	08/28	-19/02	16/06	-03/04	21/-02	16/01	-02/-13	-10/-05	14/-16	-31/27	12/02
32e	33/12	40/02	06/03	28/-21	35/-36	30/-26	18/17	03/-36	-27/-11	35/04	05/-19	18/-10	14/-20	09/-25	21/21	33/32	36/07	17/00	34/25	20/22
32f	05/24	05/13	-01/37	-01/-04	11/-03	04/14	22/22	07/06	07/-03	29/13	22/07	29/00	05/-26	32/-14	09/14	29/39	09/44	13/23	23/40	—
32g	-08/47	-23/28	08/16	-09/02	-03/18	-02/17	09/17	-01/15	12/16	-19/18	-04/22	-01/30	22/-34	08/-04	35/48	27/32	36/26	04/09	—	31
33(r)	-06/-38	-07/-17	14/33	-08/22	-09/08	-01/29	-03/01	17/08	01/19	12/-09	15/06	-13/17	-10/-14	04/-01	13/07	60/70	38/77	—	06	16
34(r)	-06/-17	-34/-14	33/34	25/19	30/15	37/32	12/-11	18/-03	34/27	08/-08	30/06	12/-06	-12/-14	-26/00	16/-16	75/75	—	50	34	25

Var.	32f	32g	33(r)	34(r)	35(r)	36	36a	36b	37(r)	38	39	40	41	42	43	44	45	46	47	48
35(r)	32	30	65	74	—	17 / -10	-12 / -05	-15 / -20	22 / 13	33 / 15	23 / -07	20 / 26	22 / 16	01 / 12	09 / 25	14 / 07	04 / 16	03 / 29	-20 / -15	13 / -12
36	13	43	09	02	01	—	-03 / -05	-03 / -14	08 / 31	27 / 35	11 / 52	06 / 03	36 / 22	28 / 27	21 / -01	19 / -09	04 / -07	26 / 14	20 / 30	17 / 56
36a	11	02	01	-12	-08	-03	—	56 / 49	-06 / 03	-02 / 17	20 / -01	-08 / 09	-16 / 30	05 / -03	02 / 24	05 / 24	05 / 27	-06 / 01	20 / 32	06 / 02
36b	-11	-08	-12	-13	-17	-10	52	—	-07 / -15	-10 / -09	00 / -11	11 / -01	-30 / -08	18 / -05	07 / -04	03 / 06	15 / 04	-02 / -19	39 / -08	26 / -21
37(r)	17	14	00	04	18	19	-02	-11	—	36 / 45	63 / 35	08 / 31	00 / 33	01 / 01	04 / 05	11 / -06	05 / 20	-07 / -04	09 / -25	-30 / -14
38	13	10	11	16	23	30	09	-09	41	—	62 / 73	59 / 70	74 / 76	12 / 16	30 / 17	08 / -07	12 / 10	50 / 33	-21 / -10	-19 / 16
39	20	-01	02	-01	07	31	09	-05	50	68	—	-04 / 25	23 / 37	-02 / 18	05 / -02	04 / -24	-09 / 00	16 / 19	20 / -18	-25 / 25
40	01	13	10	30	24	04	01	04	20	66	12	—	20 / 28	-10 / -05	17 / 10	-09 / -05	16 / 06	32 / 20	-46 / -12	-13 / -08
41	06	08	12	07	18	28	09	-17	17	75	30	25	—	34 / 22	37 / 37	20 / 24	19 / 21	45 / 33	-16 / 13	01 / 15
42	23	14	-02	03	07	29	02	03	01	12	07	-08	26	—	25 / 22	26 / 15	12 / 31	20 / -01	19 / -09	17 / 27
43	11	07	10	36	15	15	11	-03	04	20	01	11	32	24	—	86 / 82	87 / 77	58 / 53	06 / 01	44 / 08
44	06	06	-03	24	10	08	13	02	04	-01	-09	-09	19	22	84	—	82 / 61	16 / 11	19 / 25	51 / 13
45	00	-03	03	24	08	03	14	03	11	06	-07	08	13	23	83	74	—	19 / 01	10 / -24	52 / -15
46	18	12	23	34	16	21	-02	-12	-05	39	17	25	39	10	56	14	11	—	-16 / 01	-04 / 19

Var.	32f	32g	33 (r)	34 (r)	35 (r)	36	36a	36b	37 (r)	38	39	40	41	42	43	44	45	46	47	48
47	08	01	-11	-26	-17	24	26	16	-07	-12	02	-28	-01	05	03	20	-05	-08	—	53
48	15	20	-22	-10	-02	38	04	-04	-22	-02	01	-12	07	24	30	34	23	08	55	59
50	13	04	-07	16	-05	10	04	-07	00	-07	-08	-06	00	18	16	10	22	04	-08	03

References

ALLPORT, G. W. "The Historical Background of Modern Social Psychology." In G. Lindsey (Ed.), *Handbook of Social Psychology,* Vol. 1, *Theory and Method.* Cambridge: Addison-Wesley, 1954. Pp. 3–56.

ALLPORT, G. W., and POSTMAN, L. *The Psychology of Rumor.* New York: Holt, 1947.

ARONFREED, J. "Punishment Control of Children's Behavior: Conditioning, Cognition, and Internalization." Paper presented at the meeting of the American Psychological Association, New York, Sept. 1966.

BACON, F. *Novum Organum.*

BANDURA, A., and WALTERS, R. H. *Social Learning and Personality Development.* New York: Holt, Rinehart and Winston, 1963.

BECKER, W. C. "Consequences of Different Kinds of Parental Discipline." In M. L. Hoffman and L. W. Hoffman (Eds.), *Review of Child Development Research,* Vol. 1. New York: Russell Sage Foundation, 1964. Pp. 169–208.

191

BECKER, W. C., PETERSON, D. R., LURIA, Z., SHOEMAKER, D. L., and HELL-
MER, L. A. "Relations of Factors Derived from Parent-Interview
Ratings to Behavior Problems of Five-Year-Olds." *Child Devel-
opment*, 1962, *33*, 509–535.

BELLER, E. K. "Dependency and Autonomous Achievement Striving Related to Orality and Anality in Early Childhood." *Child Development*, 1957, *28*, 287–315.

BERELSON, B., and STEINER, G. A. *Human Behavior: An Inventory of
Scientific Findings*. New York: Harcourt, Brace, 1964.

BISHOP, B. M. "Mother-Child Interaction and the Social Behavior of
Children." *Psychological Monographs*, 1951, *65* (11, Whole No.
328).

BOE, E. E. "The Effect of Punishment Duration and Intensity on the
Extinction of an Instrumental Response." *Journal of Experimental Psychology*, 1966, *72*, 125–131.

BOE, E. E., and CHURCH, R. M. "The Permanent Effect of Punishment
During Extinction." Paper presented at the meeting of the East-
ern Psychological Association, New York, April, 1966.

BRODY, G. F. "Relationship Between Maternal Attitudes and Behavior."
Journal of Personality and Social Psychology, 1965, *2*, 317–323.

BRONFENBRENNER, U. "The Role of Age, Sex, Class, and Culture in
Studies of Moral Development." In S. Cook (Ed.), Research
Supplement, *Religious Education*, July–August 1962. Pp. S-3 to
S-17.

BURTON, R. V. *Some Factors Related to Resistance to Temptation in
Four-Year-Old Children*. (Doctoral dissertation, Harvard University) Cambridge, Mass.: 1959.

BURTON, R. V. "The Generality of Honesty Reconsidered." *Psychological Review*, 1963, *70*, 481–499.

BURTON, R. V., MACCOBY, E. E., and ALLINSMITH, W. "Antecedents of
Resistance to Temptation in Four-Year-Old Children." *Child
Development*, 1961, *32*, 689–710.

CAMPBELL, D. T., and FISKE, D. W. "Convergent and Discriminant Validation by the Multitrait-Multimethod Matrix." *Psychological
Bulletin*, 1959, *56*, 81–105.

CHURCH, R. M. "The Role of Fear in Punishment." Paper presented at
the meeting of the American Psychological Association, New
York, September, 1966.

CLAUSEN, J. A., and WILLIAMS, J. R. "Sociological Correlates of Child
Behavior." In H. W. Stevenson (Ed.), *Child Psychology*. The
Sixty-second Yearbook of the National Society for the Study of
Education, Part I. Chicago: NSSE, 1963. Pp. 62–107.

CRONBACH, L. J., and MEEHL, P. E. "Construct Validity in Psychological
Tests." *Psychological Bulletin*, 1955, *52*, 281–302.

CROWNE, D. P., and MARLOWE, D. *The Approval Motive: Studies in Evaluative Dependence.* New York: Wiley, 1964.

DOLLARD, J., DOOB, L. W., MILLER, N. E., MOWRER, O. H., and SEARS, R. R. *Frustration and Aggression.* New Haven: Yale University Press, 1939.

EDWARDS, A. L. *The Social Desirability Variable in Personality Assessment and Research.* New York: Dryden Press, 1957.

ENGLISH, A., and ENGLISH, H. *A Comprehensive Dictionary of Psychological and Psychoanalytical Terms.* New York: Longmans, Green, 1958.

ERON, L. D., BANTA, T. J., WALDER, L. O., and LAULICHT, J. H. "Comparison of Data Obtained from Mothers and Fathers on Childrearing Practices and Their Relation to Child Aggression." *Child Development,* 1961, *32,* 457–472.

ERON, L. D., WALDER, L. O., TOIGO, R., and LEFKOWITZ, M. M. "Social Class, Parental Punishment for Aggression and Child Aggression." *Child Development,* 1963, *34,* 849–867.

ESTES, W. K. "An Experimental Study of Punishment." *Psychological Monographs,* 1944, *57* (3, Whole No. 263).

FREUD, S. *An Outline of Psychoanalysis.* New York: Norton, 1949.

FREUD, S. *Civilization and Its Discontents.* London: Hogarth Press, 1930.

GRINDER, R. C. "Parental Childrearing Practices, Conscience, and Resistance to Temptation of Sixth-Grade Children." *Child Development,* 1962, *33,* 803–820.

HARLOW, H., and HARLOW, M. K. "The Effect of Rearing Conditions on Behavior." *Bulletin of the Menninger Clinic,* 1962, *26,* 213–224.

HARRIMAN, P. L. *The New Dictionary of Psychology.* New York: Philosophical Library, 1947.

HARTSHORNE, H., and MAY, M. A. *Studies in the Nature of Character:* Vol. 1, *Studies in Deceit.* New York: Macmillan, 1928.

HARTUP, W. W. "Dependence and Independence." In H. W. Stevenson (Ed.), *Child Psychology.* The Sixty-second Yearbook of the National Society for the Study of Education, Part I. Chicago: NSSE, 1963. Pp. 333–363.

HOFFMAN, M. L. "Power Assertion by the Parent and Its Impact on the Child." *Child Development,* 1960, *31,* 129–143.

HOFFMAN, M. L. "The Role of the Parent in the Child's Moral Growth." In S. Cook (Ed.), Research Supplement, *Religious Education,* July–August 1962. Pp. S-18 to S-33.

HOFFMAN, M. L. "Childrearing Practices and Moral Development: Generalizations from Empirical Research." *Child Development,* 1963, *34,* 295–318. (a)

HOFFMAN, M. L. "Socialization Practices and the Development of Moral Character." Paper presented at the Social Science Research Council conference on character development, 1963. (b)

HOLLENBERG, E., and SPERRY, M. "Some Antecedents of Aggression and Effects of Frustration in Doll Play." *Personality,* 1951, 32–43.

KAGAN, J., and MOSS, H. A. *Birth to Maturity: A Study in Psychological Development.* New York: Wiley, 1962.

KARDINER, A. *The Individual and His Society.* New York: Columbia University Press, 1939.

KENDALL, M., and BUCKLAND, W. *A Dictionary of Statistical Terms.* New York: Hafner, 1960.

KESSEN, W. "Research Design in the Study of Developmental Problems." In P. H. Mussen (Ed.), *Handbook of Research Methods in Child Development.* New York: Wiley, 1960. Pp. 36–70.

KOHLBERG, L. "Moral Development and Identification." In H. W. Stevenson (Ed.), *Child Psychology.* The Sixty-second Yearbook of the National Society for the Study of Education, Part I. Chicago: NSSE, 1963. Pp. 277–332.

KOHN, M. L. "Social Class and Parent-Child Relationships: An Interpretation." *American Journal of Sociology,* 1963, *68,* 471–480.

LEFKOWITZ, M. M., WALDER, L. O., and ERON, L. D. "Punishment, Identification and Aggression." *Merrill-Palmer Quarterly,* 1963, *9,* 159–175.

LEVIN, H., and SEARS, R. R. "Identification with Parents as a Determinant of Doll Play Aggression." *Child Development,* 1956, *27,* 135–153.

MARSHALL, H. R. "Relations Between Home Experiences and Children's Use of Language in Play Interaction with Peers." *Psychological Monographs,* 1961, *75* (5, Whole No. 509).

MCNEMAR, Q. *Psychological Statistics,* 2nd ed. New York: Wiley, 1955.

PIAGET, J. *The Moral Judgment of the Child.* London: Kegan Paul, 1932.

REDL, F., and WINEMAN, D. *Children Who Hate.* Glencoe, Ill.: Free Press, 1951.

RHEINGOLD, H. "The Measurement of Maternal Care." *Child Development,* 1960, *31,* 565–575.

ROSENTHAL, R. "Covert Communication in the Psychological Experiment." *Psychological Bulletin,* 1967, *67,* 356–367.

SEARS, R. R. "The Growth of Conscience." In I. Iscoe and H. Stevenson (Eds.), *Personality Development in Children.* Austin: University of Texas Press, 1960. Pp. 92–111.

SEARS, R. R. "The Relation of Early Socialization Experiences to Aggression in Middle Childhood." *Journal of Abnormal and Social Psychology*, 1961, *63*, 466–492.

SEARS, R. R., MACCOBY, E. E., and LEVIN, H. *Patterns of Child Rearing*. Evanston, Ill.: Row, Peterson, 1957.

SEARS, R. R., RAU, L., and ALPERT, R. "Identification and Child Training: The Development of Conscience." Paper presented at the meeting of the American Psychological Association, Chicago, 1960.

SEARS, R. R., RAU, L., and ALPERT, R. *Identification and Child Rearing*. Stanford, Calif.: Stanford University Press, 1965.

SEARS, R. R., WHITING, J. W. M., NOWLIS, V., and SEARS, P. S. "Some Child-Rearing Antecedents of Aggression and Dependency in Young Children." *Genetic Psychology Monographs*, 1953, *47*, 135–234.

SKINNER, B. F. *The Behavior of Organisms*. New York: Appleton-Century, 1938.

SMITH, H. *A Comparison of Interview and Observation Measures of Mother Behavior*. (Doctoral dissertation, Radcliffe College) Cambridge, Mass.: 1953.

SMITH, H. "A Comparison of Interview and Observation Measures of Mother Behavior." *Journal of Abnormal and Social Psychology*, 1958, *57*, 278–282.

SOLOMON, R. L. "Punishment." *American Psychologist*, 1964, *19*, 239–253.

SOLOMON, R. L., and BRUSH, E. S. "Experimentally Derived Conceptions of Anxiety and Aversion." In M. R. Jones (Ed.), *Nebraska Symposium on Motivation*, Vol. IV. Lincoln: University of Nebraska Press, 1956. Pp. 212–305.

STOUFFER, S. A. *Communism, Conformity, and Civil Liberties*. Garden City, N. Y.: Doubleday, 1955.

THOMPSON, SIR G. *The Inspiration of Science*. Oxford: Oxford University Press, 1961.

WHITING, J. W. M., and CHILD, I. L. *Child Training and Personality: A Cross-Cultural Study*. New Haven: Yale University Press, 1953.

WYNNE, L. C., RYCOFF, I. M., DAY, J., and HIRSCH, S. I. "Pseudo-mutuality in the Family Relations of Schizophrenics." *Psychiatry*, 1958, *21*, 205–220.

YARROW, M. R., CAMPBELL, J. D., and BURTON, R. V. "Reliability of Maternal Retrospection: A Preliminary Report." *Family Process*, 1964, *3*, 207–218.

ZUNICH, M. "Relationship Between Maternal Behavior and Attitudes Toward Children." *Journal of Genetic Psychology*, 1962, *100*, 155–165.

Index

A

Acceptance: coding reliability of, 165; measurement of, 165, (a) conscience, 104, (b) dependency, 38–39 (*see also* Affectional relations)

Admission of deviation: coding reliability, 169, 171; measurement of, 169, 171 (*see also* Conscience)

Affectional relations: and aggression, 67; and conscience, 102–107; and dependency, 37, 38–39, 40–41, (a) and conscience, 105, 107, 108; measurement of, 102–3, 165, (a) coding reliability of, 165, (b) intercorrelation of indices, 37, 40

Aggression: coding reliability, 166, 168, 170, 171; concept of, 58–61; and dependency frustration, 66; direct and indirect, 60; and disciplinary techniques, 77–82; in doll play, 65, 69, 76, 79, (a) and punishment, 76, 88; and frustration, 57, 65–68; handling of, and dependency, 46–48; hypothesized antecedents of, 55–58 (*see also* Frustration; Punishment; Permissiveness of aggression); and maternal warmth, 67; measurement of, 58–65, 166, 168, 170, 171, (a) intercorrelation of indices, 60–61, (b) methodological problems in, 89–91, (c) reliability of, 62–64, 166, 168, 170, 171; in mother's presence, and punishment, 72–73, 77–79; not in mother's presence, and punishment, 74–75, 76, 79; and permissiveness, 81–82; permissiveness (encouragement) of, 81–82; and punishment, 68–81, 83, 86–87, 88, (a) hypotheses of, 57, 68, 70, 71, 78–79, (b) and identification, 88–89, (c) and permissiveness, 82–83, 84–85, 86–87, 88, (d) physical, 72–76, 77–79, (e) severity of, 78–79, (f) sex differences in response to, 79, 88–89; punishment for, 69–70, 71, 72–76, 77; and rearing correlates, 64–89, 92–93, (a) from independent designs, 79–80, (b) from nonindependent designs, 77–79, 80; theories of, 55–58

ALLINSMITH, W., 14, 103, 117, 122

ALLPORT, G. W., 2, 132

ALPERT, R., 4, 14, 23, 35, 40, 42, 45, 48, 60, 61, 65, 66, 78, 79, 81, 82, 95, 97, 101, 102, 105, 117, 118, 119

Annoying things about child (*see* Rejection)

Apparatus factors in measurement, 9

ARONFREED, J., 122

Attention wanted (*see* Dependency)

B

BACON, R., 130, 140

BANDURA, A., 4, 5

BANTA, J. J., 14, 65, 79, 80, 97

BECKER, W. C., 4, 14, 39, 65, 66, 78, 79, 80, 89, 101

Behavioristic theory in childrearing research, 3–5

BELLER, E. K., 22

BERELSON, B., 13, 109

Bias in interview data: coder, 115–116, 142–144; nonindependent sources of data, 51, 69, 80, 114–117; social desirability, 137–140

BISHOP, B. M., 5

Bivariate analyses, limitations of, 129

BOE, E. E., 69

BRODY, G. F., 119

BRONFENBRENNER, U., 101

BRUSH, E. S., 122

BUCKLAND, W., 6–7

BURTON, R. V., 14, 65, 78, 83, 95, 97, 102, 103, 117, 122, 123

C

CAMPBELL, D. T., 9, 119

CAMPBELL, J. D., 123

Causal relationships, 49–50, 56, 102, 114–115, 146–147, 152

Child development, theories of, 3–5 (*see also* Developmental theory)

CHILD, I. L., 42

Childrearing research: methodology in, 4–6, 126; status of, 151–152

CHURCH, R. M., 69

CLAUSEN, J. A., 3

Closeness wanted (*see* Dependency)

Coding, reliability of: 142–144; aggression measures, 62–64, 166, 168, 170, 171; conscience measures, 97, 168–69, 172; dependency measures, 26, 166, 170, 171; effect on relationships obtained, 113–114, 142–144 (*see also* Reliability)

Communication of research findings, 20, 130–134

Compliance: coding reliability, 167, 169; measurement of, 167, 169

Conceptualization: and equivalence of indices, 19, 21–22, 55, 71, 77, 89–92; and measurement, 19, 21, 22, 23–24, 49, 52–54, 89–92, 134–142

Confession, measurement of, 168, 171 (*see also* Conscience)

Conscience: and affectional relations, 102–107, 108, (a) coding reliability, 168–169, 172, (b) and dependency, 105, 107, 108, (c) interpretations in the literature, 100–102, (d) sex differences in, 107; conceptualization of, 95; and dependency, 105, 107; and disciplinary techniques, 107–113; hypothesized antecedents of, 100–102; and love-oriented techniques, 109–113; and love withdrawal, 107–113, (a) and warmth, 112–113, (b) and acceptance, 27, 38–39, 102–107; measurement of, 96–98, 168–169, 172, (a) intercorrelations of indices, 98, 99, (b) methodological problems in coding instructions, 115–116, (c) validity of, 116–119; and object-oriented techniques, 107, 109–113; and physical punishment, 107, 109–113; and rearing correlates, 102–113; and rejection, 103–107; and warmth, and love withdrawal, 112–113

Conscience formation, developmental model, 120–123, (a) inadequacy of correlational data, 121–123

Consistency in findings: on aggression, 64–89; on conscience, 103–113, 123–124; contribu-

tions of methods to correlates of, (a) aggression, 70–88, (b) conscience, 113–124, (c) dependency, 49–54; criteria of, 8–10, 19; on dependency, 37–52

Construct validity of conscience measure, 116–118

Contaminated designs, 69, 77–79, 80, 114–117

Continuity in research, 1, 2, 6, 8, 10, 148–151

Correlational data: and cause-effect relationships, 126, 146–147; and developmental theory, 123, 146–147

CRONBACH, L. J., 116

CROWNE, D. P., 137

D

DAY, J., 5

Demands, levels of (*see* Restrictiveness)

Dependency: and affectional demonstrativeness, 37, 38–39, 40–41; concept of, 21–23, 53, (a) generality vs. specificity of, 22–24; and conscience, 105, (a) and affectional relations, 105, 107, 108; and handling of aggression, 38–39, 46–48; and love withdrawal, 38–39, 43–45; measurement of, 24–30, 166, 170–171, (a) intercorrelation of indices, 24–34; mother's response to, 38–39, 41–43, (a) and aggression, 66–67, (b) coding reliability to, 158, (c) measurement of, 158; and number of annoying things about child, 37, 38–39; and rearing correlates, 34–52; and restrictiveness, 38–39, 43–45;

and techniques of control, 38–39, 43–45; theory of, 34–35; and things enjoyed in child, 37, 38–39

Dependency frustration, 66

Deprivation of privileges: coding reliability, 156; and conscience, 107–112; and dependency, 38–39; measurement of, 156

Design (*see* Independent data sources; Nonindependence of data sources)

Developmental history, 120–122

Developmental theory, 2–4

Disciplinary techniques: and aggression, 77–82; and conscience, 107–113; and dependency, 43–45 (*see also* under specific techniques; punishment)

DOLLARD, J., 56

DOOB, L. W., 56

E

EDWARDS, A. L., 137

Emotionality in discipline: coding reliability, 164–165; measurement of, 164–165

Encouragement of aggression (*see* Permissiveness of aggression)

ENGLISH, A., 7

ENGLISH, H., 7

ERON, L. D., 14, 65, 79, 80, 97

ESTES, W. K., 68

Experimental approach to child rearing, methodological problems in, 145–146

Experimental evidence, interpretation in terms of interview findings, 134

F

FISKE, D. W., 9, 119

FREUD, S., 3

Frustration: and aggression, 65–68; concept of, 65–68; measurement of, 65–66 (*see also* Restrictiveness)

G

Global rating, problems in use of (*see* Bias in interview data)

GRINDER, R. C., 117

Guilt (*see* Conscience)

H

HARLOW, H., 5

HARLOW, M. K., 5

HARRIMAN, P. L., 7

HARTSHORNE, H., 95

HARTUP, W. W., 23, 34

HELLMER, L. A., 14, 39, 65, 66, 68, 79, 80, 89

HIRSCH, S. I., 5

HOFFMAN, M. L., 14, 65, 79, 101

HOLLENBERG, E., 65, 66

I

Identification: and effects of punishment on aggression, 88–89; theory of conscience formation, 120

Independency: coding reliability, 166, 169; measurement of, 166, 169; response to, 158

Independent data sources: advantages of, 52; and findings on aggression, 69, 74–75, 76, 79–80; and findings on conscience, 117–119 (*see also* Nonindependence)

Indices: adequacy of, in relation to hypothesis formulation and testing, 92–93, 123–124; equivalence of, 24, 149, 150 (*see also* Intercorrelation of indices)

Intercorrelations of indices: of aggression, 60–61; of conscience, 98; of dependency, 26–34; of punishment, 77

Interpretation of findings: directional criteria, 128–130; inconsistencies, 127–130; in secondary sources, 132–134; statistical criteria, 128–130

Interview: adequacy of questions, 17, 61–62, 140–142; consistency with questionnaire findings for measurement of behavior, 135–136, 147; procedures in NIMH Study, 14–17, (a) measurement of aggression, 61–63, 166, 168, 170, 171, (b) measurement of conscience, 96–97, 168–169, 172, (c) measurement of dependency, 26, 28, 166, 170, 171; proposed research on, 145–146; Sears, Maccoby, Levin, 14–17, 153–172; social meaning of interview items, 136–140; sources of error in, 134–144; as a tool for childrearing data, 51–52, 134–146; validity of, as measures of behavior, 117–119, 146–147

Isolation: coding reliability, 155; and conscience, 110–111; and dependency, 38–39, 44; measurement of, 155

K

KAGAN, J., 39, 42, 45
KARDINER, A., 3
KENDALL, M., 6–7
KESSEN, W., 10–11

KOHLBERG, L., 101
KOHN, M. L., 3

L

Labeling child behavior: coding reliability, 165; measurement of, 165

LAULICHT, J. H., 14, 65, 79, 80, 97
LEFKOWITZ, M. M., 14, 65, 79
LEVIN, H., 4, 13, 14, 15, 16, 17, 28, 34, 40, 41, 42, 44, 46, 47, 61, 65, 66, 77, 78, 82, 83, 88, 95, 97, 100, 102, 103, 105, 107, 109, 112, 114, 115, 122, 133, 144, 146

Love-oriented techniques: coding reliability, 155, 156; and conscience, 109–113; measures of, 107, 155, 156

Love withdrawal: coding reliability, 155; and conscience, 107–113; and dependency, 38–39, 43–45; measurement of, 155; and warmth, and conscience, 112–113 (*see also* Disciplinary techniques; love-oriented techniques)

LURIA, Z., 14, 39, 65, 66, 78, 79, 80, 89

M

MACCOBY, E. E., 4, 13, 14, 15, 16, 17, 28, 34, 40, 41, 42, 44, 46, 47, 61, 65, 66, 77, 78, 82, 83, 88, 95, 97, 100, 102, 103, 105, 107, 109, 112, 114, 115, 122, 133, 144, 146

MCNEMAR, Q., 144
MARLOWE, D., 137
MARSHALL, H. R., 45
MAY, M. A., 95
MEEHL, P. W., 116

Methodology in childrearing research, 4–6

MILLER, N. E., 56

MOSS, H. A., 37, 42, 45

MOWRER, O. H., 56

Multivariate analyses: of "antecedents" of aggression, 83; of "antecedents" of conscience, 112–113; hypotheses requiring, 147

N

Nonindependence: in coding of verbal reports, 113–116; of data sources, built-in bias, 45, 51, 69, 78, 80, 114–117

NOWLIS, V., 14, 42, 48, 57, 58, 65, 66, 79, 88

O

Object-oriented disciplinary techniques: coding reliability, 156–157; and conscience, 107, 109, 112; measures of, 156–157

Observations of behavior: interview reports and, 135–137, 140–142; problems of methods, 5, 145–146

Open-ended questions: advantages and limitations, 51; coder reliability, 51, 142–144

P

Permissiveness of aggression: and aggression, 81–82, 84–85; coding reliability, 159, 160; and dependency, 38–39; measurement of, 82, 159, 160; punishment of aggression and aggression, 83, 86–87, 88

Permissiveness of dependency (see

Dependency, mother's response to)

Personality development, theories of, 2–3, 4

PETERSON, D. R., 14, 39, 65, 66, 78, 79, 80, 89

PIAGET, J., 95

POSTMAN, L., 132

Praise: coding reliability, 156; and conscience, 110–111; measurement of, 156

Psychoanalytic theory, in childrearing research, 3–5, 56

Punishment: and aggression, 68–81, 83, 86–87, 88, (a) hypotheses of, 57, 68–69, 70–71, 79, (b) and permissiveness, 86–87; for aggression, 69–70, 71, 72–73, 74–75, 76, 77, 86–87, (a) and aggression, 72–73, 77–78; comfort after, 159, (b) and dependency, 46–48, 72–73; and conscience, 107–110, for denial of deviance, 38–39, (a) and conscience, measurement of, 159; and dependency, 38–39, 43–45; of dependency, 41–43; hypotheses of, 57, 68–69, 70–71, 79; measurement of, 69–70, 71, 77, 157, (a) problems in, 89–91; physical, and (a) aggression, 72–73, 74–75, 76, 77–79, 86–87, (b) dependency, 38–39, 44; severity of, and (a) aggression, 72–73, 74–75, 76, 78, 86–87, (b) conscience, 110–111, (c) dependency, 38–39, 44; measurement of, 76–77, 163–164

Q

Questionnaire: intercorrelation with interview findings, 32–34, 63;

in NIMH Study, 17–18, 28–29, 31, 32–34, (a) measurement of aggression, 62–64, (b) measurement of dependency, 28–29

R

RAU, L., 4, 14, 23, 35, 40, 42, 45, 48, 60, 61, 65, 66, 78, 79, 81, 82, 95, 97, 101, 102, 105, 117, 118, 119

Reasoning: and conscience, 110–111; measurement of, 155

REDL, F., 91

Rejection: and conscience, 103–107, and dependency, 104, 106, 108; measurement of, 17, 103, 165, 171

Reliability: of coding, (a) in NIMH Study, 153–172, (b) in *Patterns of Child Rearing*, 153–172, (c) of verbal reports, 26, 97, 113–114, 142–144; effect on magnitude of relationships, 144; types of, 20, 62–64 (*see also* Intercorrelation of indices)

Replication: choice of kind, 8, 9, 10, 148–151; in correlates of aggression, 64–89; in correlates of conscience, 102–113; in correlates of dependency, 34–52; criteria of, 6–9; deterrents to, 10–12; need for, 10, 11–12, 148–151; procedures for assessment of in present study, 12–13, 14–20

Research strategy, 148–151

Restrictiveness: and aggression, 67; and dependency, 38–39, 43–44; measurement of, 160–163, 169

Restrictions and demands, as index of frustration, 65–66

Reviews of research (*see* Secondary sources)

Rewards: and conscience, 110–111; and dependency, 38–39, 44; measurement of, 156; and punishment, interactive effects of, 4, 83

RHEINGOLD, H., 5

ROSENTHAL, R., 146

RYCOFF, I. M., 5

S

Sample: in childrearing studies, 13–14, 91; in comparison studies of aggression, 65; used in NIMH Study, 13–14

SEARS, P. S., 14, 42, 48, 57, 58, 65, 66, 79, 88

SEARS, R. R., (1939), 56; (1953), 14, 42, 48, 57, 58, 65, 66, 79, 88; (1956), 65, 66, 88; (1957–61), 4, 13, 14, 15, 16, 17, 26, 28, 34, 40, 41, 42, 44, 46, 47, 61, 66, 76, 77, 78, 82, 83, 88, 95, 97, 100, 102, 103, 105, 107, 109, 112, 114, 115, 122, 133, 144, 146; (1960), 101, 118; (1965), 4, 14, 23, 35, 40, 42, 45, 48, 60, 61, 65, 66, 78, 79, 81, 82, 95, 97, 101, 102, 105, 117, 118, 119

Secondary sources: problems of interpretation in, 132–134; reviews of conscience development, 101–102

Separation anxiety (*see* Dependency)

Sex differences: in "antecedents" of conscience, 107; in response to punishment, 79–80

SHOEMAKER, D. L., 14, 39, 65, 66, 78, 79, 80, 89

SKINNER, B. F., 68

SMITH, H., 119

Social desirability bias in interview data, 137–140

Social learning theory in childrearing research, 3–4, 35, 56–58

SOLOMON, R. L., 69, 122

SPERRY, M., 66

Statistical significance as a criterion, 128–129

STEINER, G. A., 13, 109

STOUFFER, S. A., 7

Superego (*see* Conscience)

T

Teacher ratings: in NIMH Study, 17–18, (a) measurement of aggression, 62–64, (b) measurement of conscience, 97, (c) measurement of dependency, 29–30, (d) and mothers' responses, 32–34, 63–64 (*see also* Aggression; Conscience; Dependency)

Techniques of control (*see* Disciplinary techniques)

Temporal factors in measurement, 50

Theories of personality development, 2–5

THOMPSON, G., 127

TOIGO, R., 14, 65, 79

Trait consistency: in aggression, 60–61; in dependency, 26–34

U

Unreliability (*see* Reliability; Coding, reliability of)

V

Validity: construct validity of conscience measure, 116–118; of interview data, 134–144; measures of conscience, 116–119; and procedural adequacy, 1–2

Verbal reports: in childrearing research, 4–5; comparisons with behavior measures, 118–119; nonindependence of coding, 113–116; reliability of coding, 113; validity of, as indices of behavior, 134–144, 147

W

WALDER, L. O., 14, 65, 79, 80, 97

WALTERS, R. H., 4, 5

Warmth: and aggression, 66, 67; and conscience, 102–107, 113; and dependency, 37–41; and love withdrawal, and conscience, 112, 113; measurement of, 17, 102, 165

WHITING, J. W. M., 14, 42–43, 47–48, 57, 58, 65, 66, 79, 88

WILLIAMS, J. R., 3

WINEMAN, D., 91

WYNNE, L. C., 5

Y

YARROW, M. R., 123

Z

ZUNICH, M., 119